A POLICEMAN'S TALE

An Autobiography

Witten and compiled by
Patrick John McNeill

McNeill Books

CREATiON

2006, 2010, 2010, 2022

Copyright
© 2006 Patrick J. McNeill (Book)
© 2022 Giles McNeill (Design)

Cover photograph
The photograph on the cover was taken in Castle Square in Lincoln by Constable Douglas Grant of Headquarters Photography Department, in 1967, soon after the Lincolnshire Constabulary amalgamated with Lincoln City Police. It was for use on the police stand that year at the Lincolnshire Show and later was featured on the front cover of the Chief Constable's Annual Report to the Lincolnshire Police Committee.

All rights reserved
This book or any portion thereof may not be reproduced or used in any manner whatsoever without the express written permission of the publisher except for the use of brief quotations in a book review or scholarly journal.

First published in Great Britain in 2006 by Patrick J. McNeill.
McNeill Books, 3 The Chestnuts, Nettleham, Lincoln LN2 2NH

Fourth Edition

ISBN: 979-8-8438-3952-9

Foreword

I am the son of a Lincolnshire police officer. The Lincolnshire Police Authority employed me from 1958 to 1992, and now they pay my pension.

This is the story of my life leading up to and through those years working for the police in the green and rural county of Lincolnshire. They were years that saw considerable changes in the lifestyle of the people of the county and in the system of policing.

The story begins early in the Second World War and goes through to the second millennium, charting boyhood, schooldays, and working life. It includes something about my family and friends and a good deal about police work.

I've tried to include a taste of the routine nature of life in the police as well as the ups and downs, especially where something funny happened.

You will learn how my distinct lack of skill on the football field as a boy translated into me being in charge of young people rock climbing, canoeing, mountain trekking and beach lifesaving. You will also discover how my love of chocolate digestive biscuits became the cause of me lecturing American university students.

The writing of this tale has been much encouraged by my dear wife, Julia, who has patiently read every word offering advice along the way.

Nettleham, March 2006

Contents

	Foreword	iii
	Contents	v
I.	Great Gonerby	1
II.	Louth	6
III.	Sleaford	8
IV.	Colchester & London	12
V.	Cleethorpes	17
VI.	Humberstone Foundation School	34
VII.	Police Cadet	50
VIII.	Pannal Ash	73
IX.	Boston	80
X.	Gainsborough	103
XI.	Headquarters CID	120
XII.	Wakefield and Spalding	128
XIII.	Headquarters War Duties	144
XIV.	Cleethorpes & Grimsby CID	151
XV.	Boston & Stamford	166
XVI.	Boston & Skegness	176
XVII.	Market Rasen	185
XVIII.	Skegness	196
XIX.	Headquarters Training	199
XX.	Headquarters Operations Room	215
XXI.	Lincoln Swift Inspector	219
XXII.	Horncastle Rural Inspector	228
XXIII.	Boston Chief Inspector	255
XXIV.	Headquarters Community Affairs Department	268
XXV.	Nettleham in Retirement	288

I Great Gonerby

The story starts with my birth on Sunday 28th December 1941, at 8:30pm at Great Gonerby, a village atop a hill on the Great North Road, north of Grantham, in Lincolnshire. Charles Dickens wrote of the hill, calling it 'a murder for chase horses'. People born in Great Gonerby are known by an old and proud tradition as 'Clock Pelters'[1]. Those born in Lincolnshire are known as 'Yellow Bellies'[2]. Therefore, this is the story of a clock pelting yellow belly, who became a Lincolnshire policeman.

Dr Giles and Nurse Moore attended for the delivery and made a charge of four guineas. I was the first child of Harold and Bessie McNeill. At the time of my birth on that snowy Sunday, my father was in Grantham Hospital with a

---

[1] Clock Pelter – Natives of Great Gonerby were said to throw mud from the village pond at the hands of the church clock to stop it, thus giving themselves more time before work began. This is quite a feat as the pond is a good distance from the church.
[2] Yellow Bellies – Natives of Lincolnshire possibly from the yellow waistcoats of the Lincolnshire Regiment (10th foot).

fractured skull, having been knocked off his bicycle while on night patrol along the Great North Road. He believes a pantechnicon struck him, after the driver failed to see him in his black uniform in the faint glimmer of his blacked-out headlights – a wartime precaution against aircraft attacks.

To assist my mother with her new child my Great-aunt Lizzie (Grandfather Pickering's sister) had come to stay at the police house beside the Great North Road. My parents occupied the semi-detached house on the left and Sergeant Newton and his family lived in the house on the other side, with the police office, for the beat, attached. The house was almost new when my parents moved in.

Perhaps I'd better set the scene a little more with some information about who my parents were. My father, Harold Douglas Roy McNeill, was the son of Joseph Patrick McNeill, a soldier, who'd joined the army when aged sixteen. My grandfather was a member of the Army Ordnance Corps and is described on his marriage certificate as a carriage smith (military). He served in Ireland (Dublin area) and as a professional soldier was one of the early ones to go to France on the outbreak of the Great War. He married my grandmother, Lily Elizabeth May, and they lived in Ipswich and then moved to 10 Alexandra Terrace in Colchester.

During the First World War, Grandfather Joseph had been gassed in the trenches and suffered poor health for the rest of his life. He was awarded three military medals, the Star 'Aug - Nov 1914', the Silver War Medal 1914 - 1918, and 'The Great War for Civilisation 1914 -1919' medal inscribed similarly S - 5371 Pte J McNeill A.O.C. He had trained as a toolmaker. Following his release from the military, he worked as a plumber, as there was no work for toolmakers. My father told me grandfather was self-taught as a plumber and he managed to obtain work, installing central heating in buildings, including a hospital, in the Essex area. Their second house in Colchester was at 76 Constantine Road. Joseph died on 16th March 1941 and have one of my father's photographs showing a newly dug grave, with fresh flowers, endorsed on the back '20/3/41'. Unfortunately, I never knew my paternal grandfather

My father was one of his parents' two children. He was born in their house in Charles Street, Ipswich. They later had a daughter Dorothy.

My mother was the daughter of Harry Andrew Pickering and his wife Edith (née Daughton). She was born in a cottage on the banks of the Catchwater Drain at Stickney Fen and was one of seven children (six surviving into adulthood). My maternal grandfather was the son of a garthman (the farm worker who is responsible for the farmyard) and had been brought up in villages near Stickney. He had worked all his life as a bricklayer.

My mother went to the village school in Stickney and her final report dated 30th March 1928, signed by Mr. A Gillett, the headmaster, was 'Very satisfactory. An intelligent and conscientious scholar'. Her marks for arithmetic were ten out of ten with a similar result for spelling. On leaving school, she went to Skegness where she worked at the Tower café on Lumley Road eventually becoming the cashier.

My father told me that times were hard when he was

young. He would be sent to the market in Colchester at closing time to do his best to obtain cheap or free fruit. He had won a scholarship because of his English to a good school but had been unable to take this up because of the cost. He started work as an office boy for a cable company that specialised in bringing electricity to areas not connected to the grid. The company, Henley Cables, sent him to Lincolnshire where extensive electrification was taking place in the early 1930s. He was based in the company office in Skegness. It was in Skegness that he met my mother.

With the prospect of marriage, a home would be needed, and married policemen were provided with houses. His uncle Leslie was a police officer in Salford. My father joined the Lincolnshire Constabulary on 2nd November 1933. He was sent to Cleethorpes and then Market Rasen. He was given permission to marry my mother from his superintendent. They were married in September 1936 at St. Luke's Church, Stickney. He was posted to Brant Broughton where they lived in a flat at the crossroads garage of Messrs Troop.

When Great Gonerby beat became vacant, together with the semi-detached house on the hilltop at the police station, my parents moved there in time for my birth in December 1941.

I was baptised in the church where my parents had married, St. Luke's at Stickney, on Sunday, 26th April 1942 with my mother's sister Win, and her husband Basil Taylor as Godparents. I wore my father's christening gown. My mother's brother George was another Godparent, and as Basil was abroad in Burma, serving in the Royal Air force,

Uncle Fred Warner stood in as proxy.

My memories of Great Gonerby are rather vague. I have photographs showing a fair-haired bright little lad playing with his cousins Roland and Basil, taking photographs, and collecting for the Red Cross. In addition, my father took a photograph of me with Sergeant Newton and a huge fish he'd caught. The fish was at least as big as me or even bigger!

It was wartime and I have vague memories of columns of army vehicles travelling along the Great North Road. Fortunately, the hardships of wartime passed me by at this tender age. Another photograph shows me in a huge (relative to my size) baby's gas mask, and a later one shows me in a gas mask which was bright red with a strange valve at the nose for outgoing air. It made me look like the cartoon character Mickey Mouse.

II Louth

My father was moved to Louth in 1944 and joined the Criminal Investigation Department (CID), as a detective constable under the watchful eye of Detective Sergeant Montgomery, known affectionately as 'Monty'

The family, with my six-week-old sister Susan, moved to a small house on Keddington Road. It was called Aaron House and all I remember is that the stairs went up to the first floor from the living room. My mother is said to have cried when she saw it, having had to leave a modern semi-detached house in Great Gonerby for something very much older and smaller.

I had a friend, Barry Coupland, and we spent a great deal of time playing on the pavement beside the road in front of the house. The pavement had a raised kerbstone that separated it distinctly from the road and we spent lots of time sitting on this raised area. I also remember hiding under the dining room table when an air raid threatened.

A Policeman's Tale

Another memory is of seeing a serious road accident outside the baker's shop, with a poor man covered in blood being carried into an ambulance. This seemed a very shocking thing for a four-year-old boy to witness, and had a great effect on me, figuring in nightmares for years afterwards. It certainly gave me a great respect for the dangers of the road, and the value of road safety. When I woke with a nightmare my mother would tell me to think of rosy apples and go back to sleep.

My mother used to take my sister and I along Keddington Road towards the village of Keddington. The lane soon led to fields beside waterway that was the old, abandoned Louth Navigation. Here we would picnic beside a derelict lock in the summer enjoying the fresh air and countryside. My mother loved walking with her children and would patiently explain the names of the hedgerow berries and other interesting wild plants and flowers.

There were some family outings, and I always enjoyed a chance to paddle in the sea or a pool. Even more, I enjoyed getting out my bucket and spade and building a sandcastle or making a canal in the sand.

Father attended a course at the Metropolitan Police Detective Training School at Hendon, while stationed at Louth. He took part in a film about the training of detectives, which led to witty comments from his Superintendent about his potential as a film star. In any event, he had passed the promotion examinations and soon was promoted to the rank of detective sergeant.

III Sleaford

Promotion for my father meant another move. This time we were off to Sleaford in the early spring of 1946. The new address was 38 Electric Station Road – a nearly new, detached house on the edge of town beside the river Slea. I well remember fishing expeditions into the field next door with my mother and sister when sticklebacks were captured and put into a jam jar. On one occasion, I fell into the river and had to be pulled out by my mother – no doubt that was what made her keen for me to learn to swim.

I also remember the floods, which followed the heavy snowfall of 1947. Snow fell somewhere in the United Kingdom every day between 22nd January and 17th March. The snow, which was chest deep (for a five-year-old), lay about for weeks. When the thaw finally came in March accompanied by rain and severe gales it caused severe problems for the town. The river Slea overtopped its banks with the melt water, and I remember going to bed one

A Policeman's Tale

evening having left my little wooden boat peacefully laying on the lawn and then finding the next morning that the whole house was surrounded by water and my boat was nicely afloat. In the town, fire brigade hosepipes were strewn across the main street pumping water back into the river from flooded basements, and it was some time before life got back to normal. The floorboards in our hallway had to be taken up because water had got into the under-floor space, and I remember gazing into the gap as discussions took place about rotting timbers.

One strange event took place at Sleaford, which looking back now seems out of character. Nowadays I love to soak up the sun, preferably on a beach washed by a warm sea. Back then however it was decided that we toddlers needed more sun than nature was providing, and I was one of lots of small children taken to the town's clinic. Having had most of my clothes taken off I was ushered into a room in the centre of which was a large bright object giving off a very bright greenish light. All round the room were little children in the same state of undress as me. I took instant fright and let out loud bellows of objection and began struggling to run away. I don't know what happened next, but I'm sure that my poor mother must have felt very embarrassed at the behaviour of her screaming son. At least no more attempts were made to give me artificial sun and I was always very pleased ever after to benefit from the natural variety.

At the age of five, I started school. The school was near the church in the town centre, and on the first morning, my father set off with me on a little seat fastened to the crossbar of his bike. There were footrests at the top of the front fork and the journey took very little time. On reaching school, we found the doors firmly closed and everyone in assembly. I was let in a little later to begin schooldays. Unfortunately, father had this habit of getting me to school late, which left a deep impression on me giving me a hatred of lateness in others and myself. After a while the twin girls, Carol, and Ann Wilby, who lived next door to us, started walking with me to school and bringing me home afterwards. All went well until one day they seemed to have gone home without me, and as a brave five-year-old, I set off on my own. Sleaford has a busy crossroads in the centre guarded by traffic lights. I never could figure out whether pedestrians were meant to walk when the lights were red or when they were green. The footpath at the crossroads is under a colonnaded walk, and I well remember stepping off the footpath, from behind one of the columns, and hearing a screech of brakes. I saw a black saloon car come to a halt, inches from my little body with a very shocked looking driver. Another lesson learnt perhaps.

During this time at Sleaford, my mother suffered from tuberculosis (TB), which she later said was caught while working at Skegness as the cashier in The Tower Café. It was always smoky, she said. This was before the days of the discovery of a successful drug treatment and when the regime of open-air sanatoria was the vogue. On 24th December 1947, my mother went off in an ambulance and was admitted to Creaton Sanatorium, in Northamptonshire, for what was to be a very long stay, leaving my father to cope with two young children as well as his work as a detective which often meant being out late into the night.

My father's work also meant another detective course at the Metropolitan Police Detective Training School at Hendon from 27th September to 4th December 1948.

My mother's long stay in the Creaton Sanatorium was to last until her discharge on 7th July 1949.

IV Colchester & London

Not long after my dear mother had been sent off to her sanatorium my sister Susan was sent to stay with Grandmother Pickering at Stickney, and I went firstly to stay with the Dennison family – Mr. Dennison was a policemen colleague of my father. A little later, I went off to Colchester where Auntie Dorothy, my father's sister, and her husband Uncle Raymond took me in. Auntie Dorothy had a son of her own, Neill, and a stepdaughter Heather, and I was made very welcome. School in Colchester was another new experience for me.

Memories from this time include going to North Street Primary School and having to cross the 'by-pass', a wide modern road. On one occasion, I was hovering at the edge of the old type of pedestrian crossing, with just road studs, and a (non-flashing) Belisha beacon, when a black police car pulled up and a kindly officer motioned me to cross the road in front of the patrol car. At school, a new custom was introduced which involved spending what seemed an eternity lying on individual straw mats for an afternoon rest. This seems a good idea to me, and I am sorry that it didn't seem to feature in the years of schooling that followed.

Another memory is of school dinners, which I usually enjoyed, except when it was beetroot, which made the gravy all red, or ginger pudding, although the custard was good. One day we had fried eggs, which I love, and of course, I ate everything else on the plate saving the best till last. Suddenly an unkind hand belonging to the supervisor clipped my ear. She took my plate away and told me how very bad it was to waste food, and that I should not be leaving a perfectly good egg. My protests were in vain, and I learned several early lessons about life from this incident. I certainly resolved to eat the best first in future, and that jumping to conclusions is not always wise.

With a growing baby son, and two other children, in a very small, terraced house it was decided that I should move to my Grandmother McNeill's home, which was up the hill in Colchester at 35 Eld Lane. Grandmother lived in an alms-house that consisted of only a kitchen and a bed sitting room. Grandmother and I shared the double bed. There was no bathroom, facilities were basic, consisting of the kitchen sink, and a flushing lavatory about thirty yards down the garden in a little row of outhouses – at least there was one to each of the alms-houses.

For reasons which are not clear to me, in January 1949 my father took me to live with 'Auntie' Marie' and 'Uncle' Hal (Mr. & Mrs. H. Dodsworth). They were actually cousins of my father, and lived at 9 The Dell, Abbey Wood,

London, SE2. This was to be a short stay, but my memories seem to say that it was full of experiences. For one thing, I caught the mumps and was confined to bed eating only very soft food like boiled eggs and being visited by the doctor to check me over and ensure I was not suffering side effects. The mumps did not seem very serious to me giving me only a very swollen neck. It only lasted a few days before I was able to resume school.

The London school seemed very different to me. There was a second storey to it and a very high wire fence surrounded the playground. The playground however was wonderful as it included a real American Wild West covered wagon, which was great for playing cowboy and Indian games. In the classroom, we had a corner where you got to play at shops with cardboard money.

A friendship developed with Jimmy Ferguson who lived on the other side of the common and I spent many happy hours at his house playing in the garden. A favourite game was making miniature canals and lining the bottom with clay we found in the woods to stop the water running away. The woods could be scary to a seven-year-old with lurking youths, who on one visit waved a knife at us. However, a visit was worth it to gather more canal-making material.

One day on the way home from school, crossing the common, I came across a group of people with a very large dog, which may have been a Great Dane. I lingered for some time and eventually made my way back to The Dell. Here I met a frantic Aunt Marie who told me she had just called the police to report me missing. I learned another lesson that day.

A Policeman's Tale

One very interesting feature of the houses in Abbey Wood I'd not seen before, was a strange wire contraption on the chimney pots of a few of them. It was in the shape of an H, and I eventually enquired (apparently, I rarely stopped asking questions), about the purpose of this strange equipment. I was told that it was television. When I asked what that was, I was properly informed that television was like the wireless, but that you could see a picture as well. Armed with this important revelation I spent a considerable amount of time watching these strange H devices to see if I could see the picture too. Alas I never did. It was only when I got to Cleethorpes, I saw the wondrous Muffin the Mule, a wooden puppet, on a television set.

Another wonder of the capital city was the trams, which ran along the main road from Woolwich. Like trains, they ran on rails, with an overhead wire, and a long pole extended from the roof of the trams to the wire. Many of the trams were very old with outside stairs and I was fascinated watching them. They were red, and the sounds they made were great, especially the bell, the sound of the motor and the squeal of the wheels against the rails at bends.

Marie and Hal Dodsworth had a son of their own, Michael. A letter from them to my parents after I'd left said that Michael had been impressed by my love of spaghetti. I think he was right; I've always loved spaghetti and baked beans.

In April 1949, my London adventure ended. My mother returned to her family and the Lincolnshire Constabulary decided that sea-air would be good for her (and this fitted in with their plans to move my father from Sleaford anyway). The force arranged that our family would swap homes with the Lake family living in Cleethorpes. It was a few weeks before I left my cousins in Abbey Wood. I wrote to my father and mother saying I was looking forward to coming to Cleethorpes and playing on the sands.

V Cleethorpes

At Cleethorpes, we lived at 32 Lindum Road. The Lincolnshire Constabulary rented this semi-detached house from the Topliss family for their officers to occupy. Many years later, I found an entry in the file for the house indicating that it was in a superior neighbourhood. The house had been built around 1920 on the Cleethorpes Boulevard Estate which was land owned by Sidney Sussex College at Cambridge. It was rendered in concrete, and the woodwork was painted in chocolate brown and cream, whereas all the other police houses in Lindsey were painted in 'county green', (a shade of pea green). This was apparently because Mrs Topliss held the old superstition that green is an unlucky colour and insisted that when the county painted our house, they used something other than 'county green'. My father was now doing shift work as a town sergeant.

It was great to be living at the seaside and the 'front' was only a ten-minute walk away from home. There was a decent garden to play in and school was reached by a halfpenny ride on a trolley bus (nearly as much fun as a tram, but without the rails). I used to walk to the bus stop outside Tasker's the Grocers and wait for the trolley buses. I caught the number eleven, which would be in a smart grey and blue livery if it were one operated by Cleethorpes Borough Transport, or carmine maroon if it were one of the Grimsby Borough Transport vehicles. The trolley buses turned around at Cleethorpes Bathing Pool, about half a mile southward from where I waited, and you could see when your bus set off. You could be confident that one would arrive every four or five minutes, and I would spend the few minutes waiting watching the waves on the sea and the ships on the estuary of the river Humber with the lighthouse at Spurn Point in Yorkshire often visible. I liked being on the top deck for the mile journey and used to get off at the top of Isaac's Hill near the library and walk the rest of the way to school. This journey passed a convenient shop, which sold liquorice, penny iced buns, kali, and other delights for a seven-year-old to spend his pocket money on.

Then into Bursar Street Infants School just across the road from the tuck shop. I was in Mrs. Hall's class. She was very keen on her nature table, which always had displays of sticky buds and other fascinating countryside items. I loved music lessons, which usually had me shaking bells or a tambourine. A highlight of the morning was the delivery of one-third pint bottles of milk, which provided welcome refreshment. We always saved the circular cardboard lids with a hole for the straw, playing games with them, just as

A Policeman's Tale

we did with cigarette cards.

The next summer, at the age of eight, I moved up to the junior school, which was on the same site in Bursar Street. The headmaster was Mr. Rudd, and I was in Miss Browning's class of about fifty children. One highlight of these days was the nature programmes that we listened to on a speaker in the classroom. The BBC broadcasts were an interesting break from usual schoolwork, and we often had the benefit of a glossy brochure to accompany the broadcasts. My school report indicated that my results were quite good but that I was rather slow.

At home, my father encouraged me to set up a caterpillar club in Lindum Road with my friends. The members included my sister, Susan, the girl from next door, Susan Tweedy, and several other local children. The object was for members to collect interesting caterpillars that could be kept in a jam jar (with a supply of appropriate food), and the brought to the club to show to other members. Some of the best caterpillars I found while visiting my grandmother at 49 Horbling Lane, Stickney, with my mother and sister. The ragwort plant grew on the banks of the local dyke, the East Fen Catchwater Drain, and this was home to the caterpillar of the cinnabar moth, a hairy black and orange grub that seemed to thrive on the highly poisonous leaves.

This was the first of several clubs, which local children arranged. We had great games in the street where the arrival of any traffic was a very rare event, usually accompanied by a raucous motor horn. Kick ball fly was a favourite, and we played 'crashing but don't' on our cycles. We chalked wickets on the fence and played cricket with a tennis ball and had fun skipping. Sometimes we tied one end of a long skipping rope to the lamppost so that more could join in the skipping. Songs such as 'Under the moon and over the stars' always accompanied this. My sister was very good juggling with two balls thrown against the wall. I used to try this too and the usual rhyme we chanted went: 'PK penny packet, first you chew it then you crack it, PK penny packet'.

When not playing in the street with friends I used to go off to the bus terminus outside the bathing pool on the Kingsway. Waiting for the number eleven trolley buses or the number six motorbuses to arrive I would ask the conductor if I could have the used tickets for my collection. Kindly ones would open the box of used tickets on the rear platform and empty it for my benefit. There were always lots of the same type, halfpenny greens, penny browns, and two-penny reds. Sometimes though there were the very odd workmen's tickets. These were white with a red circle on them and often they had several punch holes in them from several journeys.

Following wartime austerity, we had become used to rationing and the use of ration books to share out food and other essentials. Not only that, but policemen's salaries had also slipped in value compared to pre-war days when police were paid about fifty percent above the average manual wage. There was plenty of make do and mend when it came to clothes. We always seemed to have a joint of meat on the table on Sundays, which my mother would roast, however the remnants were minced up on Monday washday for a second meal. The final items to come off rationing were sweets, which were always a special treat. On the day sweet rationing ended, I visited my favourite sweet shops, Young's, and Tuke's, and found all the sweet jars empty and the chocolate gone.

Other childhood diversions involved listening to the wireless, favourite programmes being Dick Barton, Special Agent, and PC 49 with the catch phrase "Oh! My Sunday helmet!" I also enjoyed the comedy programmes, especially Ted Ray in 'Rays a Laugh' and 'Educating Archie'. This was a strange radio programme as it featured Peter Brough a ventriloquist and his dummy. Later came the delights of Dan Dare, Pilot of the Future on Radio Luxembourg. I received a postcard saying, 'Be sure to tune in to Radio Luxembourg 208 metres on Saturday, October 15th, 1955, at 7pm when there will be good news on the air for you in "Penguin Parade." With the help of my father, I managed to win the prize of the day on the children's programme with King Penguin by stumping him with the question 'What is a wash of whelks'. The large box of Penguin biscuits, marshmallows, and other goodies, which arrived in the post from the McDonald Biscuit Bakery, as a reward, was very welcome.

I was a keen reader of the Beano, and Arthur Mee's Children's Newspaper, which were delivered to us each week, and later graduated to the Eagle. I loved the Eagle with its front-page adventures of the spaceman Dan Dare, and the features inside which often explained, with wonderful pictures, technical marvels of the day.

Holidays were often spent visiting my maternal grandparents at Stickney. They lived in a semi-detached council house in Horbling Lane with a very large garden with plenty of room for several chicken houses and runs. Electricity had only recently reached Stickney and cooking was on oil stoves, while the radio ran from an accumulator that was charged weekly at the village store where my Uncle Frank worked. Great fun was had when I was allowed to accompany Uncle Frank as he toured the villages in Short's ancient van delivering groceries and collecting eggs from customers for resale. Grandmother drew hot water from the black range in the kitchen, and on washdays, a fire was laid under a huge brick boiler in the scullery to heat the water. The mangle was a great iron contraption with huge wooden rollers. Another strange matter, (to a townie like me), was the arrangement for the lavatory. This meant a visit down the 'coursey' as Grandpa called it, to an outside loo, which was a large bucket with a wooden seat on top. To add to the wonder toilet paper was squares of News Chronicle threaded onto a piece of string.

Grandpa Pickering loved his pipe and as a pensioner received tobacco money with his old age pension. I loved the smell when he opened his tin of Robin Redbreast tobacco and loved even more the ceremony of lighting his pipe. After tamping down the tobacco in the bowl, he would take a brightly coloured wooden spill from a pot by the fire and light it from the fire in the grate. He would then apply it to his pipe and after several puffs, clouds of smoke would be emitted into the room.

Bath time for me was a novelty. A long, galvanised metal bath hung on a hook in the outside toilet, and when a bath was wanted, this was brought into the living room. It was set on the rag mat in front of the range. Next water was drawn from the tap on the front of the range until there was about six inches of water in the bottom. While this was going on I undressed and when all was ready and at the right temperature I got in for my weekly bath. My sister followed me while I got my pyjamas on ready for bed.

Another ceremony was the filling of the large pot hot water bottles at bedtime. They were filled from the kitchen range and taken up to the feather beds upstairs. The beds were another novelty for me as they were the old type with brass work at the heads and feet. I usually shared a bed with Uncle Frank, while my sister, Susan shared with my mother. I liked Uncle Frank's bedroom especially the clock under a glass dome that worked with chromium-plated balls turning back and forth. In the morning, there was always the crowing of a cockerel to wake me, or the noise made by the pigs kept by the Madison's in their garden next door.

Back at school, I moved up through the years, via Miss Barrett's class to Miss Jackson's class. It was decided that our school should have a uniform during my time there. I was kitted out with a grey blazer with the red Bursar Primary badge on the breast pocket, grey shorts, and grey socks. We all looked very smart.

Another of my pastimes was train spotting and I frequently cycled down to Cleethorpes Station and watched the train movements from a vantage point behind Hawkeye's Café on the Promenade. This was a hobby that I loved, exchanging information about visiting engines with the other spotters. Friendly engine drivers or firemen seemed to like seeing us beside the lines and no one ever chased us away. I eventually bought the correct Ian Allan handbooks of engine numbers with details of all the different types. When I got home, I carefully underlined the numbers of any new engines I'd seen.

Miss Ingham, our music teacher used to give us lessons in the music room. At an early stage, she decided to sort out the singers from the non-singers. We took turns to sing a line from the nursery rhyme 'Hickory, Dickory Dock.' When it came to me, I was very nervous, embarrassed, and apprehensive. Standing up, I opened my mouth, and nothing came out. The last line was a complete blank. I was prompted and croaked out the immortal line 'Hickory Dickory Dock'. This sealed my fate for the rest of my life. I was assessed as a 'growler' and so I have always remained.

We had the benefit of Miss Jackson for two years at Bursar Street. As the deputy head, she was very strict and was a keen devotee of the cane, which she wielded powerfully. She would stare into your eyes delivering her homily on your faults, then say 'put out your left hand'. She would bring her stick down forcefully across your palm leaving it red and smarting. On one occasion, after she saw my lips pouting as I thought a caning very unjust, she delivered a second dose to my right hand and my pouting lips had to be carefully controlled thereafter. For some reason, she thought me lazy and was determined to beat it out of me. I'm not sure whether she succeeded but she certainly did her best with her stick.

Two years of Miss Jackson taught me a great deal about courtesy. She was very strong on this and took anyone to task who failed to extend courtesies where due. We learned that on buses a gentleman always followed a lady up the

A Policeman's Tale

stairs and preceded her when descending. In both cases, this would help the lady should she trip, and the gentleman would cushion her fall. Doors were always held open for ladies and seats given up appropriately. On one occasion, she must have been looking from behind the net curtains in her front window. She lived on Oxford Street which was the route I walked to school on fine days, and she saw a baker's boy lean his cycle against a wall with its load of bread in the front basket. The cycle fell over and the bread spilled out. As a courteous person, I should have picked it all up and sorted it out, but I failed to do this hurrying to school. I received an upbraiding in front of the class later that morning.

Another lesson came when we moved to the new temporary classroom on the north side of Bursar Street. The main school was an Edwardian brick construction dating from the early twentieth century, but for my last year at the school, my class was in a new building. The most startling innovations were the dark green blackboards, used with yellow chalk. Toilets were also provided in the buildings saving a long walk across the playground. The floors however were no longer the polished wood, which we had been used to, but the new-fangled Marley Tiles, a sort of shiny linoleum in light green and beige. Mysteriously black marks began to appear on the tiles and Miss Jackson was keen to track down the culprit. She selected me to stand guard over a lunch hour outside the toilets while everyone was out in the playground and asked me to spot anyone causing black marks when they came in. When she returned, she pointed out several black marks on the toilet door near my position and lots of black marks on the floor. I was dumbfounded; clearly, she had found the culprit. The black rubber stick on soles on my shoes had made the marks! She was clearly not only a wonderful teacher but also a great detective.

I joined the Wolf Cubs on 16th January 1951, becoming a member of the Yellow Pack of the Seventh Cleethorpes Group under the cub master Mr. Taplin and with Miss Boyers as the Arkela. I was taken to Craske & Smiths on Cleethorpes Road at Grimsby and kitted out with my green cap with gold braiding, green jumper, neckerchief and woggle and green sock tabs. I learned the cub law, the cub promise, the salute, and the Grand Howl becoming a 'tender pad'. Next, steps towards my first star were taken, acquiring and demonstrating knowledge of the Union Jack; various activities such as leapfrog and somersaulting, balance, cleanliness, telling the time, nature study, tidiness, the Highway Code, and very importantly tying knots. I'm still awfully glad I can tie reef knots and know how to do a clove hitch as these skills have always come in handy during my life.

An annual event was bob-a-job week, just before Saint George's Day. I got dressed in my uniform then I'd set off round the neighbour's houses enquiring whether I could do work for them to earn funds for the scouts. Most were kind enough to find me a small task or even give me the shilling, sign my card, and not require any work in return (probably glad to be rid of a small boy on their doorstep). However, the gentleman at one house demanded that I dig over his large vegetable plot, which was ridiculously hard work and took an awfully long time. My father told me later that he was a big wheel in scouting and was out to test me. I felt he got his shilling's worth from my efforts, but perhaps it compensated for the people who had been a soft touch in the other direction.

On 23rd June 1952, Bursar Primary School went off to London on an excursion by train setting off just after 6.00am. The train passed through Boston at 7.40am and reached Kings Cross at 10.30am. London Transport red busses were waiting there to take us on a tour of the sights. Highlights were the exceptionally large London buildings, and in the Cromwell Road, the Natural History Museum where I delighted in seeing the massive stuffed elephants, the rocks in the geology department, and especially a skeleton of the extinct dodo bird. The skeleton of a ninety-one-foot-long whale also caught my imagination. At the Tower of London, we saw the Crown Jewels and I was amazed to see how tiny Queen Victoria's crown was, being only the size of the palm of my hand. This was followed by a visit to the zoo where there were live elephants giving rides, and my sister Susan mounted an elephant while I took photographs on my Fullview camera. I was extremely interested in the penguins, black bears, and hundreds of tropical birds.

A few days later, on Sunday 29th June 1952 Lord Rowallan, the Chief Scout, paid a visit to Laceby where the local scouts and cubs held a rally in his honour. Lord Rowallan had a distinguished wartime military career and was Governor of Tasmania from 1959 to 1963. I was impressed that he wore a kilt with his uniform instead of scout shorts but was told he was Scottish, so this was quite normal. We cubs did the Grand Howl for him, and then while his lordship addressed the scouts, we cubs got changed into outfits representing different countries. My pack wore Japanese outfits, and I had a strange hat that I was told was authentically Japanese. We then paraded in the arena in our colourful gear before going on to give a display of how we went about passing the tests to gain our various badges and stars.

My mother encouraged me to do errands for one of our neighbours. I liked this because it enabled me to earn small amounts to augment my pocket money, so on Saturdays I would go around to 36 Lindum Road where Miss Parish lived. Her house was one of two in the road without electricity, which always seemed odd to me as gas lamps were used instead. She would despatch me to the fishmongers for cod's heads to feed the cat and to the butchers for some neck of lamb for herself. I often used to get shopping in for my mother at the same time. I'd cycle up to the butchers in Sea View Street, and then up to the fishmongers near the Market Place to get these things. On one occasion, my mother suggested that the customary reward of sixpence given by Miss Parish should be refused because she could ill afford it out of her pension. I went along with this and thanked her kindly but said no. The next thing I knew was she was round to my house talking to my mother in floods of tears. It appears that it was one of her pleasures in life to give me sixpence, and this weekly happening was re-instated immediately.

During the 1952 school summer holidays my father

introduced me to Mr. Geoff. Pass. He had a business on Cleethorpes Promenade photographing holidaymakers as they walked along. He would photograph them and give them a numbered ticket inviting them to buy their photograph later in the day. I was taken on as a summer help, and my job was to collect completed films from the little kiosk near High Cliff and take them to the processing works just off Knoll Street a short bike ride away. There the films were developed and printed and then it was my job to dry the prints on the glazing machine and sort them out ready for return to the kiosk. I used also to relieve in the kiosk and hand over the finished photographs to claimants in return for their half crowns. I earned some particularly useful pocket money doing this.

One very memorable event of my childhood began on a Friday night. The wind rose and on Saturday a whole gale was blowing offshore. High tide on Saturday evening was at 6.43pm at Cleethorpes. It was a spring tide, the highest in the month, and one of the highest in the year, but that night the tide reached a new level. Throughout the short winter day that was Saturday, 31st January 1953, a wind screamed and blew down the garden fence which divided our garden from the adjoining semi-detached house's garden. During the dark evening, while I was snugly at home, the North Sea battered the Lincolnshire coast causing great havoc, and breaching the defences, mainly sand dunes at Sutton on Sea. In the darkness, forty-two people were drowned in Lincolnshire, and 307 in total, drowned along the East Coast. Many lives were lost at sea and on the continent – 1836 in Holland. A great emergency began, although the severity was not realised immediately due to the state of communications in those days. I went off on the Sunday morning to survey the local damage. The bathing pool fencing had disappeared, and the pool was full of penny slot machines and debris washed down from the arcades on the sands of the north promenade. Many of the sea-front buildings had lost windows and walls and the devastation was considerable. The sea had washed away the ballast under the railway lines near Suggitts Lane and the promenade was scattered with wood and metal wreckage. My father was drafted off to help with the rescue work for several weeks staying at Sutton on Sea in the Bacchus Hotel, until the height of the emergency was over.

King George VI had died in February 1952; on 2nd June 1953, Queen Elizabeth II was crowned at Westminster Abbey. At school, we each set about making a scrapbook of the coronation events, and my father and I decided to order a full set of the Coronation Stamps for all the Commonwealth countries (I think there were about sixty-two countries in the Commonwealth at that time). Cleethorpes was to celebrate the event with a grand firework display and the setting fire to an old ship on the beach that would be a beacon to ships in the Humber. The coronation was a great event, and it was going to be televised. Very few people had their own television sets and throughout the land neighbours gathered around sets when invited by those who owned them. In Lindum Road Mr & Mrs Riach, the parents of my friends Keith and Dorothy Welton invited our family into their front room together with many others to view the progress of the coronation procession and the

A Policeman's Tale

events in the abbey. Unfortunately, the day was very wet, and the planned fireworks and beacon lighting had to be postponed.

There was even more excitement when it was announced that Mount Everest had been finally conquered and that Edmund Hillary had been knighted for his efforts. All the pupils at Bursar Street were presented with a New Testament as a souvenir of the occasion.

Miss Jackson was very keen that as many of her pupils should pass the eleven plus examination as possible. Passing this exam was the passport to the grammar school, which only about a quarter of children managed to achieve. Those not passing went on to the secondary modern school instead. In January, we had an intelligence test to measure intelligence quotient that consisted of what seemed to me puzzles. Then towards the end of the school year came the examination proper. My abiding memory is of the tips that Miss Jackson gave us for the essay, which we would have to write. She said that whatever the subject we should try to use some good words, avoiding adjectives such as 'nice', and 'a lot of'. We learned some first-class adjectives, and then she gave us the killer word to use. She told us to incorporate 'meandering' if possible, in our essay, as this would make an exceptionally good impression on the markers. Now whenever I write anything, my mind still wants me to use 'meandering' if possible.

Miss Jackson's school reports, endorsed by Mr. Rudd, indicate that while I was rather slow, I showed some promise, and my slowness should improve with age and experience. Whether it did or not I leave that for you, dear reader, to judge.

I managed to reach a level in the examination that sent me for an interview by the Headmaster of Humberston Foundation School. This was the local grammar school, known to most people as Clee Grammar. Colonel Thomas was fulfilling his final duties before retirement, after thirty years at the school, and he seemed determined to accept only the best. I told him I had been reading Ivanhoe, and the Black Tulip, which seemed to impress him. In any event, I was accepted as a pupil to begin in September 1953 with sixty other local boys.

In the last year at infants' school, the children in my class had a routine medical check, and in the last year at junior school, we eleven-year-olds were called for another to the local clinic. This time our medicals were much more thorough than the previous one and I found it more embarrassing too. We were offered the choice of having a parent present and I asked my mother to accompany me. This turned out to be a mistake, and the main reason for my embarrassment. I had to wait around for some time without my shirt and vest in just my shorts. Then the nurse called me into the doctor's room. Mother followed me, and she was invited to sit near his desk so she could see what the doctor was doing. The nurse weighed me and measured my height. The doctor sounded my chest, front and back, with his stethoscope. Next, I had to sit so my feet didn't reach the floor and he tapped each knee with a rubber mallet. Strangely, my foot shot forward each time and he seemed pleased my reflexes were in order. Then I had to unfasten my shorts, which slipped down, and the doctor lowered my

A Policeman's Tale

underpants. He examined me carefully with probing fingers and then required me to cough. This mysterious request I complied with, even though I had no trace of a cold. After making me cough for a second time, he seemed satisfied, and I was released to pull up my pants and shorts. I was sent on my way. Getting dressed and still blushing, I asked my mother why the doctor had tapped my knees and why he wanted me to cough. My mother said it was to see if I was developing properly. The meaning of this was a mystery to me for several years afterwards. It must be clear that I'd led a sheltered childhood up to this point.

As a reward for my efforts in passing the 'scholarship', father and mother funded a flight in an Auster single engine plane from the sands at Cleethorpes. The plane flew from the area just south of the bathing pool and operated when the tide was out taking off from the wet sand. My sister came along for the ride, and we had a great view of the pier, the gasworks, and the whole of Cleethorpes and much of Grimsby – a great experience although it was much bumpier than I had expected.

VI Humberstone Foundation School

Matthew Humberstone, Lord of the Manor of Humberstone, founded the new school I was to attend in the reign of Queen Anne. The first school opened in 1823 at Humberstone and this lasted until 'Humberstone's New Foundation' Grammar School was erected at Clee opening on 25th September 1882. Most of the school I knew opened in 1937, with the older buildings still being used. The school site was very large, with plenty of space for tennis courts, three football pitches as well as a cricket field.

Grammar School meant a new uniform and apparently lots of new rules. The letter dated June 1953 received from S.F. Thomas, headmaster, School House, Clee, enclosed several forms. These included an application form, a form of agreement, a dinner and milk form, and a health certificate form. Most had to be returned as soon as possible but the health certificate 'should be brought by the boy on the first morning of term, which begins on Tuesday, September 8th, at 9.30am'.

The letter continued: 'Your boy should be in possession of the following articles of clothing, all of which, with the exception of the boots and shoes, are supplied by the School Outfitters' and there followed details of three local suppliers of school uniforms. The list included, school cap and tie, two football jerseys (one white and the other black-and-white striped), football shorts (black), football boots, gym singlet, gym shoes, towel, light slippers for wear in school (optional), school blazer, grey flannel trousers and white cricket shirt (compulsory). As all boys are required to change either into gym shoes or into light slippers on entering the school each day, these must be brought on the first morning of term.' Other instructions in the letter required the marking of all clothing with the boy's name, and that the boy should be provided with a copy of the Bible (Revised Version) and of Hymns Ancient and Modern.

My father took me to G. Wilson & Sons, the local outfitters. In their Cleethorpes shop, at the top end of Saint Peter's Avenue, in an upstairs room lined with wooden cabinets and several mirrors I tried on my new black cap. Bob Lockwood, an inspector on the local buses, who was a family friend, donated this. I was fitted up with all the other gear and, as still seems to be the way today, room was left for some growing. Despite this, I felt quite grand in the new uniform. The black blazer with black and white piping and a splendid badge on the breast pocket seemed fine. I also imagined I was a player for 'the Mariners', Grimsby Town Football Club, in the striped black and white jersey and black shorts since these were the same strip the club wore. If only I could have played football at that inspiring level!

The new school was exciting but daunting. After leaving my shoes in the cloakroom and putting on a pair of plimsolls, I was directed to the classroom that I'd get to know very well over the coming year. There were now only thirty boys in a form, which seemed very few compared with the fifty or more in primary school. There were two forms in each year and the whole school catered for around four hundred pupils. The masters wore black academic gowns, which I later discovered was a term of their employment. Only the headmaster, Mr. C. Shaw, wore a mortarboard.

Each day, morning assembly for the whole school was impressive. The staff would assemble on the stage; the head would take the lectern, and conduct prayers and hymns followed by announcements. Remembrance services were always very moving as he read the list of fallen Old Humberstonians. We pupils had the benefit of wooden chairs with tip-up seats in groups of three formed into long lines. At the end of the lines a prefect stood ready to pounce on any misbehaviour, which they often did, issuing lines to the guilty ones. The grandest occasions in the school hall were Speech Days when a grandee would be invited to give us the benefit of his wisdom and distribute prizes. The whole school would be expected to learn and sing in Latin 'Gaudeamus Igitur', which the headmaster felt made a good impression on visitors.

Each form had its own prefect, (as well as a form master), who took the register morning and afternoon. The prefects and sixth form didn't wear uniform and seemed

A Policeman's Tale

very adult to we first formers. My form had three members who had failed to progress the previous year and were required to repeat the year. This seemed curious to me, a new concept, but also a warning that results were expected. We had individual desks, which contained all the issued books for each subject. It also kept safe your pens and pencils, gym kit and exercise books.

When I first went to Clee Grammar, we had a six-day week. One afternoon a week was devoted to sport for half the school, while the other half had the afternoon off. To compensate we attended on Saturday mornings. Our sports master was Mr. Roberts who put us through our paces very thoroughly ensuring we were as fit as he could make us and experienced in a range of sporting activities. Regular gym sessions were held in addition to the sports afternoon. Mr. Roberts was reckoned very strict and on one occasion a boy, about to take a shower after a gym session was discovered, contrary to Mr. Roberts' rules, to have been wearing his underpants beneath his gym shorts. He was required to bend over and receive six of the best from a well-aimed gym shoe on his bare bottom. After that, I think no one ever forgot when changing for gym to remove his underwear – free and easy being the order of the day.

On Monday 8th March 1954, my mother was again admitted to hospital. This time it was Springfields, the Grimsby Chest Hospital with another problem associated with her previous tuberculosis. She was to remain there for almost eight months and endured the removal of one of her lungs. Susan and I missed her terribly, and because of the risk of spreading infection, only my father was allowed to visit the hospital. The parents of one of Susan's classmates, (another Susan), Mr and Mrs Jones, cared for Susan while mother was in hospital. Mr. Jones was a schoolmaster and they lived on the corner of Sign Hills Avenue and Oxford Street, a short walk from Lindum Road. Mother returned home on Saturday 30th October 1954 to our general rejoicing.

On 29th March 1954, my father took me to the Palace Theatre on Victoria Street in Grimsby – the great comedians Laurel and Hardy were appearing. I remember they did several very funny sketches very much on the line of the films in which I was more used to seeing them appear. I am not sure but think the trip to the theatre must have been to cheer me up after something which had happened the week before at school in the gym.

While our physical education master, Mr. Roberts could be somewhat severe if you contravened his rules, as outlined earlier, he had another side to his character. One gym session, on Monday, 22nd March 1954, involved groups of us doing different activities in areas of the gymnasium. I used to enjoy wrestling and generally partnered Colin Harker who was about my own build – both of us being sturdy specimens of boyhood. After wrestling, we moved on to rope climbing, which was a great challenge to heavier boys. However, once I worked out that you trapped the rope on top of one foot with the other, I sometimes managed to get up to the ceiling of the gym. Next activity was practicing the 'western roll'. This high jump technique was in vogue in the days of sandpit landing areas before

A Policeman's Tale

bouncy rubber mattresses softened your fall. Doing the 'western roll' involved hurling yourself sideways over the bar and trying to land on two legs and arms. In the gym, this was practised over one of the wooden beams lowered to a suitable height. Unfortunately, my technique must have been defective and as I went over the thick wooden beam, my right arm struck it firmly. On landing, I seemed to have lost the use of this arm and since I could not continue, went over to Mr. Roberts. I told him of the problem and was advised to 'rub it better'. I attempted this, and the lesson ended shortly afterwards.

Into the changing room for showers, I managed to get my gym shoes and shorts off but was struggling with my singlet attempting to poke my numb arm through the opening. Mr. Roberts came over and decided that 'rubbing it better' was not working, but I managed to get my shower and to get dressed. Very soon afterwards, however, following a visit to Doctor Jones, I was at Grimsby General Hospital for an X-ray of the arm, and it turned out that the end of the radius bone in the lower arm was broken at my elbow. Long waits followed but eventually a few days later, I was anaesthetised, and my arm was set in the operating theatre. For several weeks, my arm was strapped up to my chest and I had to manage with the left. This resulted in very squiggly writing in my exercise books. Not long afterwards, Mr. Roberts visited me at home to see how I was getting on. He was very friendly, and I showed him my laboratory (the converted coal-shed) where birthdays and Christmas presents had built up a collection of equipment including a Bunsen burner and quite an impressive array of chemicals from Broadburns the chemists.

Discipline was well maintained although some masters struggled. Detentions were awarded for behaviour too serious for lines, and the next sanction was a headmaster's whacking. I suffered detention only when the whole form was detained after school for a misdemeanour if the actual culprit hadn't been identified. Boys queuing outside Mr. Shaw's office for a whacking were always interesting to the rest of us. It was rumoured that, if he gave you the cane with your shorts and pants off, you only got half of the six-of-the-best, you'd get with them on. I hated the thought of making such a choice and fortunately never had to - I've no doubt that caning deters bad behaviour and is preferable to exclusion and expulsion.

The joys of French, Mathematics, and English Literature and so on were taught by different masters and for some subjects, such as art, geography, history, manual (woodworking), and the sciences we all trooped off to the appropriate room carrying whatever was needed for that lesson. The amount of homework increased substantially over Miss Jackson's demands, and my satchel conveyed great quantities back and forth each day.

I travelled to school sometimes on the number six buses, which passed the school, and sometimes on my cycle, calling for my classmate, Barrie Watts, on the way. I always stayed for school dinners, which I enjoyed. The school had its own kitchen and the staff prepared very good meals. There were two sittings for lunch, and we dined at long tables seated on benches.

We were continually marked on our homework and

examined with regular sets of results being published. At the end of the first year the top thirty of the sixty in the year group were moved up to form 2L which meant they learnt Latin, while the remainder, which included me went on to form 2G which meant no Latin. I continued to progress through the school usually ending the year in the top three of the class and gaining a prize on Speech Day.

I made some good friends at school and spent much of my time with Michael Benson, Colin Harker, Barrie Watts, Philip Cook, Barry Flodman, and Terry Crossley. My friends Benson and Harker (for that is how we normally addressed each other) were just as keen radio listeners as I was. Our main topic of conversation was often the Goon Show, and we could often be heard imitating the characters Bluebottle and Eccles in the playground. Of course, we never ran in the playground being allowed only to walk.

Television made little impact on us until the advent of the programme 'Six Five Special' when rock and roll was introduced into the country. I was privileged to visit Michael Benson's home in Cromwell Road (not far from Lindum Road), to see this programme. We did not have a television at home, and it was always great fun seeing these black and white programmes.

Michael introduced me to classical music. He had several twelve-inch seventy-eight revolutions per minute records, and we loved to hear Tchaikovsky's 1812 Overture with its martial music and canon shots. Eventually we moved onto the Bruch violin concerto and much more besides. His father owned a reel-to-reel Grundig tape recorder that he allowed us to use, and this provided us with hours of entertainment. Saturday evenings after tea were devoted to viewing.

Other excitements and pastimes for a teenager were membership of the school scientific society and the astronomical society founded by my friend Barrie Watts. One weekend we set off on a trip to the observatory at Hull University. We took a train to New Holland pier where the train stopped on the long jetty jutting out over the estuary of the Humber, then onto the paddle steamer ferry across to the King George Dock in Hull. The observatory, since it was a daytime trip, seemed almost less interesting than the journey.

Occasional trips to the big city of Hull with the family were treats and since the Humber had yet to be bridged this always meant a trip on the wonderful flat-bottomed paddle steamers. We also had family holidays, often visiting my grandparents at Stickney or going to Colchester to see Grandmother McNeill and Uncle Raymond, Aunt Dorothy and my cousins Heather and Neill.

During my teenage years, I also continued my hobby of train spotting spending many hours at the back of Hawkeys Café on Cleethorpes Promenade near the locomotive turntable recording details of all the engines that visited the town. Weekends brought in large numbers of trip trains from the midlands. British Railways pressed into service locomotives normally employed on freight duties to cope with the huge demand. Vast crowds of holidaymakers were brought to the seaside in this way and the smoke hanging over the area of the station was always something that detracted from the supposed joys of seaside fresh air.

A Policeman's Tale

I was also the holder of a season ticket for Cleethorpes Swimming Pool. This vast pool, which Cleethorpes Borough Council listed in the annual Cleethorpes brochure as the 'largest swimming pool in the country', was oval shaped, and over one hundred yards long. It was a great attraction to the young people of the town as well as the holidaymakers. Cycling to the pool, I used to chain the machine to the railings, and go through the turnstiles clutching my trunks wrapped in a towel. The pool was quite elderly, and the changing rooms were not very pleasant with cold concrete floors. To change you entered a green painted cubicle with a short door in the middle. A very heavy wooden duckboard kept your feet off the concrete. When changed you took your clothes to the attendant who exchanged them for a numbered rubber band.

The water rarely got above seventy degrees and was usually in the fifties or low sixties. I remember Mr. Roberts, our physical education master, taking the form to the pool soon after it opened at Whitsun, and seeing '49°F' chalked on the notice board. Getting into the water required nerves of steel, and I well remember my friend Michael Benson shivering on the concrete edge turning blue as he contemplated the prospect of the cold water. Still, I suppose these things were good for us, and in those days, lots of cold showers were thought to shape the British character. In my final year at Clee Grammar, an indoor swimming pool was built but it was unfortunately opened too late for me to indulge in such luxury.

While a teenager, I carried on with summertime work, but this time for the chemist, Mr. Saunby, who had a laboratory in Cambridge Street. I used to cycle to his shop in Dolphin Street, collect films handed in for developing and printing, and take them back to the laboratory. There I would open the films in complete darkness and hang them in a long developing tank. The next stage was to wash the films and then fix the image in another tank. Drying the films in tall dryers through which warm air was blown followed this stage. When the films were ready for printing it was my job to produce enprints using an enlarger to expose the sensitive paper, develop the prints, wash them, fix them, and then dry them. This occupied many happy hours in the dim yellow light that was all that was allowed. My father used to look in on me occasionally to check my progress. When the prints were ready and sorted into little blue wallets with the cut-up negatives I'd return them to the chemist's shop.

I mentioned earlier that some of the masters had trouble keeping forms in order and there were a few incidents, which caused the headmaster a great deal of stress. Mr. Lawley, who taught what we called Scripture, but which would now be called Religious Studies, had a great problem maintaining order through all the years he taught my form. I remember him fighting one pupil and both of them falling into the stationery cupboard as they brawled. He earned an unfortunate nickname because when he was addressing us, particularly when angry, as was often the case, he ejected little bits of saliva from his mouth. He often had confrontations with the unrulier form members who deliberately set out to goad him. This always seemed very odd to me as his subject, which often meant we were

A Policeman's Tale

reading sections of the bible, seemed to be about improving people's attitudes. I used to find my form mates behaviour generally annoying but there was at least one amusing incident when a couple of pupils climbed through the hatch into the roof space above our form room before Mr. Lawley's lesson began. We had four lamps in the room, which hung from the ceiling on flex that was normally about six feet long. The miscreants in the roof began hauling up the flexes so that, to us beneath, the lamps seemed to be magically rising and falling. Mr. Lawley didn't notice immediately although everyone else did. When he did see what was happening his angry outburst was very alarming, but I'm not sure he ever discovered who was responsible. If he had there would have been more candidates for a visit to the headmaster's study for a whacking.

We arrived at school on the first day of April one year to discover that the headmasters study roof bore a rude legend addressed to 'Fatso', not only that but in the quadrangle in front of the head's study the flagpole had at its top a chamber pot. Somewhat embarrassingly for me the police officer called in to investigate these cases of wilful damage was my father, and he interviewed several of my form mates.

Many tales might be told, and mostly they are about incidents, which have stuck in my mind for fifty years. There was the time in woodwork when 'Gassy' Brewster injured himself and fainted. Not long afterwards, I managed to stick a chisel in my finger (I still have the scar) and buckled to my knees as my thick red blood welled out. When I was cycling home in the rain one day with my head down, not keeping a proper look out, I ran into the back of a parked car on Clee Road. That left another scar on my shin, which is still there. Other happenings didn't leave scars but stick in the memory. Some boys specialised in playground nastiness. A favourite was the knee in the thigh called a dead leg, and the other was the Chinese ear rub - very painful too. One form mate (who had better not be named) would creep up behind someone and give him an unpleasant surprise. My turn came waiting for lessons to resume after lunch in our form room. He came up behind me, and threw his arms round me. My arms were pinned to my sides. He grabbed the front of my short trousers, shouting 'I've got 'em', to the rest of the form. I knew exactly what he had got, and hoped the other lads didn't, but he clung on tenaciously as I whirled round trying to shake him off. Eventually a powerful elbow in the ribs made him let go. I was left to try to regain some dignity and get over the painful experience as the first lesson of the afternoon began.

The same boy was embarrassed himself not long afterwards. We were all changing for gym when the usual level of noise changed, and all eyes were directed to this individual. He had taken off his trousers. Those close to him had noticed that instead of the usual pink, his legs were a strange dark brown shade. Mr. Roberts saw the phenomenon too and, as we all turned to look, he enquired the cause. It turned out the youth had been gathering walnuts from a tree in his village and he'd put them in his pockets. Walnuts in their green cases give off a juice that stains a very dark brown. He was brown all the way down from waist to ankles and after our gym session in the showers despite vigorous soaping this didn't change. However, by the next gym session when we all looked curiously to see if he was still brown, we were disappointed to find the stains had almost faded away.

Policemen's income remained relatively low until the £1000 a year policeman in the early 1960s, when a recruiting crisis led to the government increasing police wages to £20 a week. My father, as a sergeant earned a fair amount, but with two children and a wife to maintain, money was always tight. My mother had been almost ecstatic when she was able to buy a Hoover vacuum cleaner, and when we got an electric washing machine in 1956 this was a huge advance on the dolly tub, washboard and dolly peg used for years. Often, I was pleased to receive hand-me-down clothes to wear. Uncle Frank provided some of my underwear, while Uncle John Hood passed on swimming trunks and khaki summer shorts. I was one of the last in my form to go into long trousers. This was in the third year when I was fourteen and my father used to tell me long trousers would hurt my knees. Of course, they never did. My school blazer, which fitted well at eleven years of age, got very tight. In 1957, I was 5'9¾" tall and weighed 10 stone 7 pounds. My mother decided to put my blazer badge on the jacket my father had been married in. Fortunately, this was black, and it was not very noticeable that I had no braid around the edges like the others in my form.

The years in the fourth and fifth forms were devoted to studying for the General Certificate of Education at Ordinary Level. Towards the end of our third year, we were asked to choose the subjects, we wished to take. Some subjects were compulsory, but there was a choice between arts and science subjects. We heard talks from the masters heading the various departments giving us ideas about our choices. I remember the biology master, Mr. Proctor, tempting us boys to take his subject with the promise of studying human sexual development – something that, to some of us at least, was quite a mystery - I was still leading a sheltered life. In any event I chose to study chemistry, physics, and biology, giving up art, manual (wood and metal work), history and geography. However, after completing my fourth-year studies it was decided that everyone should do history and geography once more. The history master revolted and said it was impossible to cram two years study in the remaining year, but Mr. 'Pud' Parr, the very well-built geography master, rose to the challenge. Of the eight subjects I took in the examinations, I managed to fail only the English Literature papers, achieving decent results in the other subjects. I always wondered whether failing English Literature reflected the day early in my period at Clee Grammar when Mr. Hartley, (known as Jammy), the English master had advised me that my essays should concentrate on subjects such as 'How I mend a bicycle tyre puncture' rather than something requiring more imagination. I was very pleased that I did fairly well in French and the sciences.

My days at Humberstone Foundation School ended in July 1958. I was sorry about this as it meant losing contact with a number of friends and the start of a new life working for the Lincolnshire Constabulary. Early in 1958 my parents began talking about what career I would follow on leaving

A Policeman's Tale

school. My own ideas were not very ambitious. From an early age I'd wanted to drive a steam engine and later I was keen to work a telephone switchboard. My friend Michael Benson was going to join the BBC as an engineer, but I had no real ideas. When my father told me that if I joined the police, I could retire at the age of forty-nine with a fat pension, as he described it - that seemed a promising idea to me.

The first step was to choose a police force. If I joined the Grimsby Borough Police as a cadet I could live at home, so I wrote a letter to them. A classmate, Michael Hardisty, had done the same thing. The next thing that happened was that two police officers from Grimsby visited school during a PE lesson and were seen watching our efforts and talking to Mr. Roberts. 'Dusty' Hardisty was an exceptionally good footballer and his athletic prowess in the gymnasium outshone my efforts considerably and shortly afterwards he was successfully interviewed for a place in the Grimsby Borough Police Cadet force. Meanwhile I received word that I should look elsewhere. This was the first time I became aware that this particular police force had a proud reputation in police footballing circles and was generally the winner of all the police footballing championship matches. It still seems a little odd to me that police recruiting depended more on your footballing ability than academic success, but perhaps they had got it right because the Grimsby Force had some fine officers and a high reputation.

VII Police Cadet

So, I applied to join the Lincolnshire Constabulary as a cadet. I wrote a short letter asking for an application form and the next step was a short check of my educational abilities through an entrance examination at Cleethorpes Police Station, which was administered by Sergeant Wiseman. This was a simple test of spelling and arithmetic, which I found straightforward.

I received a letter signed by Chief Superintendent Philip Knights (who later became the Chief Constable of Birmingham as Sir Philip, and on retirement Lord Knights), inviting me for a selection board on 30th May 1958. I was warned the medical and X-ray examinations and interviews allotted would occupy the greater part of the day.

The day came, and I went to the police headquarters on Church Lane at Lincoln. The headquarters was in a large house, dating from around 1920, with panelled interior and a grand staircase leading up to the Chief Constable's office.

A Policeman's Tale

With other sixteen-year-old prospective cadets I waited in a corridor leading to the 'schoolroom', which must have been at one time a rather splendid library with views over the extensive gardens, tennis courts and towards Lincoln Cathedral.

A sergeant was in charge and ushered us into the schoolroom in small groups. Large trestle tables were set up and one of the tables was on top of another one. Its side formed a screen behind which we could see just the legs of candidates being examined by the doctor. We were told to undress down to the waist and take off our shoes, and then weighed on a set of scales. Next came the all-important height check as each applicant was measured. A minimum of five feet, eight inches applied, and while this was no problem for me with a couple of inches to spare, it was something of a challenge for several others. One or two were told to return when they had grown some more. Next, we were provided with a screw-capped bottle, told to visit the small room next door and provide a sample. On returning, the sample was checked using some little rubber black and white balls, which floated at the correct levels if you were free of diabetic problems. Reading the letters on a card on the wall was my next test and I was pleased that I could read all but the bottom line with each eye.

After this test, it was time to queue up near the screened area. On being called forward the police doctor used his stethoscope to sound my chest. He checked my blood pressure and peered into my eyes with his little torch. He told me to drop my trousers. As I unfastened the buttons, memories of my embarrassment as an eleven-year-old came flooding back. This time, fortunately, my dear mother was not there to witness him slipping down my underpants, his probing fingers checking for problems, and asking me to cough twice. Fortunately, he seemed to find everything in order, and I was able to retrieve my pants and regain the privacy of my clothes.

Next, we potential recruits were taken to a clinic in Mint Lane in Lincoln for X-ray examination of our chests. Since my mother had suffered with TB, I had regularly been X-rayed in Grimsby as a precaution, and I was very familiar with the process. The worst part was always the shock of pressing your bare chest on the cold screen while the photograph of your lungs was taken.

Having got through all the medical checks it was time for interview and we waited upstairs in the wide wood-panelled corridor outside the Chief Constable's office. The Chief Constable was Mr. John Barnet, and I must have given satisfactory replies because a few weeks later I received an offer of employment as a police cadet with an enquiry as to my starting date.

My father wanted me to start immediately after leaving school, but I thought I should have a two-week break before beginning work. Consequently, I started work on Monday, 11th August 1958. Fortunately, I was given a lift to Lincoln from Cleethorpes in the Land Rover, which travelled regularly from Cleethorpes police station to Headquarters.

My first introduction was to Sergeant Tony Taylor and Miss Fairchild who was a civilian clerk. They formed the administrative department, and I was to be their office boy. I had a desk and an ancient pre-war black Imperial

A Policeman's Tale

typewriter. There was a telephone in the office connected through a switchboard downstairs to the outside world and the rest of the police force. In addition, an internal intercom connected the offices of headquarters, and this was a wonderful affair with a row of keys to depress for each office. It allowed you to talk to several people at once if desired.

One of my duties, shared with the cadet in the Accounts Department, was to visit all the headquarters offices collecting and distributing mail and papers. This soon gave me a good idea of everyone working there and regular entry to everyone's office from the chief constable downwards. Learning to make myself useful, Chief Superintendent Philip Knights (later The Lord Knights, CBE, QPM, DL) congratulated me when I changed the blotting paper on his hand blotter. He said a cadet had never previously done this for him, so I chalked this up as a good mark.

Robin Leak was the Accounts Department cadet and he had joined six months before me, so he was able to show me the ropes. One duty was in the mailroom where we sorted the copious quantities of files, and mail for other parts of the police force as well as mail destined for the post office, Lincoln City Police, and the county council. There were pigeonholes with labels. The labels bore the names of the superintendents in charge of each of the ten divisions and since the mail was addressed usually not to them by name, I needed to learn who was in charge of each division.

A good fun part of the job was using the franking machine. This had to be filled with sticky red ink and metal levers set for the right amount of postage. Then the package was put on a platform, pushed towards the 'works' while turning a handle with your other hand. Regular readings of the meters on the machine were needed and details had to be put in the register. When the machine had nearly run out of credit one of the accounts clerks had to take it to the sorting office to be filled up.

Each evening either Robin or I set out with a large bundle of mail for the post office, then down the hill to the County Offices with more mail, followed by a cycle ride across the city to the Sessions House which was the Headquarters of the City Police. After that, I used to push my cycle up Lindum Hill, perspiring freely, glad that my hat had little holes to let out the steam, on my way back to my lodgings.

While I was in the Administrative Department, a regular Friday duty was to accompany Sergeant Taylor to the National Provincial Bank in Castle Square. This was after Miss Fairchild, and I had carefully calculated how much in change we would need for each of the staff pay packets. At the old half-timbered bank, we would draw around eighty pounds in notes and change, which would be carefully put into an old leather Gladstone bag for the journey back along the Bail to Church Lane. In the office, we would count out pay for the staff including, my own which amounted to about three pounds and ten shillings and put it into little brown pay packets with a green printed payslip.

When first arriving in Lincoln I was allocated lodgings at 18 Good Lane, not far from Headquarters, and a short walk down Newport. I found the front door of the terraced house in the side passage and knocked. Miss Ayto, my

A Policeman's Tale

landlady, conducted me up the stairs into the front room that contained a brass bedstead, rather like my Grandmother Pickering's, a washstand, a rush mat, and startlingly to my eye a large chamber pot. This was the first indication that there was not a handy bathroom, which I'd been used to most of my life. In fact, the lavatory was outside the back door and my morning wash was at the kitchen sink. I washed shirtless, while Miss Ayto fried the bacon for breakfast! It meant that I was always in danger of being splashed with hot fat but also that I only got a proper wash at weekends when I went home to Cleethorpes. This was really a matter of Hobson's choice. My wages were three pounds and ten shillings. Lodgings cost two pounds ten shillings or three pounds ten shillings if I stayed the weekend. The train home to Cleethorpes cost sixteen shillings or the Lincolnshire Roadcar bus a little less.

This left just enough money to pay for the regular haircuts, which were mandatory and a few other necessities. I chose to travel home each week, sometimes by bus and sometimes by train. The train was relatively swift, but the bus visited all the villages in the Wolds taking over two hours to travel the thirty-five miles to Cleethorpes. Returning to Lincoln on Mondays meant an early start to be in the office for 9am. I caught the 7.15am Birmingham train from Cleethorpes Station. The carriages were pulled by a steam engine, which reached Saint Marks station around 8.20 am. Then I had a quick walk to Saint Mary's Street where waiting corporation buses conveyed me up the High Street, through the Stonebow, along Silver Street, up Lindum Hill, passed the cathedral and then into Church

Lane. I used to arrive almost exactly at 9am.

Sometimes the journey home would be by train, and, even though this was more expensive, the speed was very welcome. For some reason going home was always on a diesel multiple unit train in its dark green livery. I always enjoyed sitting immediately behind the driver, watching his actions, observing that he correctly responded to all the semaphore signals. Nowadays I'd be called an anorak or geek, but these terms had not been invented in 1958.

After some time in Good Lane another cadet, Malcolm Baxter, who was working in the clothing department, visited me. Malcolm had the enviable ability to remember the collar number of every member of the uniformed staff of the force. This was because of his duties in Laundry House in Church Lane where great quantities of uniforms were stored for issue to force members. After his visit to my digs, we compared notes on our lodgings. I complained that the food often had dog hairs in it and that I could never get a proper wash. He told me I had a very rough deal compared with him. The clothing department was housed in the same building as the training department. They were the ones who allocated lodgings and Malcolm undertook to help me find somewhere better to live.

Eventually it turned out that my Aunt Lil had a friend in Rasen Lane, who in turn had a friend who was kindly disposed to taking in a sixteen-year-old lad and looking after him. So, I moved to 76 Rasen Lane, the home of Mrs Ashworth, and her husband Edgar. Mrs. Ashworth had been the matron of the old workhouse in Burton Road. Her bed making skills were wonderful and I was now treated to

A Policeman's Tale

a wonderful double feather bed with every corner beautifully tucked in. Even better, there was a proper bathroom, and I could even take a shower or bath. The garden was huge, and Edgar was a keen gardener. My mother had tried to pass her green thumb on to me and I was always keen to help in the garden.

I spent over a year at the Rasen Lane lodgings and was very well looked after. Often, I visited the friends of the Ashworths who lived across the road at the corner of Cecil Street, and we'd watch television together.

After six months, I moved departments, as it was policy to give experience in various aspects of the force, starting work in the Enquiry Office, which doubled as the Firearms and Aliens Department.

Apart from dealing with infrequent callers at the office counter, my main work was with the firearm and shotgun licensing system. Mr. Strong, a civilian, who sported a green eyeshade, was in charge. The main feature of the work was the need for accuracy with meticulous recording of details. All the records were handwritten and every effort to use a beautiful clear style was encouraged. We used black ink and old-fashioned pens, which had to be regularly dipped in inkwells. The details of restrictions on the holding of firearms were carefully copied into each certificate before it was sent out, and sometimes this was my task.

The complexity of firearms legislation made the work difficult, but I learnt a lot with Mr. Strong. There was sufficient work for two cadets in the office, and the other cadet was known by the nickname 'Nimrod' Johnson. He was one of the unfortunate cadets who did not make it as a career leaving to become an outfitter with Hepworths. Nevertheless, 'Nimrod' was always great fun to be with.

On one occasion, a caller at the Enquiry Office presented a large cardboard box, which he put on the counter. Looking inside I saw a handsome large, brown-feathered chicken, which looked at me with a glint in its eye. The caller said he had found the chicken in Church Lane and had brought it in as found property. Now the police have always had plenty to do with lost and found property and there are extensive procedures. I set about filling in the details of the chicken, where and when it was found and the details of the finder in the appropriate register in triplicate. When I'd finished, 'Nimrod' recommended I consulted Mr. Strong about the next step, since we could not really keep the chicken in the found property cupboard. Mr. Strong took one look at the chicken and exploded.

The rules were quite clear he exclaimed. The only livestock the police accept was dogs, not cats, budgerigars, rabbits, chickens, or anything else – just dogs. I was instructed to take the cardboard box into Church Lane and find somewhere to deposit the fine-feathered fowl. I suppose this was another lesson learned. I never found out what happened to the entry in the register. Over my police career, the word 'Escaped' often appeared in registers when livestock had been mistakenly accepted or a found dog had proved too troublesome to keep.

We were given regular schooling in police law and had to study in our spare time. We also had to write a diary of our daily doings and present this for checking at regular intervals. Each month we had a training day, usually under

A Policeman's Tale

the guidance of Sergeant Stanley Reames. He was a kindly man to we youngsters. One of his favourite expressions when guiding us through our law studies was to tell a tale about Joe Soap, the name he gave to whichever lawbreaker he was using to illustrate the lecture he was giving, and we always looked forward to hearing the details of the mythical Joe Soap's criminal activities or motoring sins.

The usual pattern of training days was for us to be paraded in front of headquarters in the yard while the Chief Constable inspected us. Sometimes we were sent for a brisk run around Church Lane and Eastgate, after which Mr. Barnett would question us on current affairs in the world. He told us we should read either The Times or The Daily Telegraph and not some inferior newspaper. We would have a law lecture sometimes by Inspector Charles Everitt who was in charge of the Training Department and in the afternoon might be drilled to improve our marching skills. Inspector Everitt had a wooden leg following a wartime injury and he was a hard taskmaster. Sometimes he would give us the law lecture and quite often, he would walk up and down our lines as we stood on parade minutely inspecting our uniforms for blemishes, checking the sharpness of the creases in our trousers, and the degree of shine on our shoes. We wore navy blue battledress blouses when I first joined, and these were always difficult to keep smart. He not only checked our appearance but also was keen to see that we stood to attention correctly and were a credit to our uniform.

We were required to sign up for evening classes in typing and shorthand. These were held at Lincoln Technical

College on College Street at the bottom of Lindum Hill. Shorthand proved very difficult for me, probably because I had little need (or inclination) to practice it, and very little remains with me beyond the first couple of lessons even though I persevered for several months. However, typing was different. My father had encouraged me to type on his machine at home and of course, I had a machine on my office desk. I enjoyed typing classes. Most of the students were young women and, since most of my fellow cadets dropped out fairly soon after starting, I was left as the only male in the class.

My touch-typing skills improved gradually, and I enjoyed the sessions when we were required to type in time to Victor Sylvester strict tempo waltzes. Eventually I passed my first typing examinations and even received a book prize for my efforts. A moment came when I typed a request asking the Chief Constable for permission to accept this gift, which he graciously granted. A prize-giving evening at the Technical College followed on 9th March 1960, when the London Editor of the Encyclopaedia Britannica made an entertaining and witty speech. Even better, there was a buffet supper to enjoy after I had received my ten-shilling prize voucher to buy the book of my choice. I chose one called Letter Writer which has proved very useful.

During my cadetship, I gained a certificate in First Aid and attended a two-week course for cadets held at the West Riding of Yorkshire Police Headquarters in Wakefield from 6th to 18th July 1959. After the opening address by the chief constable, Captain Sir Henry Study, C.B.E., the course concentrated on improving drilling skills, and knowledge of

A Policeman's Tale

police law with much reference to the policeman's bible Moriarty's Police Law. There were also daily sessions at the Sun Lane Baths in Wakefield. These were very old Victorian swimming baths where we cadets were put through our paces learning the rudiments of lifesaving practicing towing each other up and down. I managed to gain the Royal Life Saving Society Intermediate Certificate for practical knowledge of rescue, releasing oneself from the clutch of the drowning and for ability to render aid in resuscitating the apparently drowned. Together with daily physical training and self-defence sessions, there was sufficient activity to ensure I returned much fitter than when I had started.

I moved around departments at Headquarters and eventually reached my goal of a place in the Information Room. This was where the senior cadets worked under the guidance of a sergeant, two constables, and several civilian clerks. The Information Room was the place where 999 calls were received and where radio cars were despatched to incidents. The walls were lined with huge magnetic maps of the whole county and the radio desk occupied the bay window area overlooking the gardens and cathedral. The headquarters switchboard was in a separate room and during daytime, this was usually worked by one of the civilian clerks. However, we cadets learned to operate not only the switchboard but also the radio. Perhaps my youthful ambitions were already being fulfilled.

It was shift work, usually 8am to 3pm or 2pm to 10pm. The cadets were expected to go through the Police Gazette and The West Riding of Yorkshire Police Reports carefully noting details of all the wanted criminals. Each name was checked against our records to discover whether the individual had been checked in the county. An index strip was placed on display boards, known as Stripdex panels. Our job was to keep these up to date and remove strips when criminals were caught. Another cadet or one of the civilian clerks, Miss Jean Mawer, Miss Jean Bentley or Miss Phyllis Langley, checked our work to ensure accuracy and woe betide us if we missed an entry or made an error. We also indexed stolen vehicles by their registration number and checked to see if they had been seen in the county.

I enjoyed using the radio to call the patrol cars. It was often my job to do the half hourly location check noting down where each car was and which way it was heading. In bad weather, we took details of conditions, such as visibility in fog, or depth of snow. We also operated little lights showing whether cars were engaged on an incident or taking refreshments. Remembering which call signs represented the cars in different parts of the county was quite an undertaking. The police wavelength was also shared with Lincoln City Police, and with the three county fire brigades for Lindsey, Kesteven, and Holland. It was interesting hearing the fire crews report in from fire scenes. Often their requests were, 'Make pumps three' when they needed more assistance putting out a major fire.

We cadets were sent regularly to watch the proceedings at the Lindsey or Kesteven magistrates' courts held in the old prison building in Lincoln Castle. These were always interesting occasions beginning with the usual applications for extensions to drinking hours, speeding offences, and

A Policeman's Tale

then moving on to defended cases. These were often cases of driving without due care and attention, or not having a driving licence, and were good learning experiences for a prospective police officer.

Towards the end of October 1959 Mrs. Ashwell decided that because of her continuing ill health, she could no longer accommodate me, and I had to set about finding new lodgings. I spent a morning checking out various addresses but finally settled on an address in Cecil Street quite close to Headquarters. My new landlady was Mrs. Kilner and I moved in on Monday 27th October 1959.

The work in the information room continued to be interesting – it was much more like real police work rather that the office work of other departments. For instance, on Friday 13th November 1959 a prisoner escaped from Lincoln Prison. I was working from 2pm to 10pm but my shift that evening went on until the early hours of the next morning. We put into operation our Scheme A and later Scheme C. These were planned checks at predetermined points, mostly on the county boundary and necessitated lots of radio messages and phone calls to get officers into position with full details of the escaped prisoner. Mr. Barnet, our chief constable appeared with Mr Felix Sayer, the City Police chief constable, to oversee the operations. The prisoner, who was called McCandless, had been tracked to a road near the prison by the police dogs where they had lost the scent. It was thought a car might have picked him up. I was needed to operate the telephone switchboard until nearly 1am at which time I was allowed, somewhat tired, off duty.

Diversions from the usual course of events were provided by the need to visit the shopping area in Bailgate for a supply of three pounds of tea to keep us all refreshed, or to Bigger's Shop to buy some new beakers for the staff.

There were various social events to lighten our days including whist drives in the schoolroom, and a highlight was the headquarters dinner and dance held at the Eastgate Hotel (later to be called The Lincoln). One of the guests was the Chief Constable of Birmingham, Philip Knights, who remembered me from the days when I had changed his blotting paper when he had been our chief clerk.

My duties in the Information Room ended on Sunday, 15th May 1960, and the next day the van from Scunthorpe Divisional Headquarters arrived to take me to my new posting. Picking up my luggage from my digs, we set off for Scunthorpe where I was shown round the police station, then on to 35 Rowland Road where I met Beattie and Gordon Panton who were to provide a home for me.

My work was in the Borough Office. This is the front office of the police station. Visitors and enquirers are received, and details of incidents are reported. I found much of the work similar to that in the Headquarters Enquiry Office, but there were some additional features in a working police station. Often callers produced their driving licence or insurance certificate and if they were correct, I recorded the details. One example was a caller telling me her pet tortoise had been crushed by a builder's lorry and was in pain. She had failed to contact the Royal Society for the Prevention of Cruelty to Animals and wondered if the police could help her with her tortoise. I

A Policeman's Tale

advised her to contact a veterinary surgeon. Another call reported a fight in a local hotel between two women. Three policemen were sent to sort this out and they reported that the women had been fighting over a man. When I noted this in my journal the inspector commented 'lucky chap'. One morning a man called at the office window and asked to speak to an educated policeman. He would not say any more than this and eventually he departed saying that he would go to see the sergeant at Kirton in Lindsey.

I soon got involved in training police dogs. A volunteer set off to walk over a pre-arranged route across fields. Usually, you dropped a few items along the way to encourage the dog. Then you hid and waited for the dogs to follow your scent and find you. Sometimes I laid several tracks, especially if the young dog Sentinel was being trained.

Tuesday 22nd May 1960 was a red-letter day for me. I took a day's annual leave to go home to Cleethorpes for a second shot at the driving test. I managed to pass the test for Group A vehicles and was given a pink slip showing my competence to drive. The first test had been a miserable failure, not helped when the examiner while travelling along the busy shopping thoroughfare in Grimsby, Freeman Street, shouted for me to make an emergency stop. I looked in the mirror and slammed on the brakes of the elderly Austin Big 7, and the examiner grabbed the chain running along the top of his passenger door. Unfortunately, this chain operated the door catch. The door, (which was hinged at the rear), began to swing open and my examiner was nearly lost!

The Scunthorpe Divisional Cricket team must have been desperate one day in June 1960 to select me. Nevertheless, I found myself travelling with the traffic sergeant, Sergeant Tyreman to Goole. We batted first and I managed to get one run not out. We were all out for forty-eight. The best part was the after-match tea.

My stay with landlady Beattie and her husband Gordon was enjoyable. Beattie was learning to drive and now I had my driving licence I was qualified to accompany her and give her driving lessons. We had some good trips in her old Austin Ten. Usually, I drove to an old airfield and then let her take over. On one trip while I was driving the oil feed to the oil pressure gauge behind the dashboard came loose. From the end of this copper pipe came hot black oil spurting all over my light stone-coloured trousers. It was very disconcerting and very uncomfortable to say the least, and Beattie was most concerned. When we eventually got back to Scunthorpe, she tried very hard wash the oil out of my stained trousers. They never quite recovered, but fortunately, I suffered no permanent damage.

In July 1960, I received a new uniform tunic in place of the battledress blouse I'd been wearing since starting as a cadet. This made me look much more like a policeman and I felt very smart.

Not long after this, my father offered to sell me his Austin Big Seven. The car was somewhat elderly even then having first hit the road in 1938. He had bought it for forty pounds and generously offered it to me at the same price. I accepted and became the proud owner of my first car. I polished the black paintwork assiduously and even ensured

A Policeman's Tale

the engine block was painted a beautiful shade of apple green. I had to keep the back seat inflated by blowing up the tube inside the cushion. When winter came, it was necessary to turn on the tap under the bonnet, which fed water through a pipe that heated a small area around the driver and passenger's knees.

My time was spent in the Borough Office, in the Administrative Office, relieving on the switchboard, as well as attending Assizes, Quarter Sessions, Magistrates' Courts, Inquests, and training days. Often, I was privileged to act as observer in one of the patrol cars and I always enjoyed this. Sometimes I'd go out to help with a country village fete or some other event where manpower was needed, and I continued helping with police dog training.

For a week, 10th to 17th September 1960 the force sent me off to the Training Ship Foudroyant moored in the harbour at Gosport. This ship had been captured from the French in the Napoleonic wars and now was used to train young people in basic seamanship as well as giving leadership training. The joining instructions indicated that 'all activities will be competitive', an indication that I was to be tested for qualities of leadership and character with an overall assessment being made at the conclusion. It was advised that participants were likely to need 'Sealegs', a brand of seasickness tablets – so I had been warned. I soon learned how to sling my hammock from the hooks in the beams supporting the deck above. The actual process of getting in the hammock was harder to master, and when you were roused in the early dawn, by the shout "Show a leg", it was even more difficult to get out feeling like a banana.

Moored alongside the Foudroyant were three gigs, two sailing lifeboats, a petrol driven launch and a large diesel launch.

Rising at 6.15am, we rowed a gig to the Dolphin Pontoon on shore to collect the morning milk and other supplies. This was followed by a good wash after the strenuous rowing, and then we breakfasted before beginning the day's round preparing for a three-day sail around the Isle of Wight. I remember swimming in the harbour and doing exciting sailing practice beneath the gunwales of a vast aircraft carrier in Portsmouth Harbour. We learned to take depth soundings, do chart work, including taking bearings, use a sextant, and work out the meaning of buoys. We did a practical 'man-overboard' exercise, and then there was a practice expedition in the diesel launch "Scott-Paine" to Yarmouth on the Isle of Wight. A highlight on the Sunday morning was a conducted tour of Her Majesty's Submarine "Truncheon", followed by Divine Service at the naval shore base, H.M.S. Dolphin. Eventually we set off on our epic voyage passing the Nab Tower and other nautical landmarks heading for Cowes and then to Yarmouth where we spent the first night in harbour. The weather gradually deteriorated, and it was mainly poor throughout each day. Our sailed whaler was accompanied by the launch "Scott-Paine" where we did the catering and much of the navigation. The second day took us round the Isle of Wight by the Needles, and Saint Catherine's Point Lighthouse, reaching Bembridge harbour on the east side of the island where we spent the night. The final seven miles back to Portsmouth was made the following morning

A Policeman's Tale

arriving in time for dinner. I had got very wet during this voyage but suffered no ill effects and avoided the dreaded seasickness although my good friend Cadet David Leachman spent most of the time lying down with acute seasickness.

The whole experience was very enlightening, giving me much food for thought, and introducing me to a new mode of life and cadets from other areas.

I returned to my duties at Scunthorpe. On Friday, 7th October 1960 at 2.40pm, I received a call from the Information Room asking for the Mobile Police Station, which was kept at Scunthorpe, to be sent with some men to Horncastle where there were serious floods. Alas, I was not included in the contingent. My task was to visit the model traffic area near the police station and break it to the young cyclists that their session had been cancelled because Constable Reg Woods had been called away to drive the Mobile Police Station to Horncastle. It was only when I got back to my lodgings that evening that I saw on the television news the great damage the floods had done in Horncastle. Next day following enquiries from the public about the safety of relatives in Horncastle, I discovered that an elderly gentleman had died in the flooding.

On 13th October, Inspector Cranidge called me to his office to ask me whether I wanted to become a police constable. When I replied, 'Yes, sir', he gave me an application form for appointment to the Lincolnshire Constabulary. The next day Sergeant Jordan set about checking particulars of my height, weight, and chest measurements. He endorsed the application form to the effect that I was five feet, ten and a half inches tall, weighing twelve stones and seven pounds and my chest measured 36 and 38 inches when I breathed out and in.

On the following Monday I paraded at Headquarters with the other cadets. With five of them, I waited outside the Chief Constable's office for an interview. Three of us were called in and Mr. Barnet told us that that we were young, and a constable's job carries a great responsibility, but that he had no hesitation in sending us to the training school. He told me that I had a good assessment from the Foudroyant course. The other two, who included my friend David Leachman, were deferred for the present – perhaps his seasickness had counted against him in the leadership stakes.

After lunch, we three were taken to see the Police Surgeon, Doctor Pole, at his surgery. He gave us each a thorough medical ensuring we were in good health, satisfying himself that we were fit to serve for at least thirty years in a demanding job. For the second time I passed his checks and went on to be X-rayed once more at the Mint Lane clinic. Events moved swiftly and on 21st October I received a memorandum from Chief Superintendent A. R. Drury informing me that I would be appointed to the force on 28th December 1960, and that I should report to the Number Three District Police Training Centre at Pannal Ash near Harrogate on 14th November to begin initial training.

Another trip to Lincoln followed to issue a helmet, staff, handcuffs, whistle and to fit uniform and I was allocated the number 54. (This number, I discovered later, was available for me because the previous holder had had to resign, while his predecessor had fathered eight children). Eventually I handed the number on to Constable Keith Duke who was under my command at Lincoln). Documentation took place with the recording of personal details and history. I signed forms for membership of the Lincolnshire Constabulary Mutual Assistance Scheme (in which members contribute a day's pay following a death in service to support the widow), the Saint George's Orphan Fund, and the Police Convalescent Home Scheme. Conditions of service were issued to me, and I was pleased to note that constables started on £510 per annum (approximately £9/15s/6d per week) rising, after nine years' service, to £695 per annum. A pension of half pay was payable after twenty-five years or two-thirds of pay after thirty years when I would reach the ripe old age of forty-nine. Hours of duty would be eighty-eight in a fortnight performed in eleven daily periods of eight hours with (usually) time off for overtime performed. In addition to three days' rest each fortnight I would be entitled to seventeen days leave each year. Twenty-one conditions were set out governing, it seemed, every aspect of my life.

I was about to start my real police career not as a constable but while still a cadet. This seemed great initially, but I soon discovered that I would only be paid as a cadet until my nineteenth birthday at the end of December. This meant no boot allowance among other things even though I had to fix myself up with two pairs of stout police boots. I went off to the Australian Boot Company in Sincil Street in Lincoln to find some good boots ready for the next part of my life in the Lincolnshire Constabulary.

The joining instructions for the thirteen-week initial course at Pannal Ash indicated that the training centre was about two miles from the centre of Harrogate and that all students should arrive by noon. Uniform including greatcoat, staff and handcuffs with boots was to be taken and uniform would be worn at all times during school hours. Gym shorts and vest, with white gym shoes, were specified, together with swimming trunks, rugby and football kit. Force forms were also to be brought along together with notebooks and exercise books. The prescribed textbook for the course 'is Moriarty's Police Law (15th Edition)' said the joining instructions – fortunately, I was already quite familiar with much of this tome.

The best bit of the joining instructions seemed to come at the end where we were told we could have weekend leave beginning at noon on Saturdays but must return by 11.30pm on the following day, Sunday.

VIII Pannal Ash

Because I had a car, I was immensely popular with my fellow new recruits and together we all drove up to Pannal Ash. My old car would do no more than forty miles an hour, given a flat road and a fair wind, but we got to the training centre in good time and were instructed where to put our suitcases and shown our beds. I was billeted in L dormitory, a long room on the third floor of the old grey stone main building which had once been a public school. The room contained a dozen beds. The long rows were broken up into pairs of beds, then a short partition, and along the middle of the room was a long row of wardrobes so you couldn't see the beds opposite you. In the winter weather, we soon came to call our accommodation 'ell below zero' (after the popular film about the Arctic).

A neat parcel of blankets and sheet was on the bed, and we soon learned that this was our bed pack to be made up each day in a precise way. We discovered very quickly that when 'stand by your beds' was barked peremptorily at us before an inspection, woe betide any of us if our bed packs were not extremely neat and up to scratch.

The training centre held several hundred new recruits together with some returning after twelve or eighteen months for short refresher courses called 'continuation courses'. A percentage was teenagers, mostly former cadets like me. Some had worked in other areas and were aged up to the then current age limit of thirty. Many of the older ones had been in the armed forces and this meant that my sheltered existence was now clearly at an end.

It began with the songs they sang. They must have been learned and passed on over generations in barracks, but they were new to me and often, although I knew the tunes, the words I'd never heard before. There was one all about the quartermaster's stores, and something about a bridge in the moonlight. Not only did I learn new songs, but also the ex-forces people seemed to describe everything in a particular way calling for somewhat repetitive, but colourful adjectives, which I certainly cannot repeat in this document. At least they knew all about bed packs, and more importantly, they were all experts in 'bulling your boots'. We quickly found that we had only twelve weeks left to achieve a very high shine on our black boots before passing out parade day, and that by then we should have boots shining like mirrors. This revelation heralded much spit and polish, and I learned the technique of a daily application of boot polish and cold water, which eventually resulted in this glass like perfect shine. There was much argument about whether Kiwi or Cherry Blossom boot polish achieved the

A Policeman's Tale

best effect, and whether spit or cold water was better. Even the army men did not agree on this.

Everyday there was morning parade when we all stood in our greatcoats on the parade ground and were inspected. Any deviation from a high standard resulted in a parade at a very early time known as 'jankers', followed usually by what was effectively guard duty by the main door of the training centre. This was not too bad a punishment, as the door was traditionally known as 'definition doorway'. We each were issued with a booklet containing around one hundred legal definitions which all had to be learnt by the end of our thirteen weeks. The duty at the door gave an excellent opportunity to hone up your knowledge of these words and even forty-five years later, I can still recite some of them. For instance, if you ask me which animals injured in a road traffic accident require the driver to stop, I will say 'any horse, cattle, ass, mule, sheep, pig, goat or dog' without a second's thought. One unfortunate side effect of this learning was that in later years when legislation changed it was difficult to unlearn the old definitions and substitute new ones. I was always much happier with the Larceny Act 1916, than the new-fangled Theft Act of 1968.

We were well fed and provided with a bar room and recreational facilities. I have never been much of a drinker but experimented with the fashionable drink of the time, black velvet (which then was made of a half pint of Mackeson stout and a half pint of cider). Since I was only on cadets pay, I had to be careful about bar expenses and somewhat envied those on more than twice as much with full probationary constables pay. Snooker was popular and

I had a few goes, but the 'expertise' I'd gained in Michael Benson's front room years before was no match for many of my contemporaries.

Weekends were great opportunities to explore the surrounding countryside and even take a trip to Leeds. It snowed while I was at the training centre. On one of my trips around the snow-covered hills of Yorkshire I discovered the old Austin was not able to get up one of the steeper inclines. The wheels were going around but the car was not moving. I got out and pushed with the engine running and the wheels spinning. A little pushing got the car moving and I was able to jump back into the driving seat before it set off on its own.

Another outing was to the City of Varieties theatre in Leeds to see an old-time music hall show. One of my classmates met his uncle in the theatre bar, we were both treated to black Balkan Sobranie cigarettes, and I was given a double brandy – probably my first ever.

Law lessons filled much of the day, and these were punctuated by practical sessions. Each lesson had a set of objectives, which needed to be learned, and in the practical sessions, we took turns to be 'the policeman'. Often the practical involved staff members, perhaps assisted by experienced constables from the continuation courses. You would supposedly be on patrol in City Square when something would happen. For instance, a car would drive up and an old rug would cover the number plate. The luckless constable chosen for the exercise would have to go through the correct procedures in the middle of a circle of his classmates. One lad correctly asked the driver for his

A Policeman's Tale

driving licence, and then (as was the practice for our benefit) read it out. He clearly was not familiar with Yorkshire place names and pronounced the town the driver had come from as 'Gooley'. The practical was suspended for several minutes while we all regained our composure, and he was gently told that the place was Goole.

Keeping us all fit was one objective of the course and there were regular physical training and self-defence sessions in the gym or outside. We did the usual team things and 'up the wall bars go' was a regular feature, of the instructor's schedule. There was also football and rugby, and we were taken by bus into Harrogate to do lifesaving practice in the local baths. Cross-country running was also scheduled, and I remember returning from several miles pounding across fields to be looked at by Bob Barry, the physical training instructor. He asked why I was not covered in mud like most of the others. I told him I'd avoided the mud by going around it. His Scottish explosion was partly unintelligible, but I understood I had to go back over the course and get muddy. I returned sometime later, suitably muddy, and getting the mud off my body in the showers, but much washing of socks and gym kit followed. Bob Barry later became a good friend when I used to play badminton with him at Grimsby Police Station, but I never forgot the 'muddy' episode.

We had a short break for Christmas. Then my birthday falling three days later called for extra celebrations. Not only was I nineteen years old, but I was also appointed as a probationary constable, and very importantly, I began to receive proper constable's pay – a considerable boost to my finances at the time as I had my Austin car to run. Petrol was very expensive at around four shillings and sixpence a gallon, so you only got four gallons to a pound when you filled your tank. How times have changed!

At the weekend was New Year's Eve. In my family, this had never been celebrated and we had often complained about the racket made by all the ships on the river Humber sounding their hooters at midnight. However, this time it was to be different as many of the northern forces represented at the training centre had been advertising for recruits in the Scottish papers, so we were to celebrate Hogmanay this time with whisky in paper cups and the singing of Auld Lang Syne. One of the Scots wore his kilt while I stuck to my familiar pyjamas.

As the end of the period of initial training approached, we sat difficult examinations to test us in what we had been taught. Failure was not to be contemplated and we all worked hard to ensure good results. I was also tested in the swimming baths and passed the Royal Life Saving Society's examination entailing a thorough knowledge of the 'Unigrip' method of rescue proving efficiency in rescuing a person in danger of drowning. I still possess my certificate but regret that I never emulated my father who held a bronze medallion for lifesaving.

Eventually the great day of the passing out parade arrived when my parents and sister, Susan, were able to see our prowess on the parade ground. We marched smartly and performed manoeuvres to the sound of a military band. Then our guests were able to look around our classrooms. We had practiced our self-defence and other gymnastics for

A Policeman's Tale

this day and our guests were invited to admire our athletic abilities in the gymnasium. Later in the main hall, they were the audience for a special session of 'Twenty Questions' in which the contestants had to guess a police law item. I was selected to be a team member and received a book prize for my efforts. When the day ended with the address by our inspecting officer, it seemed that I about to taste my first real duties as a police officer.

Another phase of my life was over, and I learned I was to be posted to Boston under the command of Superintendent John Osgerby.

IX Boston

On Monday, 13th February 1961, I found myself reporting to the Police Divisional Headquarters in West Street, Boston. I discovered that this police station was part of the town's municipal buildings, which also housed the council chamber and the usual council offices. I was directed to 66 Skirbeck Road, where I met my new landlady and her husband, Mr. & Mrs. Smith. Mr. Smith was a trained tailor and had a workshop at the rear of the house where he altered skirts and trousers for various shops in the town. The front bedroom where there were two single beds was allocated to me. Another officer, Peter Naulls, occupied the other bed, but he was not on the same shifts as me.

I'd been told that my first shift was to be early turn the next morning, so I set my alarm clock for five o'clock and had an early night. The alarm clock went off on that dark February morning, and I switched it off and went back to sleep, only to wake half an hour later realising that I had to

A Policeman's Tale

get up and get moving. I was going to be late and emerged from the house, into the darkness of Skirbeck Road, just after 6am to find Sergeant Greenhalge cycling towards me.

He asked me why I was not at the police station at a quarter to six as I should have been, and I mumbled my lame excuses. Yet another lesson in life was being learned and I was very fortunate that he decided to give me another chance before putting me on a report.

Quite soon, I discovered that I'd needed to buy a bicycle (for which an allowance would be paid). I was sent off to the local cycle shop on London Road, where I became the proud owner of a sturdy roadster with dynamo lighting, a smart chain guard, and a capacious saddlebag. I was riding this back towards the police station when I encountered Sergeant Terrence Flynn. He was a large officer with a black moustache and a stentorian voice. He eyed me up and down and enquired why I was not wearing cycle clips. I pointed out that the machine had a chain guard and that my trouser bottoms were in no danger. He was not satisfied and made it clear that I should immediately return to the cycle dealer and get myself properly equipped. I never ever rode that cycle without appropriate clips again.

Sergeant Flynn was the scourge of young probationary constables, and he caused my next embarrassment. For the first couple of weeks an experienced constable accompanied me wherever I went, but Sergeant Flynn soon decided that I should be sent out on my own. He drove me in the police van to the Fenside council housing estate in Boston one Sunday afternoon and told me to patrol the area until five o'clock. I did as he asked exploring the area, bounded on one side by the river Witham and fields on the other. I managed to deal with everything that came my way until around half past four when I thought I'd better head back to town. I had overlooked the need to provide myself with a map of the town, and no one seemed to have put up any signs indicating the direction of the police station. After several fruitless sorties in promising directions, I had the humiliating task of asking a passer-by to direct me to the police station!

Night duty was a novelty for me and getting used to staying up all night and trying to be wide awake while trying the handles of all the shops and businesses on my beat took considerable effort. You were warned that should any shopkeeper report the next day that their shop had been left unlocked all night, or even worse been broken into, and you had not found it, that trouble for you would ensue. It was usual practice to check each of your properties twice, once before refreshments, and again afterwards. You soon learned all the back alleys where properties could be approached and the likely points where a burglar would try to get in. Your mentor showed you the spy holes in the post office and bank frosted windows where you could just see the safe door and it was a point of honour always to check these several times.

When Sergeant Flynn took the shift, he would wait in the parade room until fifteen minutes before the shift started at ten o'clock, then take out his pocket watch from the little pocket at the front of his trousers, and holding it out on its silver chain, would announce the time and tell us to synchronise our watches. Then he would check that all those due to report for duty were present before giving us our beats, the route cards for the night, and warn us of any special matters which would need our attention. He would see that we knew the time of our forty-five-minute refreshment break. In our turn we would tell him whether we needed time in the station to prepare any reports or deal with other paperwork. Of course, he suspected that most of us would rather be in the police station, where it was warm and tea was available, than out on our beats. Getting time to do our paperwork was always a struggle with him.

One of his specialities was to be close to the police station at the end of your shift and should you approach the police station any sooner than five minutes before shift end, he would send you off to some far place to teach you a lesson. Needless to say, he was not the most popular of our sergeants.

One market day he came up to me as I was talking to two stallholders. He told me to go with him and when out of their earshot he told me that I should not be idling and gossiping while on duty. I pointed out that at the training centre we had been instructed to talk to local businessmen, turnkeys (whatever they were), and people with local knowledge, so as to increase our own local knowledge. He did not seem impressed with this explanation.

One of my probationer colleagues was fond of playing practical jokes on Sergeant Flynn and he told me that he liked to climb up the fire escape on the West Street cinema. When the sergeant emerged from the police station opposite, he would toss an apple core or something else in his path to startle him. Sergeant Flynn was the last officer I knew to wear the old style of tunic with a stand-up collar worn without a shirt. He wore this tunic on nights and presented a very old-fashioned appearance.

I got on well in my lodgings and was very well looked after – the only drawback being the shared room and the disturbance of someone going on early turn when I was trying to get some sleep. I spent lots of time looking at television, which was still in black and white in those days. The news programmes were from Norwich where Anglia Television was based and their logo of a silver armoured knight on horseback remains strongly in my memory. There was a great outcry when their service was switched to Yorkshire Television a few years later. The town also had two cinemas for entertainment and there was an outdoor swimming pool.

There were three beats. The small pool of town patrol officers had to keep them manned round the clock. These beats were the Market Place beat, the Bargate beat, and the West Street beat, all of which covered the shopping centre in the middle of Boston. We made points set out on our route cards at regular intervals. The strange thing I discovered during my initial period of patrolling with an accompanying experienced officer (meaning a few more month's service than I), was that the points were usually at public houses (of which Boston had a very adequate supply). Unfortunately, several of these had been demolished years before and the places where they had been had become shops or offices, or sometimes just a piece of spare ground occupied by parked cars, so there was no visible confirmation that you were at the right place when the

A Policeman's Tale

sergeant making the point complained that you were some yards away from where you should be. When asked why new points had not been created or renamed it was pointed out that this was quite unnecessary, as everyone knew where, for instance, 'The Loggerheads' pub had been. The town centre points were not at telephone kiosks, as the outlying beat points were, as we had a system of lamps to alert us that we were needed. One of these red lights was on the Assembly rooms and could be seen from all over the Market Place. One was on top of the police box in the cattle market in Bargate, and the other was on the side of the Municipal Buildings, which housed the police station in West Street. In this way we could receive directions to incidents and be informed of crimes such as details of stolen cars or escapes from North Sea Camp Borstal Institution within a few minutes.

One of the regular daytime duties for town patrol officers was to deal with the traffic congestion in the Market Place. A magnificent lamppost, with five lamps, stood in the middle of the Market Place where the road to the docks diverges from what was then the main A.16 Grimsby to Stamford road. The junction was complicated by turns to Fish Hill in front of the Assembly Rooms. Additionally, the road south went over a pedestrian 'zebra' crossing, and then the Town Bridge. This bridge was one of only two bridges over the Haven, as the river Witham is known where it is tidal. Duty at The Five Lamps was needed regularly for the morning and evening rush periods as well as very frequently most of the day on Wednesdays and Saturdays when the market was full of stalls.

I soon got used to waving my arms for prolonged periods. The trick was to look for the driver's intentions signalled by their trafficators or by hand signals. On summer Saturdays, when holidaymakers were heading to and from Skegness, traffic was often queued for two or three miles on both approaches to Boston and the poor officer at the Five Lamps had to expedite clearing this as best as he could. Another officer would be placed in the middle of the Town Bridge zebra crossing to stop pedestrians impeding the flow. A third officer would manually operate the traffic lights on the south side of the Town Bridge where Sleaford traffic joined the flow. The three of us would try to get the vehicles moving and reduce the frustration of hundreds of drivers wondering why they were always delayed in Boston.

Of course, this was thirsty work, but fortunately, there was a little café, known as The Busman's, down Church Lane just beyond the Assembly Rooms where a quick cup of tea could be obtained. Of course, you had to find someone to relieve you on traffic duty first. Sometimes Superintendent Osgerby or one of the Inspectors would appear and give you a ten-minute break. However, if Sergeant Flynn found you in the café, he would want to know why you weren't attending to your duty.

One of the problems on the zebra crossing was that on market days huge numbers of people sought to cross the road from Fish Hill to Boots the Chemists and your job was to hold them back for as long as reasonable. Quite a few would engage you in conversation during this process and even worse happened if you saw the legendary Bertie Wilson

A Policeman's Tale

approaching. Bertie was a small-time rag and bone dealer. He was usually drunk or at least well-oiled and he never took any notice of the officer stopping pedestrians crossing and continued his merry way over your crossing. Of course, this posed a dilemma for the officer. If you let him get away with it the other pedestrians would see no point in obeying your outstretched arms. If you pursued him the traffic immediately stopped as a continuous stream of people crossed the road. I did report Bertie at least once and, on another occasion, years later helped Constable Foley bring Bertie in a drunken state to the police station.

The weekends brought another problem for the Boston police. The town attracted huge numbers of young people from places as far away as Peterborough to the Gliderdrome dance hall. The Malkinson family, owners of the next-door football stadium, home of Boston Football Club, operated this dance hall and each weekend the stage was occupied by a well-known singer or band. The Market Place would become a seething mass of people, intent on seeing a famous performer and often trouble occurred. The late shift would provide several officers on overtime until 1am to augment the strength of the night shift, and quite often all of us were fully occupied dealing with disorder. One night, I remember, vainly trying to dispel a large group of people marching around the marketplace singing 'Michael Row the Boat Ashore'. As they approached me a gap opened up, they passed around me, and carried happily on their way.

At New Year, even more problems arose, as it had become the tradition for the brave (or foolhardy) to climb the Five Lamps. This was done as midnight approached and the whole marketplace was full of people intent on seeing the fun (and preventing the police stopping the fun). The police often circled the five lamps and a battle developed between potential climbers and supporters and the police. Needless to say, the cells were often full after New Year's Eve and sometimes there were quite a few injuries to both police officers and members of the public.

One winter's night I had been sent onto the beat that covered the edges of the town. This meant using your cycle and making sure your lamp batteries were in first class condition. Your issue lamp was a black metal affair with a switch on the top and two sliders at the front allowing you to show a red or green light in addition to the normal white light. The lamp clipped onto your night belt adding to the general clutter of handcuffs and truncheon. Just as with all the other beats, you were in possession of a route card that bore the letter of the day. There were three variations of route so that the villains would not be able to work out where you might be at any particular time. The points on the card were at half hourly or forty-five-minute intervals and at each point was usually a telephone kiosk where you waited for five minutes in case the office constable at the police station wished to send you to an incident. You could also be fairly certain that at one of the points during each half of your shift a sergeant or inspector would visit you and sign your pocketbook (ensuring that you kept it up to date). This outlying beat had a series of places to check and, unlike the other beats, you had to sign a book at the end of your shift indicating the time you checked each property. Some

A Policeman's Tale

of the places were extensive with lots of doors and windows to check and it was quite a task to get them all done and still be at your point at the correct time. In addition to the regular checks the police were expected to visit the houses of people away from home to make sure they were in order.

Around 3am on this particular night, I had to check a house that had a field on the left side. I got off my cycle and was walking down the long drive with high leafless trees on either side, little moon to give any light, approaching the darkened detached house, when I heard very disturbing noises to my left. It sounded like someone with a flatulence problem, and the noises were not only rude but made me fear that a whole gang of villains was moving around the unoccupied house. The moon came from behind a cloud and suddenly all became clear. Hungry sheep were munching the remains of a turnip crop in the adjacent field and the noises were their crunching and the vapours produced by their digestive systems. It was with some relief that I finished checking the house.

The long winter nights were made easier by a few ruses soon learned from wise old colleagues, some of whom had served in the old Boston Borough Police, which had amalgamated with the Lincolnshire Constabulary in 1947. In the marketplace was a doorway with a set of wooden stairs leading to an upper storey. This dark, but warm corner was an excellent place for a young constable when frost was on the ground to sit on the top step and keep a watchful eye on anyone abroad in the night. There were also night watchmen at some of the garages and works in the town that would gladly share pot of tea with you in exchange for a visit to check on their welfare and an exchange of news.

We had two police boxes where there was a police phone and a desk where handwritten reports could be completed. You could get an accident booklet written up in one of these boxes without having to beg for time at the police station. Both had excellent heaters. The one at the cattle market had an electric heater while the one at the Assembly Rooms had an oil-filled radiator beneath which the flames of gas jets sent up a heady lot of fumes. One morning at the end of a night shift around 5.30am I set about a little paperwork in the Assembly Rooms box. The next thing I knew was the incessant ringing of the phone in the box rousing me from my slumbers. As I picked up the handset my watch indicated 6.15am and the office constable was anxious to find me and sign me off duty. Perhaps it's as well he did as the dangers of carbon monoxide were less well known in those days.

Soon after I arrived in Boston, the police dog handlers discovered that I was familiar with their training methods, and I was asked to volunteer to help them train their dogs. We set off to the outskirts of the town and were soon out in the fields. The wheat had been harvested and the fields were full of stooks – little stacks of about six or eight sheaves of wheat drying in the late summer sun. I set off in my usual fashion, leaving odd items such as a handkerchief, along my trail. At Scunthorpe I used to hide in a hedge or ditch, but the fenlands are not wooded, and hedges are usually replaced by very deep ditches with water at the bottom, so I was stumped for a hiding place after my mile

A Policeman's Tale

or so hike. The obvious place suddenly struck me, and I lay prone in the middle of one of the stooks pulling the end sheaf back over my feet and peering through the straw out of the one at the other end.

After a pleasant lie down, I heard the sound of barking and knew that Constable Johnny Bush and his Doberman pinscher must be nearing the end of the trail. I couldn't see them but within seconds the panting of the dog was close by and a rustling near my feet meant that the dog had successfully found me. Now since the aim is to find the person who might be just a lost child or elderly woman the dog is supposed to signal success by barking to bring the dog handler to the scene. However, 'Faust' decided to make sure he'd got a live find and made straight along the inside of the stook and bit into my trousers finding tasty flesh beneath. The dog barked, I shouted, and Constable Bush ran up administering clouts to the dog and slipping on its chain.

Next came the undignified removal of my trousers and pants in the middle of the cornfield to examine the damage to my anatomy. I couldn't see the damage without a mirror, even though I could feel the pain, but I was assured it was only minor and I would survive – thank goodness. Needless to say, I was a bit reluctant to help train 'Faust' again as he seemed to have developed a taste for me, which was not welcome.

One mystery, which puzzled me for a while, was the sight of uniformed constables cycling towards the docks. I'd never seen any of them at the police station and eventually found out who they were. They were members of the Dock Watch. This consisted of about six men with their sergeant who were responsible for looking after the large dock estate owned by Boston Corporation. They were not police officers but had every appearance that they were. We were pleased with this arrangement since it lessened the work of the regular officers and every now and then they were very helpful to us. The area of the docks was huge with cargos of timber, fertiliser and grain stored all around. Additionally, there was a large trade between Boston and the continent in live cattle and a lairage on the docks was maintained to house beast prior to shipping. There was constant movement of not only rail traffic to the docks, but also large numbers of lorries passed through the Market Place, adding to traffic congestion there.

One experience that I found unpleasant, and which was always the most unwelcome duty was attending post-mortem examinations in the case of sudden or accidental deaths. The first one always sticks in my mind. I was sent to the mortuary at the old Boston General Hospital. This was down by the docks. Round the back of the hospital was the separate small brick building which housed a lead lined slab and on this slab was an eleven-year-old boy who had died while playing on a building site. His mates had been rolling him around in a large concrete sewer pipe that had hit another one and broken. The examination of this poor child was an experience necessary for a young policeman but one I'd very much prefer to have avoided. I saw the broken skull bones that had caused his death and learned much else about human anatomy. Of course, I had to attend lots more of these examinations during the course of

A Policeman's Tale

my career, but the first one will always stay with me. I suppose it was mainly the death of a youngster that I most regretted but even when the subject was much older it always seemed very sad to me that finding the cause of death was so necessary.

Usually following post-mortem examinations, I had to attend the Coroners Court with its ancient rituals. I remember calling out before the start of proceedings, 'Oyez, Oyez, draw near all persons having business with Her Majesty's Coroner concerning the death of X'. On the other hand, much of what followed was much less formal than at the magistrates' court with the aim of putting distressed relatives of the deceased at their ease.

Each month probationers attended a training day. Ours were held at the old workhouse in Skirbeck Road, just a few yards from my lodgings. We spent the day parading, having lectures on law, and doing short examinations. We also had to prepare ourselves to discuss a set police law subject in a group.

My landlady, Mrs. Smith, introduced me to an annual custom, which I had no knowledge and hadn't experienced before. This was samphire gathering. Samphire is a sort of fleshy seaweed, which grows on saltwater mudflats. I had tasted samphire at Grandma Pickering's on one of my visits with my mother and had enjoyed it. You took the little branches of samphire that had been pickled in vinegar and used a fork to pull the flesh off the twiggy stem before eating it with bread and butter. At that time, I had no idea of where it came from. With my landlady, some stout Wellington boots, and plastic bags we set off to Frieston

Shore. This is where the edge of the Wash meets the public highway by a high dyke to keep the sea off the Fenland. Over the bank stretched miles of muddy creeks that we explored with quite a number of others on the same mission in search of samphire. The plants grow in the shallow water of the creeks to a height of eight or nine inches and they are easily uprooted. We filled our bags and went back to the car, cleaning off as much mud from our boots and legs as possible. Back at my digs, Mrs. Smith boiled the samphire in vinegar until this great delicacy was ready to be put in jars to be enjoyed later. This was my first sortie on to the marshes and I could see that they needed to be treated with respect. Whenever police activity was called for on the marshes searching for missing people or escaped prisoners from North Sea Camp, we always called in an expert marsh guide to help us avoid problems. The most well-known of these was a man called McKenzie Thorpe who guided wildfowlers on the marshes, including famous names such as James Robertson Justice, the film actor. 'Kenzie Thorpe was said to be a rogue, but he certainly knew his way around the wild parts of the Wash.

While at Boston the force was subject of an inspection by Mr. Peck, Her Majesty's Inspector of Constabulary, and this year, it was the turn of the Boston Division to be given scrutiny. We became used to Quarterly Instruction Classes that were similar to this inspection when the Chief Constable would visit us and put us through our paces, however when the HMI visited, we had to move into a higher gear. For the formal parade, we stood in our best uniforms in the car park at the back of the Municipal Offices

A Policeman's Tale

and Mr Peck with members of the police authority walked up and down our lines inspecting our appearance and talking to individuals.

Then we all went into the courtroom that formed part of the buildings and were addressed by Mr. Peck. Next came the command 'Stand up the probationers.' This meant that about half a dozen of us stood at the back of the wood panelled courtroom. The first question came to me. 'Tell me the definition of stealing,' said my interrogator. This was a relief, as it is one of the first things I learnt at the training centre. I shot back 'A person steals, who, without the consent of the owner, takes and carries away anything capable of being stolen.' My mouth closed at this point, and I was asked, 'Is that all?' So, I carried on, "Notwithstanding, that being a bailee or part owner thereof he fraudulently converts it to his own use or to the use of another person…' I managed to blurt out the full words of section one of the Larceny Act 1916 to the satisfaction of the HMI but to the relief of all my senior officers who were always anxious that someone would let them down. Of course, each part of the definition has its own separate definition and my probationer colleagues had to cope with giving the meaning of the words 'takes and carries away' and so on. I am sure the HMI has every expectation that all the probationers could answer his questions and that the demonstration was simply to impress the lay members of the police authority.

From 3rd to 15th December 1961, I was instructed to attend an intermediate continuation course for probationary constables. These courses were intended to build on initial training now that some experience of police duties had been gained. Because of lack of space at Pannal Ash my course was to be at Bridgend in Glamorganshire. Another constable from Lincolnshire was assigned to the same course and this was John Walkley.

I'd known John from my days as a cadet. He had also been a cadet, stationed at Cleethorpes. My father had mentioned John several times before I first met him. This was because he had joined the cadets after first being articled to a solicitor and secondly because he was the only married cadet in the force. He lived close to my parents in a flat in Seacroft road at Cleethorpes with his wife, Anne. Quite often we had both travelled together to Lincoln for training days in the Cleethorpes police van. We agreed that I would provide the transport for our trip to Wales. I had never undertaken such a lengthy trip in my car before and when the Sunday arrived on which we were to set off there was thick fog blanketing the whole country. Fogs in those days were much more serious than these days. Smoke from factory chimneys, houses, and railway engines developed very thick 'pea soupers' that made visibility almost impossible. We undertook our journey wrapped in thick clothes and warm scarves. We had to open the windscreen to obtain any sort of view of the road, peering for the white centre lines. The car heater was ineffective, and our arrival saw us in need of intensive thawing out.

The culture shock of being the only two Lincolnshire policemen in this Welsh training school was considerable. The strange pronunciation of words was one thing we had much fun with. Our instructor seemed to need to refer to budgerigars quite often, but he pronounced the word with emphasis on the 'i', which we found quite amusing. One of my classmates also had a pronounced stammer, which made it impossible for him to answer questions. I wondered how he performed in court in the witness box. It turned out he had got into the force 'because he was somebody's son'. On reflection though, so was I!

Parades were once again a feature of our daily life with much drilling and stamping of feet. However, our drill instructor surprised us one day by saying that we would do whistle practice. It was a novelty, as my own whistle had never been blown in anger. This presented a few problems as traditionally each police force had its own way of keeping whistles. Lincolnshire officers always had all, but two or three links of the whistle chain concealed, but other forces had loops of chain on display. In any event as the instructor called 'one' we grasped the chain. On 'two' we pulled out our whistles to the full extent of the chain, and on 'three' put them to our lips. 'Four' was the signal for a hearty blow, and on 'five' we put them away. The first try was marred because many of the whistles had fluff clogging up the works, but after a few repetitions, we all became accomplished at the task.

It was explained to us that one of Her Majesty's Inspectors of Constabulary, while carrying out his inspection of a Welsh force, had discovered that many officers couldn't blow their whistles when needed because of excessive fluff. This had determined that 'something must be done.' Quite a few years later (with the advent of personal radios) Lincolnshire Police decided whistles were redundant and we were allowed to stop carrying them and to keep them as souvenirs. I still have mine and it is inscribed 'The Metropolitan Lincoln County Constabulary'.

Much of the time was spent once again on police law sessions and physical training. The training centre had previously been used as a Royal Ordnance depot. It consisted mainly of wooden huts and there were a great many fire hydrants around giving a clue to its former use. There was a bar and some recreational facilities, but we were also expected to use our spare time studying and also bulling up our boots to a high shine. One evening not long before lights out I was sitting on my bed in my pyjamas carefully polishing my boots when the revellers from the bar began heading back to the dormitories. A group passed through my dormitory singing rugby songs and in a very merry state.

On seeing me with my tin of Cherry Blossom, one of them began talking about what they used to do in the army. This appeared to involve black shoe polish, toothpaste and delicate parts of a young man's anatomy. They surrounded my bed and it seemed that I must be their candidate for this ceremony as they debated whether to take me across to the shower room. To put it mildly I didn't find the prospect of their attentions appealing and my clenched fists, jutting elbows and crossed legs were an indication that resistance would be met. Fortunately, none among them laid the first hand on me and they all went off looking for a more compliant victim for a blacking - a lucky escape for me.

At the weekend, there was much, more free time and a tour of the winter countryside appealed. I managed to see something of Cardiff and of Barry Island.

The exam at the end of the course I had expected to be

A Policeman's Tale

quite fearsome, like the one at Pannal Ash. It seemed that it would be because standard questions were set at all the training centres. However, the day before the examination we had several 'revision' periods. It was very strange to discover next day that the revision had covered exactly the questions in the papers we sat, and everyone got at least ninety-eight percent correct. My view was that the northern police forces represented at Pannal Ash were able to select much better qualified recruits than those in the south and Wales. I still feel, even now, that I was being fair in this assessment.

The long journey home with John Walkley in those pre-motorway days turned out to be a repeat of the journey down as once again the country was fogbound.

Back at Boston Christmas was approaching and I was on night duty in my heavy Melton wool greatcoat. I had checked the gasworks path, which was a long dark passageway leading towards the river and had crossed over onto the riverbank so I could see the road that goes over the Sluice Bridge. This bridge crosses the river where the Witham becomes tidal and is one of the only two bridges that crossed the river in those days in the Boston area. Policemen are trained to make themselves as visible as possible during the day. For instance, you always walk on the outside edge of the pavement, and when you stay still you choose a prominent position so that the maximum number of people can see your helmet. On the other hand, at night you walk on the inside of the pavement and stand in dark corners so that you can see what is happening, and people up to no good don't see you. In any event I was doing just this when over the Sluice Bridge, which was lighted by quite good street lighting, I saw two figures approaching me. They seemed to have large white bundles under their arms. I waited and as they got almost up to me, I saw that the bundles were four turkeys. It was obvious that these two were planning splendid Christmas dinners.

Stepping forward to enquire about the origin of the turkeys, they saw me, dropped the birds in a cloud of feathers, and legged it down the 'Gassy Path'. I gave chase, but in my greatcoat was unable to keep up. So, I went back, picked up the turkeys (with not a little difficulty) and made my way to the nearby telephone box, inserted my two pence, pressed button A, and contacted the police station. The CID was very interested in my turkeys and Detective Constable Sharpe (an old Boston Borough officer) examined their necks. He pronounced that only two villains were in the habit of killing turkeys in this manner and named them. Very shortly we were round to their homes on the Fenside Estate and had them both in custody as I recognised them.

On Friday 2nd February 1962, I sat the Police Examinations Board qualifying examination for promotion in educational subjects. We were examined in English, Arithmetic, Geography and General Knowledge. The examinations were held in the Civil Defence Headquarters lecture room on Skirbeck Road where our training days were held. The first exam started at 9.45am and we finished at 5.20pm. Quite a hard day, but fortunately my education had prepared me well for the task. I remember writing enthusiastically about building a bridge across the English

A Policeman's Tale

Channel for the General Knowledge paper painting a glowing picture of the wonderful views of shipping as you drove over it while acknowledging the danger which might be posed to those ships by the massive piers holding up the bridge. This was the first promotion hurdle, and the police law examination could only be taken after several years' service. I passed the examination with 289 marks out of 400. This qualified me for Inspectors rank for which the pass mark was 240, and I was very pleased to hear some time later that Sergeant Reames had confided to my father that my marks had been the highest in the county.

My car was kept across the road from my digs at the bungalow of my Aunt Margaret and Uncle Bert (my mother's brother). Unfortunately, my faithful 1938 model, Austin Big Seven, which had served me well and to which I'd given loving attention, even to the extent of painting the engine block a shade of apple green, failed its Ministry of Transport ten-year test. The kingpins were worn, and it was going to be very expensive to renew them. A replacement was needed and so under my father's guidance we secured, for a little over one hundred pounds, an Austin Eight from his favourite garage, Askew & Sons, of Cleethorpes. This car dated from 1947 and was a considerable advance in that it could achieve fifty miles an hour. It had a navy-blue body and black wings and seemed a great improvement on my previous transport.

On 22nd February 1962, I received an order from Superintendent J. W. Osgerby: - 'You will remove from Boston to Gainsborough for town patrol duties on Monday, 5th March 1962. Suitable lodgings will be found for you and arrangements for you to be conveyed in a police vehicle made unless you wish to remove yourself in your own car.'

X Gainsborough

I went north to Gainsborough where lodgings had been found for me in a large detached Victorian house close to the old former toll bridge over the river Trent. The house seemed full of lodgers; I was shown to a very large bedroom, on the first floor, at the front of the house overlooking the main road. The room contained the usual furniture and a double bed. This seemed very satisfactory, but then I learned I was to share the room and the bed with Robin Bertram, another policeman I already knew. Our shifts were often different, and this meant we didn't always share the bed at the same time.

Robin and I became good friends over this period, and I even visited Robin's home at Burton Coggles near Grantham being entertained by his parents. At that time, this bed sharing arrangement didn't seem at all odd, but as times changed Robin delighted in telling colleagues that he and I had been bedfellows for a while, bringing a blush to my cheeks. When our landlady suffered medical problems and decided she no longer wanted lodgers, we again found joint accommodation in a bungalow on the edge of town in Mayfield Avenue. These digs were very good even though we had to share a bed once again.

The bedroom was at the rear by a deep railway cutting. At first the rumble of trains was disturbing, but as time wore on, they were not noticed. One feature of these lodgings was that central heating was fitted. This worked from a coke stove in the kitchen, and I delighted in getting it really hot during my stint of stoking early in the morning. I suppose this marked the transition for me from the first twenty or so years of my life when frosty mornings meant icy windows, freezing bedrooms, and rushing to get into clothes before turning blue with cold. The wonderful modernity of central heating had arrived in my life, and I thought it was wonderful.

Not long after my arrival in Gainsborough, I was on night duty when I encountered a fourteen-year-old boy at 4am and checked him out. His story was plausible, but I kept a discreet eye on him and after he'd gone into the public toilets, I heard loud bangs. I investigated. He was stealing the coin box from one of the cubicle doors but when he saw me, he bolted himself inside, so I had to climb over the wall to get him out. This was no mean task in my thick greatcoat, helmet, and other gear. I was walking him under arrest to the police station when he managed to break away from me. My winter uniform hampered giving chase yet to my amazement I caught him up and we both fell on the ground with me on top. At this point my sergeant who

A Policeman's Tale

was having a ride around in the Land Rover saw us, so I got help to cart him back to the police station. This was just as well because I was severely out of breath.

When he appeared at court, after hearing the details of his exploits, including several other thefts he admitted, they sent him to an approved school. A few months later we heard he had run off from there and we started looking for him. With another officer I went round to his house. While I knocked on the front door my colleague went round to the back. There was a scuffling and noises from round the back as the boy's mother opened the front door. I ran round to the back just in time to see the youth legging it over the garden fence and across the field. He had jumped out of his bedroom window onto the tiles of the kitchen roof and evaded my colleague. Once more I began to chase him but couldn't catch him. His mother proudly told me that he had won the cross-country running championship at his approved school before running away from there. In the kindliest tones I could muster, I asked her to let us know if he returned home (with little faith that she would).

A couple of hours later I managed to beg the Landrover from my sergeant and set off to tour the village of Morton to look for the run-away. In Morton was a large unoccupied manor house, Morton Hall, with extensive grounds. Driving to the front of the house I quietly began a search. There was a large heap of hay around the side of the hall that looked disturbed, so I began to prod it. Suddenly my quarry leapt out, but before he could run away, I collared him and slipped my handcuffs on him. I took him to my vehicle and fastened him with the handcuffs to the side straps of the Landrover canvas. We went back to Spring Gardens to await his return to approved school.

The local magistrates' court at that time was in the same building as the police station on the first floor. We constables not only gave evidence in the cases we brought, but on court days, one officer had to stand in the court to keep order. One court day I was assigned to this duty when a man was in the dock and, much to his disgust, the justices announced a custodial sentence. He didn't take kindly to the prospect of a cell in Her Majesty's Prison at Lincoln and began an escape bid. The officer who'd brought him up from the cells was unable to restrain him, and as the officer at the back keeping order I went to help. I was amazed at what followed. I'd been trained in all sorts of restraint methods but was quite unprepared for the power of a young man who didn't want to be held. His arms, legs, head, and teeth were his weapons and eventually six police officers were scuffling with him on the polished linoleum, slipping about on the court floor. We managed to restrain him, handcuff him, and take him down to the cells. No doubt their worships on the bench had enjoyed the show, but I was in a very dishevelled state, as were my colleagues.

One of the great freezes of the twentieth century arrived on 22nd December 1962 and went on until 4th March 1963, so it lasted 73 days during which period there was frost on every single night, while the temperature remained below freezing by day and by night on more than 30 days, even in southern England. Fortunately, the thaw when it came was very slow and no flooding resulted. Night duty on compacted hard snow with icicles in abundance became the

A Policeman's Tale

norm. Night duty was for seven nights from 10pm to 6am and came around every four weeks. Three complete sets of night duty came and went during this freezing weather. Our uniforms were usually plenty warm enough as they included a heavyweight wool Melton overcoat. Keeping my legs warm was the main problem and I found other officers had solved this by wearing pyjamas under their trousers. I tried this and it was a great help. We had to give up patrolling the outlying areas on our cycles as it was too dangerous, and those officers qualified to drive the station Land Rover used this instead. Sergeant Gerald Parker, the traffic sergeant, had tested me soon after arriving in Gainsborough. If you have ever driven a Landrover you will know that the steering is very highly geared so that turning a corner takes much more turning of the steering wheel than in a normal motorcar.

The test started in the back yard of the police station in Spring Gardens. The road was very narrow with a narrow pavement on the side furthest from the yard and none at all on the side where the yard was situated. Abutting the pavement were terraced houses. One of my probationer colleagues had taken his Land Rover test a short while before me and he'd managed to run into the houses opposite the yard because he'd not turned the steering wheel quickly enough. Fortunately, I was aware of this and passed the test. The Land Rover was a great vehicle, especially on ice and rough terrain when you could engage four-wheel drive and a lower set of gears if needed. I enjoyed driving up the steep bank of the river Trent and trying out the vehicle's abilities on rough ground.

Being an approved driver of the Land Rover meant I could take my fellow probationers each month to Scunthorpe for our training days. The journey was always a good opportunity to catch up with all the news and gossip, and on arrival to swap tales with the Scunthorpe probationers.

My stay in Mayflower Close came to an end when the landlady decided to take a long trip abroad, so I had to find new lodgings once again. This time I went to the north end of town to a terraced house in Melrose Road, near the fire station. These lodgings were not very pleasant, and I soon started searching for somewhere more comfortable. I found Mr. and Mrs. Wells, who lived in Campbell Street, with their teenage daughter Bronwyn, and they offered me their back bedroom. I was very well looked after at these lodgings. During my stay there the annual uniform inspection came around. This annual event entailed your inspector visiting your home and checking over all your uniform and deciding what need replacing. This inspection was by Inspector Charles Watkinson. He counted my shirts and collars, trousers, tunics, coats and everything else, and then his eyes lighted on the book on my bedside cupboard that was about meteorology. Engaging me in conversation he asked about abstruse meteorological terms such as cols, warm fronts, anti-cyclones and so on. He had been in the Royal Air Force and had trained in the metrological section. It was a link which I found made it very easy to get on with him thereafter, and he proved to be a good friend.

My sergeant was called 'Jock' (since he was a Scotsman) Ingles. He was an experienced officer and a good mentor

A Policeman's Tale

for young constables. One night the red lamp on the Market Place wall came on, and, going to the phone in the passage nearby, I was told that a body had been found in the River Trent and I was to go and deal with it. I walked along to the wharf where I found Sergeant Ingles and another officer with the faithful police Land Rover and the police canvas shroud. They ushered me over to the body telling me to fish it out of the water. As I began my attempts in the dim torchlight, suddenly I realised that the pale face and hair I could see belonged to a shop window mannequin. My two colleagues were only just containing their merriment. Even with their practical joke and laughter I still I felt very relieved that I hadn't got a real dead body to sort out.

Regularly we had to check a tea warehouse quite near where the 'body' had been found. This was at the end of a long, narrow, dark passage with high walls on either side. We tried to approach most premises without using our lamps, which would have warned anyone up to no good of our imminent arrival. The lighted shopping street was left behind and going into the passage one's eyes took time to adjust. One night I was venturing down the passage peering into the darkness and listening for suspicious sounds, when something heavy landed on my shoulder. The shock was great but when I felt the soft fur of a black cat the relief was even greater.

Sergeant Ingle's wife worked at the Wolsey factory up the hill. This was on the route of the outlying beat that we covered on a long cycle ride. On nights after 2am there were only two constables covering the town. One patrolled the town centre and the other set off on the thirteen-mile cycle ride, checking a long list of properties that required signing for at the end of the shift. A book was kept for this purpose. Sometimes you would head off to the village of Morton north of Gainsborough and sometimes towards Lea to the south. Both routes involved climbing a significant hill. The most difficult checks were Roses sports club, the Wolsey factory and the golf club, as these were off the beaten track. The Wolsey factory made men's underwear and Sergeant Ingles was rumoured to be a tester for these. Around the factory were bales of off-cuts of cotton material, sometimes exotic looking leopard skin prints and so on and we speculated about what our sergeant might be wearing as a test for the company.

When I had this route on night duty, I used to buy a carton of milk from the milk-machine in the town centre and put it in my saddlebag. Then when I got to the golf clubhouse I'd sit in a comfortable wicker chair on the veranda, sometimes watching the sunrise, and the rabbits playing, drinking my milk, and thinking idle thoughts about beautiful Lincolnshire and other things.

Superintendent Leslie Kirby (we called him Rip) sent me an order on 24th July 1962 to attend a final course at the West Riding Constabulary Divisional Headquarters, Wood Street, Wakefield commencing on 19th November 1962. It promised an advance of £5 per week to cover the cost of lodgings and subsistence. Yet again Pannal Ash was full of initial trainees, and they had farmed us out for the fortnight's training. I remember little of this course with one exception. During the middle weekend we were free to

A Policeman's Tale

amuse ourselves and when someone suggested the local wrestling on the Saturday afternoon I went along. I had seen wrestling on the television occasionally, but it was an eye-opener in the flesh, with beefy men in trunks running about the canvas ring, bouncing off the ropes and apparently assaulting the referee when they didn't agree with him. The most exciting bit was when one wrestler picked another up and threw him over the ropes. He got tangled in the ropes and was trapped dangling over a poor woman in the front row. When his trainer and the referee got him undone, he promptly ran over to the ropes on the opposite side of the ring, bounced off them and flew horizontally feet first into his opponent flooring him. I couldn't make up my mind whether all this had been rehearsed for our entertainment or whether it was true sport. I was glad that I'd not had a front seat because it all seemed very dangerous to me and not at all like the time, I'd spent wrestling with Colin Harker years before at Clee Grammar in the gym.

The two-week course was successfully completed, but while at Wakefield I was told of another order in my pigeonhole back at the police station. This asked me to note that I had been nominated to attend a local driving course commencing on 3rd December 1962 for three weeks, and that I should report to Headquarters at 10am on that date taking my current driving licence with me. Again, it said that lodgings would be found.

It was a foggy day when I reported to Headquarters in Church Lane, Lincoln, and met the two other officers on the same course as me. Sergeant Peter Ben Watkinson, a short well-rounded officer, took us into the schoolroom (which was very familiar to me) and told us we couldn't go out in the police car because of the fog. The fog persisted for three days so we spent much of the time polishing the black Ford Zephyr patrol car inside and out. Not only were all the usual places polished but so were all the things under the bonnet and under the wheel arches – it looked beautiful.

Our instructor must have become tired of all the polishing, I think, because on the third day he announced we'd go out and that he would drive. He took us to a little café at Dunholme Holt beside the main Lincoln to Grimsby Road (the A46), at a slow pace peering into the fog. We were glad he seemed to be able to see where we were going. Drawing into the forecourt I noticed white painted boulders marking the car park edge, but I don't think Sergeant Watkinson did for the next thing was the front of the patrol car struck one of the boulders. We stopped, and there was an awkward silence. We had our cup of tea and went back to Headquarters where we had another long polishing session getting out the scrape marks from under the front bumper of the patrol car.

Things improved the next day as the fog had cleared and we each took turns to drive. Gradually we covered all aspects of driving safely and at speed. We ventured all over the county following our instructor's orders as he sat beside us carefully watched by the other two in the back. We were regularly debriefed on our driving. The objective was to 'make progress' which involved driving as fast as the conditions allowed in accordance with the guidance in the manual 'Roadcraft' which was the bible of advanced drivers in the police force. Peter Ben's idea of progress was not

A Policeman's Tale

always mine. Coming over the top of Caistor Hill at the start of the long downhill Caistor Drag he ordered me to 'put your ***** tab down'. I complied; the car accelerated nicely towards the one hundred mark on the dial. There was traffic ahead and a bus coming up the hill. I took my foot off the accelerator and Sergeant Watkinson took off his flat police cap and started hitting me with it repeating more vehemently his order to 'put your ***** tab down.' Somehow, I managed to negotiate all the hazards and lived to tell the tale. Driving at speed needs great concentration and judgement I discovered.

After the course, I returned to Gainsborough. I had successfully completed my probationary period and was appointed a full constable on my 21st birthday on 28th December 1962. After more driving experience accompanied by an advanced police driver, I was tested on 18th February 1963 by the traffic superintendent. Passing this test, I was now approved to drive all police vehicles with the exception of the mobile police station without further supervision.

The effect of this was that I became the reserve patrol car driver on my section and when the regular patrol car driver was unavailable, I got to take out a powerful police car on traffic patrol. Gainsborough Division covered a huge area, from Cherry Willingham in the south to Scotter in the north. I had a new beat to learn and lots more property to check on nights when explosive stores and other vulnerable properties had to be visited.

During the cold winter weather in the early months of 1963, with Constable Bill Murray, my section's regular driver, I got several opportunities to patrol with him. He encouraged me to try out my skid control technique. We chose the old airfield at Dunholme Holt where there were wide concrete runways covered in ice and snow. Whizzing about with wheels spinning we practiced turning into the skid in the approved manner and were doing well until one skid resulted in the patrol car sliding quickly sideways towards the edge of the runway. At the edge was a hard-frozen ploughed field and, when our offside tyres made contact, the tyre walls were pushed in, and the air escaped (since they were tubeless tyres even then) leaving us with two flats. This posed a dilemma since, while we had one spare, we needed a second. We decided to walk to the garage at Dunholme Holt to use their airline to blow up one of the tyres. However, it was a long walk and every half hour one of us needed to be at the radio in the car to report our location to the Information Room. We waited for the next location call, then hoofed it rapidly with our deflated tyres to the garage, got our air, and legged it back as quickly as possible. The next location call came, and we gave a very slight and not too untruthful situation to the operator. It was just as well we were not needed operationally during this embarrassing episode.

Traffic patrol took me to lots more accidents that foot patrol had. I was regularly completing accident booklets and submitting files. One night I was sent to a five-vehicle accident on the A46 at Swinderby (well off my area of patrol) and found a dreadful scene with upturned vehicles and serious injuries, but fortunately I was only needed to assist with traffic control. On another occasion I went to an accident where a retired schools' inspector from Scotland had left the road and collided with a tree. I went to see him in hospital and found him with his jaw wired together. He gave me a statement and it seemed he'd fallen asleep at the wheel having driven the hundreds of miles down from Scotland. I was getting the file together when the hospital notified me the injured driver had died, so my file became a Coroners file, and I had another inquest to attend.

One night I decided to practice my high-speed driving technique at about 3am down Tillbridge Lane which is a nice straight, though narrow, country road from Scampton to Sturton by Stow. I had got up to about 112 miles an hour when my nearside wheels struck a long puddle at the edge of the road. This upset the car's smooth progress and I just avoided a catastrophe. My confidence was a little shaken for some time after this.

The summer of 1963 approached and Robin Bertram, and another officer Tony Cade, who had been a lodger with us when I first arrived in Gainsborough at 1 Bridge Road, discussed with me a joint summer holiday. We decided to fly to Jersey and preparations were set in hand. My pay and allowances in 1963 were about £46 every four weeks. I spent about £16 on lodgings and another £20 on other expenses such as running my car, swimming, books, and papers, leaving savings of around £10 a month to pay for holidays.

My summer wardrobe needed updating I decided, and on night duty, there was plenty of time for window-shopping. In Gainsborough town centre, a good menswear shop had a dummy in the window wearing a beautiful

'Banner' short-sleeved shirt. It had grey and maroon vertical stripes. When they were open, I found they had my size and I bought it. In the window of a shop in St. Peter's Avenue, on a rest day trip home to Cleethorpes, I saw some orange swimming trunks on another dummy. They looked very snazzy to me, just right for my first overseas holiday, so I went in.

I told the salesman I wanted trunks like the ones in the window. He measured my waist, opened a drawer, and produced a pair to try on. I followed him upstairs to a changing cubicle. He gave me the trunks and closed the curtain. After I put them on, he called me out to look in a long mirror. He looked me up and down and didn't seem satisfied. He ran his fingers inside the material, smoothing the edges around my legs, and then slipped his hand down the front of the trunks, arranging things, he said, to give a neater appearance. He invited me to admire the result in the long mirror. I thought they looked fine, but he suggested I try on a blue pair.

I stepped into them as he held them out. Then once more he fussed around giving me very personal attention. It was dawning on me that he was enjoying himself more than I was and decided to beat a quick retreat with my orange trunks. Whenever I returned to that shop, I was careful not to try anything else on - perhaps off-the-peg clothes are a safer bet nowadays.

This fuss was soon forgotten as the trip to Jersey drew near and excitement at the prospect of flying off to one of the Channel Islands mounted. We were transported in a small (by modern standards) propeller driven British

A Policeman's Tale

European Airways plane to the airport on Jersey. The three of us stayed at the Pomme d'Or Hotel in Saint Helier. This was a large hotel with 172 bedrooms with splendid public rooms.

We used the excellent bus service run by the Jersey Motor Transport Company to get around the island seeing the sights such as the underground military hospital at St. Lawrence. The Germans using Russian slave labour in the Second World War had built this. It covered four acres and was hewn out of solid rock taking two and a half years to complete.

In addition, I enjoyed visiting the old castles, Neolithic tombs, and especially the beaches. As a keen swimmer I found the water disappointingly cold, but the weather was kind, and I was able to do some sunbathing. We hired cycles to tour the island, and the narrow country roads were a pleasure to ride along.

I also enjoyed walking around the town of Saint Helier looking in the shops and popping into museums.

We had a wonderful holiday. It was a change from the family holidays I'd enjoyed before and gave me a taste for travel abroad. I resolved to repeat the experience as soon as savings allowed.

Back at Gainsborough, I resumed my duties. The two major Gainsborough employers were Marshalls and Roses. Marshalls made heavy caterpillar tracked tractors, while Roses made packing machinery mainly for cigarettes. When the hooter blew at 5pm the constable on duty in the town centre had to position himself in the centre of the main road outside the works exit and prepare himself as thousands of cyclists set off in a great crowd dispersing north and south while you stopped the traffic to ensure their safety. Some of my duties took me into houses near Marshall's works and I discovered that the conditions in which some people lived were totally appalling. Filth and mess were in abundance in a few homes, and I gained an insight into why some people don't have a civilised upbringing.

While I was at Gainsborough the Central Electricity Generating Board were building power stations across the river Trent. They built three of these power stations and Gainsborough was full of workers at the sites. Many of them lived in a common lodging house near the Town Bridge. Visiting this lodging house was a regular duty and I had to get used to the Irish brogue of the occupants. Mostly they addressed me as 'sir', which had never happened to me before. One night while patrolling near the common lodging house a lady approached me and she was crying. She was wearing a nightdress and began to explain to me the difficulties of her marriage. In short, her husband was beating her, and she didn't know how to cope. I was quite unqualified to give her advice but went to her house. There I saw her sleeping baby in a cot and met her husband. He was a very short gentleman from Pakistan and as I began to question him, he picked up a baby's pottery feeding vessel and smashed it against his forehead. This knocked him unconscious. Now I had a new problem. I sent for an ambulance, which helped resolve matters for then.

Often on night duty, I had to go to the Town Bridge spanning the river Trent to mount a check for an escaped prisoner or criminals making a getaway out of the county.

A Policeman's Tale

The county boundary ran along the centre of the river so that the middle of the bridge was technically the end of my jurisdiction. There was often talk that the best way to sort out a troublesome drunk was to walk him over the bridge to the Nottinghamshire side so that another police force could sort out the problem. Of course, I never did this, but the temptation was great.

My police duties were being split between foot patrol in Gainsborough and traffic patrol duty throughout the whole division. This mix I enjoyed thoroughly, whilst I enjoyed most getting out in the patrol car. Late in 1963 we were sent one of the very latest Ford Zephyrs – a Mark IV. Unlike the previous three-gear models the new cars had four gears. They were also much bigger and were also being used in a television programme called 'Z Cars' which was very popular. We had a great deal of difficulty manoeuvring our new car in the confined space of the police station yard and garage. In addition, depending on which of the three patrol cars you were assigned to, you had to remember whether you had three gears or four. This was vital because fourth gear was in the same place as reverse on the old cars and a false move would see you take the back out of the police garage.

On 19th March 1964 my new Superintendent, Mr. Eric Darnell sent me an order to remove to Headquarters for duty in the CID on Thursday 2nd April. It was time to pack my bags once more and bid farewell to all the people I'd got to know in Gainsborough over the previous two years.

Patrick J. McNeill

XI Headquarters CID

Moving to Lincoln put me back on familiar territory. I reported to Headquarters on Church Lane where I'd started my police career in 1958 as a cadet. Now, almost six years later, I found little had changed as I entered the oak panelled entrance hall with its ornate lamp lighting the way up the elegant stairs to the Chief Constable's office, and the bronze engraved plates on the walls listing the members of the Lincolnshire Constabulary who'd fallen in the two world wars.

I was to work as the CID clerk in the large room next to the Information Room where I'd last worked. First, I met Detective Sergeant Fred Fisher who was to be my direct boss. He gave me an outline of my duties. Detective Chief Superintendent Bill Kettleborough with Detective Chief Inspector Tommy Wells as his deputy headed the department. Two Detective Inspectors, Tom Lake, and Joe Cammamile worked in Mr. Wells's office and had

A Policeman's Tale

responsibility for north and south Lincolnshire, respectively.

My duties were not far removed from some of those I'd done as a cadet. It was my job to compile the daily Lincolnshire Crime Information. This was a circular on bright yellow paper sent to each police station in the county as well as to nearby stations in surrounding forces, and to the headquarters of forces in our region. It set out details of the more important crimes throughout the county and gave details of the suspects we wanted arrested. Great care was taken to ensure accuracy and to ensure that when suspects were arrested a cancellation appeared to prevent a false arrest later.

After compilation, Detective Sergeant Fisher vetted the draft and I'd get it typed up on a wax Gestetner stencil ready for printing. The stencil was checked again at this stage and then I got it printed and distributed in the mailing system. Fred Fisher was meticulous about accuracy in every aspect. He also had responsibility for explosives licensing and this area of police work was completely new to me.

Another of my jobs was gathering crime intelligence, indexing it, and circulating details to interested parties. I was constantly on the telephone to the various stations of the county checking facts and finding out additional details.

The Information room staff that checked other forces publications to see if criminals mentioned were known in Lincolnshire shared the CID General Office. There were about six of us in the room. I was the only police officer, with a cadet, and several civilian staff. We seemed to be a lively bunch and got on well together.

Another of my jobs was to maintain an index with detailed descriptions of all the bicycles stolen in the county. I kept another index of found cycles, spent long hours, and strained my eyes trying to match up the found and stolen cycles. If I had a triumph in this area and restored a missing cycle to the owner, it resulted in the crime being marked 'No Crime', thus reducing the county crime statistics. When a cycle was found, it meant the thief didn't intend to keep it, so it fell outside the definition of theft and was therefore no longer recorded as a crime.

Behind my desk were long rows of files on where blue crime reports going back several years were stored. Each report was a summary of the steps taken to investigate a crime together with the comments of senior officers. If anyone needed to know the progress of an investigation, this was the source of details. Also kept in the office was the Headquarters Crime Complaint Book. This registered in triplicate every crime reported to the police and the Home Office required every police station to keep such a book. The pages were all printed with a number. I soon learned that sometimes Her Majesty's Inspector of Constabulary required a crime to be tracked through from recording in this book to its conclusion. It was vital that proper recording took place and a crime number allocated so that a paper trail could be established through to the blue crime report. This procedure became very important to me when I first became a sergeant some years later.

Detective Superintendent Bill Kettleborough was in charge of football in the force, presiding over the county team and watching the matches of divisional teams with

A Policeman's Tale

great enthusiasm. His own days in football boots were long gone, but he encouraged everyone still capable of running with the ball to get involved. When the Headquarters team was short of a player, I found myself kitted up on the field at St. John's Hospital, the mental hospital at Bracebridge Heath. I didn't make a name for myself, but shortly afterwards had some luck in the Headquarters draw for a Football Association Cup Final at Wembley. Mr. Kettleborough got two tickets each year and we entered a draw for them. I happily went down to London with the cadet who had drawn the other ticket to see Preston North End play West Ham United, captained by the famous Bobby Moore. The final score was Preston North End 2, West Ham United 3 with Hurst scoring the winning goal in the final minute.

My lodgings this time were temporarily in Hereward Street, but after a little while I found some good accommodation at Bracebridge Heath next to the water works at 'Burnside', on the Grantham Road with Mrs. Hardy, a widow. I had a front bedroom with a single bed, and she looked after me very well. A drawback was the closeness of the Royal Air Force base at Waddington. Sometimes it seemed my bedroom was near one end of the runway as great Vulcan bombers practiced their manoeuvres, or engine tests were run. The roaring of the huge jet engines took some getting used to as they were so loud, but as had happened when I lived by the railway line at Gainsborough, I became accustomed to the disturbance.

A drawback of being at Bracebridge Heath is that it lies about six or seven miles from uphill Lincoln, where I'd always previously lodged. My car was a necessity to get to and from work. The Austin Eight of 1947 vintage, which I'd had since leaving Boston a couple of years before failed its Ministry of Transport ten-year test and I was faced with a large bill for repairs. I opted to look for a fresh car and this time found another in the form of an Austin A55 that was for sale on an open-air dealer's site near Lincoln. On 2nd June 1964, I put down a deposit of £20 and it was mine to drive away. A couple of days later I settled with the balance of £195 and bought a vehicle excise licence for £5.10s.0d. This seemed expensive at the time but the price of a gallon of petrol was only 4s. 5½d (about 23 pence in decimal coinage). While it seemed a smart car to begin with, problems soon surfaced and almost at once, the shock absorbers needed replacing. As oil was being used at an alarming rate, I had to spend £40 having the cylinders rebored. Visits home to Cleethorpes on rest days saw me regularly driving round to Messrs. Askews on Grimsby Road for yet more attention to my 'wheels'.

Most rest days, I travelled to Cleethorpes, which I still regarded as home. When my father retired as training sergeant at Cleethorpes, he became a police civilian clerk in the administrative department. My parents had moved along Lindum Road from number 32 to number 43 on the other side of the road. This had been enabled by the kindness of Mrs. Topliss and her son Harold who both had become family friends. A room was still provided for my use on my days off and the attractions of Cleethorpes were still great. I always enjoyed a visit to the bathing pool on the sea front or in winter a trip to Scartho Baths at Grimsby.

A Policeman's Tale

Often in the summer, I'd help by mowing the lawn and perhaps then relax sunbathing in the garden.

One day, as I was soaking up the sun in the back garden at 43 Lindum Road, my friend Susan Tweedy arrived with her long-time pen pal Janez Zupancez from Slovenia in Yugoslavia who was visiting England. He'd arrived with virtually no money and Susan's father, George, had had a tough time convincing immigration officials that he should be admitted to the country. George, who'd been the Grimsby Town goalkeeper, was a forceful character and eventually Janez was allowed to stay providing the Tweedy family guaranteed to pay his way and see he returned home. We quickly decided that my new car would be great for a jaunt out and before we knew it, we were bowling along the Lincolnshire countryside finding ourselves in Lincoln viewing the wonderful sights of the castle and cathedral.

We had a picnic in the Minster yard by the statue of the famous poet Tennyson. Many years later, after Slovenia had become an independent country, I met Janez again when he returned to England, not as a poor student, but as an ear, nose, and throat surgeon, attending a conference in Nottingham.

I enjoyed my time at Headquarters and since there was a relatively small pool of officers to call upon, I was in demand to play tennis during the summer, enjoying trips round the county as well as playing locally in Lincoln on the West Common. This was permitted in duty time if you were representing the police and made a nice change from the hot office. I even got paid mileage money for using my car to transport team members, so I was not too reluctant when someone suggested I could make up the numbers for a game. In my spare time, sometimes I went to Boultham Baths for a cooling open-air swim, and at Cleethorpes on rest days tried out ten-pin bowling.

At the end of October 1964, I had the pleasure of accompanying my friend Michael Benson on a journey to Northern Ireland. We drove in his Mini to Stranraer, caught an overnight ferry to the emerald isle, and arrived at the home of his fiancée's parents in Carrickfergus. I was best man for Mike and Jan's wedding and found the experience quite exciting but nerve wracking when it came to making the best man's speech. I flew from Belfast to Manchester after the event to return home. The airfare was £4.16s.0d. with a further train fare of £1.11s.0d. from Manchester to Cleethorpes. It had been around this time that I began keeping a notebook of my expenditure and it is a goldmine of information about what seem now to be very low prices.

Back at work, I learned it was proposed to send me to Nottingham to join the new regional drug squad that was operating from there. Officers on the squad assumed the appearance of 'druggies' and hung about in low dives trying to obtain evidence to mount a raid to arrest groups of drug dealers. I was flattered to be considered but felt very inadequate and unprepared for such a task. I spoke to Mr. Kettleborough and voiced my fears and the next thing I knew was that another officer was under consideration for the job. That other officer may have been more suited, but it led ultimately to a very sad conclusion for him, and I was always glad that I spoke up and was not the one who had all the problems which surfaced for my colleague.

A Policeman's Tale

My objections can't have been taken amiss however as I was instructed that I should attend a Junior Detective Course at Wakefield beginning on 23rd November 1964. This signalled the end of this short spell at Headquarters.

XII Wakefield and Spalding

I travelled up to Wakefield on Sunday 23rd November 1964 with the two other officers from Lincolnshire on the same course. They were Neville Gurnhill from Gainsborough and Mick Turner of Cleethorpes who were both glad to use my car as transport. Once more, I had a list of joining instructions with items to take. This time I found I needed to buy new football socks and shin-pads since it appeared we would be expected to keep fit in body as well as exercise our minds learning legal principles.

My car also turned out to be useful, since the lodgings allocated were at the far end of Wakefield, entailing a longish trip back to the detective training school at Bishopgarth. Two of the officers lodging with me were from British Guyana and we became good friends corresponding after they returned home.

The course was tough and dealt with law in much greater detail than I had previously studied. The essential items to learn for each category of crime were the 'points to prove'. This is a very good system since it concentrates the mind of the detective on what he had to find evidence of in a particular case. This applies just as much to a simple theft, as to a rape, murder, or complex fraud. We covered the lot and were examined on our progress.

The only area I felt was not covered adequately related to interviewing technique. This was an area where I needed more experience.

Christmas came and went, and we had a break, but were back at Wakefield for the New Year. I remember that at around 11.30pm at my lodgings we gathered with our landlady to celebrate the arrival of 1965. She had kindly provided copious amounts of alcohol and she seemed to think I needed a constant supply of blackcurrant and vodka. This was a novel mix for me and seemed quite benign. I cheerfully sang Old Lang Syne with the rest of them, but soon afterwards, the room seems to be moving gently around. I made it up to my room and with difficulty got into bed. It seemed that I had to hold on tightly to the bed to stop it going round and round. If it stopped, the ceiling started to gyrate instead. I must have dozed off eventually, but the next day, New Year's Day, I had to be up early and off to Bishopgarth. My thick head taught me to beware of strange mixes supplied by kindly landladies.

Some months before I'd known about the CID course, I'd entered my name for the qualifying examination in police subjects for promotion to the rank of sergeant. This exam was held on 13th January 1965. Because I was away from my own station arrangements were made for me to sit the examination in number three court, West Riding Court House, Wood Street, Wakefield. The examination began at 9.45am and lasted until 4.25pm. Three areas were covered. These were 'Traffic Law', 'Criminal Law', and 'General Police Duties with Elementary Administration'.

The fact that I was on a CID course was a great help in the crime paper, and my recent traffic patrol duties helped with the traffic law. Some months later, I learned that I had been successful in the exam and the way was clear to attempt the inspectors qualifying examination when I had the necessary length of service.

The course at Wakefield was completed on 30th January 1965, and I received orders to report to Spalding Divisional Headquarters for CID duties on the following Monday.

At Spalding, I was welcomed by Detective Sergeant Keith Martin and introduced to the rest of the detectives. Detective Constable Tony Curran was to be my mentor in this new job, and he hailed from Liverpool with an accent to match. He had a very good reputation as a detective, and I learned much from him.

Lodgings had once more been arranged for me and I was very lucky to be assigned to Mrs. Scott, a widow, who lived at 'Daffodale' in Alexandra Road, Spalding. She had another lodger in the next room to me, and these changed while I was there. The first was a keen rally driver who drove a green Mini Cooper. He had a crash helmet and leather gloves with holes in the back and looked the goods. After him came John Thorne who was a tall ginger headed chap, and a reporter on the local paper. I got on very well with him and accompanied him to football matches that he

A Policeman's Tale

was reporting. It was this way that I got to spend a Saturday afternoon watching Holbeach Tigers. John later joined the BBC as a regional correspondent, and I enjoyed watching him report from all corners of the country over the years.

Steve Colby was the next lodger at 'Daffodale'. He'd joined the police as a cadet and was stationed at Spalding like me. We became good friends, and he even took me with him to his judo classes where he did his stuff on the dojo in his traditional white judo outfit. We also regularly went swimming together at the open-air pool on Pinchbeck Road. The police social club paid for sessions for local officers, and we had great fun at these. I visited his home at Foul Anchor near Tydd Gote and, he invited me to be the best man at his wedding to Jonnie on 25th March 1967. I was delighted to accept.

Soon I fell into the routine of Spalding CID. Each morning the sergeant farmed out crimes to us to investigate and we did what we could to track down the perpetrators during the day. In the case of a burglary, this usually meant visiting all the surrounding properties to discover whether anyone had seen anything suspicious. It was then that I discovered just how many houses are empty in the daytime because the occupants are out at work. No wonder that a high proportion of house burglary offences occurs in daylight.

The late evening for members of the CID seemed destined to be spent in public houses. This was not to my taste, I found, and to my mind usually a waste of time. Usually, the only people present were the detectives and the landlord of the pub. This gave us little chance of getting any useful information from criminals or informers.

I was assigned to the task of watching the local prolific burglar, Gordon Grenville Creasey. He lived on a private housing estate in Spalding, not far from my lodgings. I used to bike around his estate looking out for him coming and going. He did most of his crime outside Spalding however, and I soon became convinced that he knew whom this cyclist was that often seemed to pass his house. About 20 years later, I encountered him again at North Sea Camp, which was by then an open prison. I was talking to the governor in his office when he suggested we have a cup of tea. A few minutes later in walked Gordon Grenville Creasey with a little tray with tea and biscuits. I don't know whether he or I was most startled.

One case I got involved in was where the male deputy matron at the local geriatric hospital was stealing amphetamine pills from the dangerous drugs cabinet. With Tony Curran, we searched his home and found large quantities of the pills, and some large tins of tobacco that seemed to have come from a United States air force base. We notified HM Customs & Excise. They have far greater search powers than the police and with their assistance we soon got to the bottom of the criminal activity of our deputy matron.

Some four months after starting in the CID, I had realised that this work was not really for me. I hated the pub sessions and found the task of confronting some of the criminals in their homes unpleasant. When Superintendent Walden called me into his office one day early in June 1965 to discuss a complaint he'd received, this all came to the

A Policeman's Tale

surface. The complaint was that I'd slammed a house door on leaving after talking to a youth about criminal damage. George Walden seemed to think me somewhat intellectual and not suited to mixing with the criminal classes, deciding to transfer me to town patrol duties in Spalding town.

Although I'd bought a collection of suits for my plain clothes duties, I felt a sense of relief at this news. Therefore, it was back to shifts again in uniform, but once more, I was the section reserve mobile driver, so I got lots of opportunities to drive patrol cars.

I had a holiday in August 1965 in North Wales when my parents and I toured around Snowdonia staying in bed and breakfast accommodation. A special event was going up Mount Snowdon on the rack and pinion steam railway and finding a café at the top selling a pint of beer (even though they charged an extortionate half-a-crown –12½p - for a pint).

After my holiday, back in Spalding one warm summers day, I got up after night duty around two o'clock in the afternoon and decided to have a bath. The bathroom was downstairs off the living room. It contained just a bath and hand basin, with a frosted window into the kitchen. The kitchen was a lean-to extension, with glass all round, on the back of the house. Mrs. Scott and the other lodger were out so I had the house to myself. I ran the bath and got undressed, then before getting in, had a call of nature, so I set off for the small room that was through the living room. Into the kitchen I went, and then the loo (which must originally have been outside in the yard), emerging a minute later ready for my bath. Unfortunately, in that minute, two

Salvation Army officers had come to the back door making a collection. They were in their distinctive uniforms with the lady wearing a navy straw bonnet and the man wearing a uniform cap. They were rapping on the glass of the door. They saw me just as I saw them. The startled expressions on their faces, as they saw me in my birthday suit only a few yards away, was what I noticed next. I shot into the living room and took refuge in the bathroom, as they beat a quick exit. I never heard any more of this incident, but the Salvation Army didn't make any further visits while I was there. I decided to I'd better buy a dressing gown.

In the autumn, my CID experience was to prove valuable. On Saturday, 16th October 1965, I was on mobile patrol in East Elloe, which is the area around Holbeach. My shift was the 10am to 6pm day shift and at lunchtime, I parked my patrol car in the yard at Holbeach police station. I put the kettle on and opened my box of sandwiches. After a short while, Tony Curran drove up in the little dark blue Ford Anglia that Spalding CID used. He told me that the body of the postmistress at Moulton Chapel had been found that morning, taken to Holbeach Hospital, and that an alert mortuary attendant had found a stab wound in the back of the body. It looked as though we had a murder on our hands. The next day, Sunday, I was roped in to help man the murder incident room in the police caravan parked near Moulton Chapel Post Office. Teams of detectives and uniformed officers began enquiries and searches of the area. Very quickly, it became clear that a local man had been seen walking towards the post office early on the morning of the crime. He was not at home to be interviewed. Details were

A Policeman's Tale

circulated and a 19-year-old youth, Dennis Young, from Whaplode Drove, was arrested at Skegness at 10.20pm on the Sunday evening. The knife he had used was found in a cistern at a public toilet in the seaside town.

Enquiries in the village continued for some days and I carried on assisting in the murder enquiry room.

In February 1966, I was reading the Police Review that was delivered to me every Friday when I saw a little advertisement at the back. The Association of Civil Defence Officers invited police officers to accompany them on their annual cruise aboard M.S Dunera. The price seemed very reasonable, and I made a booking. The next step was to apply for my first passport.

In my pigeonhole in the parade room at the police station on 15th February 1966, there was a pleasant surprise. It was an order from Superintendent Walden to cover for the absence of the Admin Sergeant. He was away on a course from 28th February to 11 March and I was to be Acting Admin. Sergeant. I enjoyed the fortnight discovering the mysteries of the imprest account for the payment of expenses, and many other duties of the department. Not only that, but I got to wear two stripes on my sleeves for the two weeks.

On 26th March 1966, my sister, Susan, married David William Marshall at Saint Peter's church in Cleethorpes. I was an usher and used the portable cassette recorder that I'd bought to celebrate passing the promotion examination, to record the ceremony and the church bells afterwards.

Meanwhile I was continuing my duties, foot patrol in the town and quite often on mobile duties either on the East

Elloe car or the West Elloe car. One summertime treat was to pull up beside a field of strawberry pickers and with their permission pick a punnet of strawberries to enjoy during my shift. This was just one of the perks of the intensively cultivated fenland around Spalding. One night shift while checking the wilds of Gedney Drove End marshes, a wildfowler invited me into his little black hut where a very pleasant glass of parsnip wine was on offer. Of course, this was long before the days of the breathalyser, thank goodness.

My own car had given regular trouble and it had been expensive fixing it. Patrolling in Spalding, I saw a white Wolseley 1500 displayed on a garage forecourt. I fell in love with it, especially the walnut interior trimmings and the lighted badge on the radiator. On 9th June 1966, I made a down payment of £180 and entered into a hire purchase agreement to pay £10.4s.0d. a month for the next two years. While this car was a little smaller than the A55, it was a very good runner and served me well for several years until attacks of rust, especially in the area under the bonnet, made me change it.

By this time, I'd started getting together suntan oil, sunglasses, and deck shoes for my cruise. I sent off for a pair of red sailcloth swim shorts by mail order. My old camera was well past its best and I mentioned my forthcoming holiday to the clerk in the Trustee Savings Bank in the Sheepmarket at Spalding. He kindly loaned me his half-frame 35mm camera to try out on my holiday. I bought a couple of Agfacolor slide films and was all set. My parents agreed to take me in their car to Liverpool to join

A Policeman's Tale

the ship on Saturday 20th August 1966.

The cruise was great fun and we covered 2,971 miles visiting Vigo in Northern Spain, Madeira, and Oporto before returning to Liverpool. I had a berth in Cunningham dormitory and met a group of young men, becoming good friends with several of them. One of them was Colin 'Taffy' Edwards, and I got to know him very well.

I thought Santiago dela Compostela with its great baroque cathedral, a place of pilgrimage for hundreds of years, was a wonderful place. Madeira with its terraced volcanic hillsides, full of flowers, and producing the great Malmsey fortified wine was spectacular. Even though the beaches were simply black volcanic ash, the lido was great for swimming and sunbathing. When M.S. Dunera returned to the docks at Liverpool on 3rd September, we'd all had a wonderful time both on board the ship and touring around seeing the sights in the countries we'd visited.

It was back to work on my return to Spalding. Another case with a post office connection started while I was on patrol near Holbeach. One dark and foggy night, on 7th October 1966, I was called to the Post Office at Tydd Gote, which is right on the Lincolnshire boundary. At 11.50pm that night the postmaster, Mr. Archer, heard a noise downstairs, got out of bed taking a poker from the kitchen fireplace, and went into the shop. He switched on the light and saw a man silhouetted against a glass door. He recognised the man but didn't know his name because he'd been in the shop earlier in the day. While phoning for the police, the man dived over the counter and Mr. Archer hit him on the head with the poker. The offender then threatened the postmaster with a bottle before running off.

Arriving at the scene somewhat later because of the thick fog, I found Cambridgeshire detectives already there. While I spoke to the postmaster, they searched the area and found Joshua Gray of no fixed abode wandering in the fog. In the lights of the post office, I saw a wound on his head where the poker had struck him. Arresting him, I took him back to Spalding police station. He was later committed for trial to the Quarter Sessions.

Not everything I dealt with went smoothly, and one cold winter's day I was sent to a car on fire out in the fens. I arrived to find the local fire brigade in attendance, and they had dealt with the fire. All I had to do was fill in a 'fire card' with details and be on my way. The lane was narrow, and the dykes were exceedingly deep. The fire engine blocked the way ahead, so I tried a three-point turn. When there is only ten feet to play with this is a difficult manoeuvre. Suddenly I found my front nearside wheel hanging in midair over the dyke bank. I contemplated what I might do next. I needn't have worried because several of the firemen just lifted up my car and in no time, it was back on the road facing the way I wanted to go. Unhappily, while all this was going on a gust of wind blew my flat cap off and you guessed it – it went in the dyke. No bother, for the firemen were in their waders – one of them went in and fished it out for me. I have great respect for firemen, and this was a great example of their capability to help in an emergency (even though it was of my own making).

While out in my patrol car I suppose I seemed ready to

A Policeman's Tale

respond always to whatever incident required police attention. Certainly, the powerful Ford cars we drove were impressive to look at and I always hoped the crew seemed just as impressive to the public. However, one day I was driving happily through Pinchbeck just north of Spalding when the engine coughed and died on me. This highly maintained motorcar wouldn't restart, and it dawned on me that I'd run out of petrol. I tried to keep this shameful information secret, as news of it would undoubtedly dent my (probably imagined) image as a highly competent traffic patrol officer. The sad thing was that some wag in Operations Room let the whole county know. I never forgot to check the fuel gauge before setting off on patrol again.

Another embarrassment happened on night duty during the quiet hours before dawn. It was the normal thing to be at a given point at a particular time so that a supervisory officer could meet you if he wished. These points for traffic patrol cars were made once before your meal break and once afterwards and were allocated to you before beginning your shift. This particular night I'd a point on the divisional boundary at the bridge at Surfleet on the main road between Spalding and Boston. I parked up near the bridge over the river Glen, just off the main road, for the fifteen minutes at around 3.30am. and settled back to await a visit. I must have dozed off, for the next thing I knew was the sound of a revving car engine and the sight of the Boston Patrol car disappearing up the road towards Boston. It was unusual of them not to have a word on the boundary, and I soon discovered the reason why. The contents of my car boot were carefully placed all over the road behind my car. I had to spend some time gathering road signs, shovel, brush, camera, and the rest of my equipment from the road and putting it back in the boot. No doubt the two Boston officers had a great laugh at my expense.

Another duty which traffic patrol officers were given was following diplomats from iron-curtain countries when they passed through the county. Theoretically, we disguised our patrol cars so that it was not obvious that they were police cars. However, the disguise took the form of two pieces of black card fastened with rubber bands over the police signs on the car roof. This left our blue light, silver bell (this was the days before sirens), and loudspeaker as obvious indicators of the fact that we were driving a police car. When assigned to this duty you parked at the county boundary and waited for the diplomatic car to appear. You were issued with details of the expected route and any areas they were not supposed to visit (usually in Lincolnshire they were expected to avoid Royal Air Force bases). On one occasion, the two Czechoslovakian military attachés arrived from Norfolk on the A17 road from Kings Lynn and I met them south of Sutton Bridge. I followed their car and they seemed to find their way down the road beside every airfield on the eastern side of the county all the way to Grimsby. I radioed Headquarters, reported this each time, and was instructed just to keep following them. On arrival at Grimsby, their destination was the Royal Hotel, which I knew had been demolished several months before. They seemed very nonplussed on discovering the empty space where the hotel should have been, and eventually I took the

A Policeman's Tale

initiative leading them to another hotel in the town for the night.

One night I was parked up at my point at around 3am, at the telephone kiosk at Sutton St. James, when the radio spluttered into life, and I was sent to Postland near Crowland not far from the Soke of Peterborough boundary. A fatal road accident was reported, and I made all speed to get there – quite some distance, reaching 100mph on the straight bits of road. At the scene was my section sergeant who'd travelled down from Spalding. A car was in the dyke, the ambulance had already been loaded with the body of a young man from the car, and I followed the ambulance to Peterborough Hospital where he was certified dead and placed in the mortuary. Work finished there I returned to Spalding as it had gone 6am and my shift had ended.

Next day I went in for my shift to learn two startling facts. Firstly, the next crew of my patrol car had discovered there was no oil in the sump at all - no doubt due to my high speeds. Secondly, a farmer had reported an injured man had appeared at his farmhouse door mid-morning. He had been flung from the crashed car and slowly made his way across fields to the farm seeking help. We had not seen him in the dark, but it was a good lesson of the need to ascertain the number of people in a crashed car.

One day while I was on foot-patrol found me at the Johnson Hospital where a farmer had been brought in and pronounced dead on arrival. Sudden deaths are always thoroughly investigated by the police and a report for the coroner prepared so this was my task. First, I went with the body to the mortuary and almost immediately, a woman arrived announcing she had been asked to lay out the body. This was something I'd never heard of at the time, and I was curious about what it meant. I soon found out as she asked me to help undress the poor fellow on the slab. He'd only died very shortly before and there was no problem getting his things off. I was struck that although he was dead, he looked fitter than I was. She went about her task and shortly afterwards the mortuary technician arrived to begin preparations for the post-mortem examination. He thanked me for helping and told me that getting started quickly was always useful and much easier than trying to deal with a body once rigor mortis had set in.

At 1am one morning on the A.16 road outside the Mailcart public house at Spalding I was doing what we called a road check. I stopped a nice car heading into town and the driver wound down his window. It was the singer, Ronnie Hilton. He had been doing his act at the seaside resort of Skegness earlier in the evening and was on his way home. I wished him well and sent him on his way - I should have asked for his autograph on reflection!

Extract from his obituary in the Guardian 22 February 2001 "Ronnie Hilton who has died, aged seventy-five, was one of those 1950s vocalists whose career coincided with rock 'n' roll's 1956 onslaught on the ballad-dominated hit parade. But for a time, Hilton was a star - strictly for home consumption - with nine top twenty hits between 1954 and 1957, that transitional era between 78 and 45rpm records. A quarter of a century later he became the voice of BBC Radio 2's Sounds of The Fifties series.

Hilton's approach owed much to the "nice 'n'easy" style

A Policeman's Tale

of Americans such as Bing Crosby, Eddie Fisher, and Perry Como. Together with the likes of Dickie Valentine and Michael Holliday, his was the kind of voice and style to which youngsters smooched as they edged across those dance floors not yet vibrating to Bill Haley's Rock Around the Clock and Elvis Presley's Blue Suede Shoes."

My days at Spalding were ending. The government had determined that the police forces of the country would be made more efficient by a reduction in their numbers. They required the amalgamation of smaller forces. The Lincolnshire Constabulary, a force of around eight hundred men, was to join with Grimsby Borough and Lincoln City forces to create a new force serving Lincolnshire that would be 1800 strong.

The ten police divisions existing in Lincolnshire were to be re-organised. Boston and Spalding Divisions would amalgamate, which meant that there would no longer be a superintendent at Spalding. Similar combinations of divisions were happening throughout the force, coming into effect on 1st April 1967. Our Superintendent, Gilbert Walden decided he would retire. He decided that the last divisional Instruction Class would be an opportunity to photograph most of the members of the Spalding Division. We all lined up in the back yard of the police station for the photographer with the Chief Constable, Mr. John Barnet.

Patrick J. McNeill

XIII Headquarters War Duties

On 17th April 1967, I was moved back to Headquarters joining the Training Department. With the amalgamation, there was going to be sufficient work for a dedicated clerk in the department dealing with war duties and emergency planning. I was to gather the various tasks from those doing them currently and set up the job ready for the appointment of a civilian clerk.

This time lodgings were down the hill at 1, Ashlin Grove, a very large Victorian house, accommodating a few long stay lodgers like me. There were others, usually police officers on training courses, who would stay for just a week or fortnight. I got to know lots of them – often giving lifts up to Headquarters in my car. One lodger was a printer with the Lincolnshire Echo. He used to work the hot metal linotype machines preparing the print for each evening's edition. He was a fan of the Theatre Royal and I joined him for several outings to see repertory company productions

A Policeman's Tale

like 'The Long and the Short and the Tall', 'Entertaining Mr. Sloan' and 'Blythe Spirit'.

We long term lodgers soon learnt about the bathroom on the first-floor landing, which had a door with a full-length glass panel. The glass was frosted, patterned with seashells and little yachts and reasonably opaque. However, we discovered, when we stepped out of the bath, one or other of the two young daughters of our landlady had an eye at one of the yachts in the glass. An experiment we did revealed that in this position, a clear view could be had of the goings on in the bathroom. Since the door was just by the bath, the little dears had been checking that we were putting on plenty of shampoo and possibly something to do with the birds and bees as well.

My work progressed well in an office in the former Lincoln City Police station on Church Lane. This building had originally housed a small fire engine and was equipped with several cells. I soon learned the ropes and amassed a great collection of files. Many related to the air-raid warning system intended to give four minutes warning of a nuclear attack. I had to arrange for regular testing of the 'carrier system' linking police stations with the national warning system. Main police stations in turn had a means of sending messages to speakers installed in works and village post offices all over the area so that local warnings could be given using hand sirens and maroons. The system also allowed for the sounding of power-driven sirens and these all had to be maintained and tested. My files contained details of all the maintenance contracts and tests. Faults were often. Sometimes a bird had nested in the siren or there was faulty wiring or relays. All these problems had to be put right, and retests arranged.

There was also a system of coastal flood warnings using sirens. These needed public tests so that audibility could be checked.

I also had to look into the serviceability of gas masks carried by police patrol cars and stocked at each police station. Many were left over from World War II. We were told these gave no protection against radioactive dust, so a withdrawal was arranged. A couple of cells, next to my office, were full of old gas masks, and my problem was to dispose of them. I soon discovered that burning them produced masses of black smoke from the rubber content.

I visited Grimsby Police Station and the Sessions House in Lincoln to view and audit their gas masks and had to condemn many of them, arranging for replacements. Another task involved finding storage for the explosive maroons that would be issued to all warning points. The maroons fired three charges into the air, which then exploded with the Morse code signal for D. This was to give warning of imminent radioactive fallout. With Superintendent Steve Vessey, head of training, I visited the old airfield at Dunholme Holt, where a brick building seemed suitable for keeping explosives, being a long way from any other building. Despite all our arrangements, we never actually took delivery of more than a few demonstration maroons.

I was asked to help with a photograph needed for the Lincolnshire Show held in June 1967. They wanted a full-size display picture of a policeman, and it was decided that

A Policeman's Tale

I filled the bill. In Castle Square in Lincoln, I posed by the police pillar while Headquarters Photography Department did their stuff. The picture that resulted is on the cover of these memoirs. It was also used later on the cover of the Chief Constable's Annual Report to the Police Committee.

On Thursday 6th July I was happily working among my gas masks and files relating to air raid sirens, I was phoned up and told that I was need for some real police work. A petrol tanker had been heading down Lindum Hill in Lincoln when its brakes failed.

The tanker was fully laden with fuel and the driver, knowing what might happen, had got to the left-hand bend at the bottom of the hill, just before the traffic lights, next to the Sessions House (Lincoln Divisional Headquarters), and run his offside wheels along the wall separating the two carriageways. This had demolished the wall, but it had slowed his tanker down somewhat. Unfortunately, it had tipped over and was lying on its side with petrol running out of it just a few yards before the traffic lights. The petrol was going into the drains, heading down towards Broadgate and probably out into the river Witham. A highly explosive situation had developed, and a single spark would have caused a great catastrophe.

I was given a personal radio set (the first time I'd used one of these) and stationed near the Adam and Eve Public House at the top of Lindum Hill to divert traffic. Fortunately, the fire brigade and police action avoided a worse disaster. Shortly afterwards all tankers carrying fuel were prohibited from using Lindum Hill.

After this excitement, my thoughts were turning to

holidays as I'd been sent details of the Civil Defence Officers Association cruise for 1967 and I liked what I saw. I made a booking and, in the meantime, went on a visit to London for a reunion with some of the friends made on the 1966 cruise. I'd enjoyed using the camera loaned to me for the previous cruise and I bought a Minoltina S 35mm camera of my own ready for my holiday.

M.S. Dunera sailed from Tilbury on 17th September heading for Gibraltar, 1302 miles away. We saw all the sights there and went up by ski lift to the top of the rock. The Barbary apes seemed very friendly and used to meeting visitors. It was interesting to see lots of cars in Union Jack colours and signs in the form of red, white, and blue bunting of the recent referendum voting overwhelmingly in favour of staying under the British crown. Looking round the shops was enjoyable and noticing the red pillar-boxes, together with policemen wearing helmets, just like mine, made me feel at home. With friends, I went to the beach enjoying the warmth and wonderful sunshine.

The same day we set sail across the Straits to the exotic delights of North Africa, travelling just thirty miles. In the evening, we took a trip to the Rif Hotel for a splendid dinner including couscous followed by the charms of a belly dancer. She invited me to join her on the floor and copy her movements. Having tucked up my shirt to display my belly, I discovered that it was far more difficult than I expected, but in true British fashion, I did my best so as not to let the side down. I made my companions laugh as I gyrated to the eastern melody. I should think she thought I was hopeless, but perhaps she was used to that.

A Policeman's Tale

The next day I'd booked an excursion tour by bus to Tetuan. We visited the old town seeing the mosques, fountains, and a castle. Then we had a look at the Kasbah. A highlight was a dye and tanning works where leather was prepared and set out in the sun to dry, in vivid reds and yellows. Later it would be made into pointed slippers and other handcrafted goods. Afterwards there was time to soak up the sun with friends on the beach in front of the Rif Hotel.

The next port of call was to be Lisbon, and we travelled the 288 miles taking about 48 hours for the trip. I spent much of the time on deck sunbathing and sometimes watching the dolphins playing in the bow wave of the ship. A good vantage point was the fo'c'sle right at the front of the ship. Another diversion was a show put on by a professional producer who roped in likely performers. I was in the chorus for a South Pacific spoof we did, miming to 'There is nothing like a dame' in an American sailor's outfit.

More fun was had in a crossing the line ceremony. Although we didn't actually cross the equator, there were traditional celebrations. The cruise director lined up several lads and lasses, including me, by the swimming pool. We had a good audience. King Neptune was to visit us, and we all needed to be made presentable apparently. Therefore, we were lathered with a mixture that was more like porridge than shaving foam. Not only was my face and head covered but so was everywhere else, including having half a bucket of the sticky stuff shoved inside my shorts. After being 'shaved', I was thrown unceremoniously into the swimming pool. The passengers who'd gathered round seemed to find this amusing. The water didn't actually remove all the gluey mixture and I had to wait for a vigorous shower to get it off.

Lisbon was an impressive and wonderful city. The tour to Sintra to see the summer palaces of the Portuguese kings was memorable, as were visits to the seaside towns of Cascais and Estoril.

We returned to Tilbury on 30th September 1967 having covered 2,644 miles.

After a second great cruise, it was back to work in Church Lane.

My job was to train a replacement civilian clerk and when this had been done, and she was able to carry on the work, a move for me was arranged. I was to go to Cleethorpes to replace Keith Rodgers, the CID clerk, who was becoming a regular detective.

XIV Cleethorpes & Grimsby CID

On 13th November 1967, I moved to the CID office at Cleethorpes Police Station. This was great, because for the first time in nine years I could live at home with my parents at 43 Lindum Road.

Very quickly, I found that the work revolved around the accurate recording of details of crimes in the important divisional crime register. Each crime was allocated a number by me, and brief details entered. My job was to ensure that the investigation was progressed, and this progress was noted in the register. I saw to it that the crime report made out by the investigating officer arrived on time after seven days, that it was submitted to Headquarters, and then returned in due course. I had to ensure that each crime was shown as 'detected', 'undetected', or 'no crime'. If an offender was caught, I had to put details in the register and show what happened to the offender by way of court process, caution, or some other disposal.

At the end of the month, a statistical sheet was completed summarising crimes by category and explaining any rises or falls in numbers. This had to go to Headquarters to compile force statistics for the Home Office.

There were plenty of files to maintain and generally, I acted as the link for officers out in the division doing their crime enquiries.

When starting at Cleethorpes I knew that it was unlikely to mean my staying there long, because the division was due to amalgamate with what had become the Grimsby Division on 1st January 1968. Part of my work involved preparations to move all the Cleethorpes files to Grimsby Police Station.

Most of the officers at Grimsby were from the former Grimsby Borough Police force that had amalgamated with Lincolnshire Constabulary on 1st April 1967. It was a little like going into the lion's den. They had their own ways of doing things and some of the 'county' ways were not welcome. For instance, whereas in the county our usual way of dealing with offenders was to report them for summons, in the borough everyone seemed to get arrested – a novel approach to me, but having many advantages, especially for obtaining fingerprints and completing files.

At Grimsby, I fulfilled a similar role in the CID Admin office, but here there was a sergeant in charge. He was Detective Sergeant Peter Cook, and we had two civilian clerks and a shorthand/typist to help with the work. First, my main job was to sort the large number of crime complaints and ensure they all had been allocated for

A Policeman's Tale

investigation. Next, I recorded them in the Crime Register, and passed details to one of the clerks who produced the daily Divisional Crime Information. This was a listing giving details all the crimes, so that the officers of the division could see what was happening each day.

Meanwhile a press conference was being held by one of the superintendents and I often needed to supply details of crimes for his benefit.

Once all this had been done and it often took all morning and into the afternoon, I had to sift incoming crime reports and ensure they were dealt with. The Grimsby division was the busiest division in the county and when I was there, we recorded more than two thousand crimes a year. These needed statistics prepared and analysed. This was all done by hand. Later a computerised system was introduced, with all the expected problems of a new system, but this simplified the analysis of the statistics. On the other hand, when a query arose someone still had to look at all the files to find out why there was an anomaly. One good thing, which soon became apparent, was that trends in crime could be identified more quickly and areas where high crime rates were occurring identified.

Great changes had occurred in the leadership of Lincolnshire Police and George Terry became our Chief Constable. Nationally a new policing scheme was being adopted and in came the notion of crime & intelligence collators. These supported local officers assigned on a permanent basis to each area of a town, as had always been the case with rural beats. Alongside this development, motor patrols using panda cars supported the local beat officers. A large fleet of these panda cars was purchased by each police force and the initial colours of turquoise and cream were a novelty.

My long-time girlfriend, Susan Tweedy, had succumbed to the charms of one of my old form mates from Clee Grammar School, Chris Warren. As luck would have it my sister's friend, Julia Boyers, responded kindly to an invitation to go out with me, and we began regular trips out in the Wolseley 1500 for ice-creams on a Sunday to Appleby's at Covenham. Evenings were sometimes spent at the Wheatsheaf Hotel, listening to a piano and drums combination as soft background music to a pleasant drink and conversation.

With the arrival of spring, we began tennis sessions, as Julia was a keen player. Later I joined the St. Columba's church badminton club. This was on Weelsby Road, Grimsby, and we played many enjoyable and energetic games there. Badminton was also played in the ballroom of Grimsby Police Station on a thick green mat that we laid out each time. Julia and I often played with Bob Barry who was back at Grimsby from the training centre. His cry in a Scottish accent of 'Come on Pat' will always stay in my memory. This was a good venue despite the low ceiling, but at least there were good changing facilities with showers, which were very welcome, especially on warm summer days.

We sometimes went to see David at his Cuxwold Cricket Club and enjoyed picnicking afterwards. Susan, my sister, always provided a good picnic. Once we'd parked in a field by a barn, sheltering us from the wind, when a herd of cows came to see what we were doing. My dear sister became

A Policeman's Tale

agitated and called on David and me to get rid of them. 'Do something' she shouted in alarm – no mean task.

Early in 1968, my eye had been taken by an advertisement for 'Bachelors Abroad', a holiday company specialising in arranging travel for single people. I got their brochure and booked a Club Mediteranée holiday in Yugoslavia at Sveti Marko. This was the height of the 'swinging sixties'. Flower power was abroad, and I understood that at Club Mediteranée the order of the day was Tahitian style, living in straw huts, and paying for drinks with beads (actually plastic 'poppets' worn as a necklace). I began to gather holiday gear, including a mask, snorkel and flippers and Polynesian print swim trunks.

The holiday was from 10th to 25th August 1968 and the flight was to Dubrovnik, by bus to Kotor in Montenegro, and then by caique (a local fishing boat) to the island. A great welcome party of holidaymakers awaited us on arrival all dressed in pareos, beads, and bright costumes. The cas (hut) allocated to me and two other English 'Bachelors Abroad', was called Hernie. It was basic, but we only needed it for sleeping. The scenery was magnificent with wonderful mountains on the nearby mainland. The water was warm and great for snorkelling, and I learned to water-ski, achieving a certificate for my efforts. The trick and art is to remember to keep the arms straight and bend the knees as you whiz across the waves. Some of the staff put on wonderful displays of water-skiing technique. Several of them abreast would do jumps off ramps or would mount shoulders often carrying colourful flags to add to the wonderfully exciting spectacle.

The activities were all free and there was no problem finding someone to have a game of boules on the beach. The food cooked by French chefs was marvellous starting with a wonderful breakfast in the open-air restaurant. I loved yoghurt with honey and almonds followed by hard-boiled eggs. Lunch was also excellent, and in the evening, a splendid dinner was provided. After that, the staff of gentil animateurs would put on a show.

If you got hungry in the day, there were open-air barbeques where local speciality cevapcicis could be bought. These were little meat savouries that I thought delicious. Drinks needed to be bought, except at meals, and the coloured beads round my neck, provided the currency. I took a trip to the mainland to see the old walled city of Kotor, walked the walls, and looked in several of the old churches.

The atmosphere of Club Mediteranée appealed to me. It seemed a great way to see another country, soak up the sunshine yet do all sorts of activities that otherwise you'd have little chance to try.

On going back, to work at Grimsby Police Station I soon gained a new boss in my office. D/Sergeant Cook was promoted to Inspector on town patrol and John Braithwaite took his place. While his job was to oversee my work, much of his time was spent preparing cases committed to Grimsby Borough Quarter Sessions. The Detective Sergeant, who'd handled the case initially, usually prepared trial cases. Additionally, there were cases where an individual was sent for sentence, or which had originated in the uniform department, or even from the British Transport

A Policeman's Tale

Police. The CID Admin staff looked after these additional cases. Some of it was farmed out to me, especially making checks into the social and work history of the offender. I used to ring employers to find out their opinion of offenders so that the recorder or judge had an independent assessment to use when sentencing. In addition, our office handled all the paperwork concerning criminal records and fingerprints that had to be returned to Scotland Yard and the regional bureau at Wakefield following the conviction of an offender. Patricia Hawken handled much of this work.

I'd happily done this work for over a year when it was decided that it was time for my sergeant, John Braithwaite to take on one of the teams of investigating detectives. A replacement was needed in the CID Admin. Office and Chief Superintendent Darnell came to see me. He told me I would fill the position on an acting basis. Then an hour or two later he returned and said I'd do it on a temporary basis. This was a huge difference. Acting officers usually revert to their former rank, but temporary ranks usually convert to the confirmed rank. I was very pleased. My promotion to temporary sergeant took effect on 27th March 1969. I was 27 years old, with 8¼ years' service.

Even better news swiftly followed and a full promotion with effect from 10th April was announced in force General Orders.

My new job meant that I took over the task of liaising with the Quarter Sessions and later the Crown Court. One of the most pleasurable parts of the job was seeing that a solicitor was contracted to represent the police (as prosecutors), and that in turn the solicitor briefed the counsel of our choice. Regular trips to various solicitors followed and I formed several friendships with them. I'd get a brief prepared for them and then take it round and discuss any intricacies so they could ensure counsel knew all the details.

I spent a considerable amount of time delving into two heavy tomes. One was Oke's Magisterial Formulist, and the other was Archbold's Criminal Pleadings. With the aid of these volumes, I could set out the charge against the offender correctly and set about providing details of the evidence. The next task was to provide an accurate history of the offender. This was simplified if he'd often been in trouble with the police, although that could complicate it, because histories were available from previous appearances. The main essential was accuracy and I spent long hours clearing up discrepancies and verifying facts.

This was necessary because when Quarter Sessions started, and later Crown Court, I had to go into the witness box, swear to tell the truth, and then present the history to the court. Often defence or prosecution barristers would question me and ask me to elaborate, and occasionally the recorder or judge would do the same. On one occasion, I had an offender with a conviction in Leith that had been difficult to check out. I always attempted to get information about the crime that had led to a previous conviction. This time I'd telephoned Leith to find out about a housebreaking, but they'd been unable to tell me anything. When I reported this to the judge, he uttered the famous phrase "The Leith Police dismisseth us". In this case, it was quite true, and there was laughter in court.

My other task in court was to ensure details of the sentence passed was accurately recorded. When there were several concurrent with consecutive sentences, sometimes suspended for a period, it was often difficult to get down exactly what the judge had decided.

Meanwhile my dear sister, Susan, and her husband David, presented me with a niece –Bridget Sarah Marshall, who was born on 9th April 1969. On 13th July 1969, I attended her baptism at St. Peter's Church, having the honour of being chosen as one of her godparents. The other two were Norman and Rosemary McVicker. This was an opportunity for a great family get together and we celebrated the event at Susan and David's House at 23 Pearson Road, Cleethorpes, after the church service.

Julia enjoyed swimming as much as I did. She was also keen to have a day on the beach and sometimes we'd take a trip to Mablethorpe and picnic on the sands. Another favourite outing for both of us was to the open-air swimming pool in Jubilee Park at Woodhall Spa. This was always a treat as open-air swimming pools have gradually declined in number.

In August, I went off to North Wales for a break, staying at Colin 'Taffy' Edwards parents' house in Ruthin. We visited Caernarfon Castle where preparations were in full swing for the installation of Prince Charles as Prince of Wales. We saw a Son et Lumiere show in the evening at the castle. I enjoyed a tour of Anglesey and climbing the 'bonkin' as Taffy called the hill Mulvami, near Ruthin.

Back in Cleethorpes, Julia and I had decided that we

would take a holiday together that year. We booked with Club Mediteranée flying on 1st September 1969, by Caravelle to Nice for an overnight stay and then on to Bastia in the north of Corsica. Our village was at Santa Guilia just north of Bonifacio on a most beautiful bay with a lagoon behind the beach. The huts were substantial if still a little basic. Once again, the facilities were great for sport, classical music, and evening shows. The food was also exceptionally good.

With friends, Mary, and James, we wanted to hire a car to tour the island but the government restriction on taking currency abroad presented a problem. At the time, you were only allowed to take £10 each on holiday, and the deposit to hire the car was £40. A kindly holidaymaker overheard our discussions about how to surmount this difficulty. She was the wife of the producer of 'Coronation Street', and the currency restriction seemed not to be a problem for her. She proffered £40 in £10 notes, and we borrowed it gratefully. It enabled us to hire a small Renault car and travel through the mountains and sweet chestnut woods, seeing the rocky calanches on the way to Ajaccio. There we saw Napoleon's birthplace and then went on to see more of the lush scenery. We finished with an evening meal in one of the high mountain villages.

On another trip we visited the town of Bonifacio where the French Foreign Legion were based, seeing the wonderful cliffs of wind-eroded sandstone with houses perched perilously on top. This holiday ended after three weeks on 22nd September 1969 after a superb Corsican break.

Back in England, in early November, I was invited down to Saltdean, near Brighton, the home of Mike, and Jan Benson. They were about to have their new son, Richard John, christened and I was again honoured to be asked to act as godparent.

In my spare time, I'd been studying for the inspector's examinations. I took these in January 1970 and passed. Subsequently on 6th May 1970, I was confirmed in the rank of Sergeant.

Because I had become the CID Admin sergeant, someone was needed to replace me. Martin Ward was chosen to do this, and I got on well with him. Martin was an excellent worker, and he later became a Detective Inspector.

Our new chief constable, George Terry, was certainly a new broom and suddenly expenditure on communications within the force increased dramatically. A force newspaper, 'Alert', was introduced and regular updates in the form of more frequent general orders were issued. A force public relations officer, Tony Diggins, was appointed, and so was a welfare officer. Many other changes were introduced, with a view to bringing Lincolnshire Constabulary into the second half of the twentieth century. Eventually George Terry moved on to Sussex and Laurence Byford took his place.

Holidays in 1970 included a trip up to the west of Scotland with Taffy Edwards in June. We visited Oban, took a sea trip around the Isle of Mull on one of MacBrayne's vessels, and saw Fingal's Cave on Staffa. I had only known this because of the Mendelssohn overture of that name, and it was exciting to see the black basalt columns of rock around the sea washed cave entrance. On the same trip, I visited the monastery of St. Columba, on the island of Iona, a fascinating remote site where early Christianity began in our islands.

Another holiday with Julia at the beginning of September saw us flying from Heathrow to the Greek Island of Corfu in the Ionian Sea. We stayed in the Club Mediteranée village at Ipsos on the west of the island a short distance by caique from Corfu town. Once again, we were accommodated in straw huts and bathroom facilities were open air. The huge range of activities on offer together with the marvellous food and brilliant weather made for a great holiday. My favourites were water skiing and dinghy sailing, and I managed to obtain a certificate of sailing competence. We hired a scooter and travelled as far as Paleocastritsa, which called for riding over the mountains to the other side of the island. The trip was well worth it as the scenery was stunning. While on Corfu we were close to Mount Pantocrator and had good views of the mountains of Albania. One morning at dawn, we found the roof of our cas shaking and experienced our first earthquake – fortunately only a minor one. Another enjoyable trip was to see the Achilleon – built as a summerhouse for Kaiser Wilhelm and now a casino. One of the sights is the cricket pitch in front of the old governor's palace in Corfu town. This lush green square is a surprise in such a setting, and I remember sitting at one of the cafes nearby trying out my Greek to order a drink of Coca Cola.

A Policeman's Tale

In October 1970, the CID staff organised a trip to Holland to see Amsterdam. We sailed from Immingham across the North Sea overnight, giving us a full day in the interesting city. A tour of the sights took in the royal palace and a visit to an Edam cheese dairy. We saw windmills galore and funny little lift up bridges, plus lots of interesting parts of the city. Our journey home was again overnight, and in the morning, I enjoyed a close-up view of Spurn Point at the mouth of the River Humber.

The government of Sir Edward Heath had appointed the Radcliffe-Maud committee. This enquiry into the set-up of local government reported that new counties should be created, including Humberside. The boroughs, and areas of countryside surrounding, Cleethorpes, Grimsby, and Scunthorpe, together with Brigg and the Isle of Axholme would no longer be part of Lincolnshire. This meant a new police force being created to cover Humberside and effectively a reduction in the size of the Lincolnshire Constabulary down to 1200 officers. This was due to take effect in 1974 on 1st April.

Meanwhile, as the implications of this sank in, I continued my social life. Julia's birthday on 23rd March 1971 was celebrated in style at the swish Dakens Restaurant in Grimsby Market Place.

I was sent on a Sergeants Refresher Course to Horncastle in April, where we brushed up on our law, and devoted time to man-management and leadership subjects.

Holidays in 1971 included a trip up to Scotland with Taffy, staying on the Isle of Skye and then three weeks from

27th August to 17th September, on my own (Julia was hard up at the time having bought a new car) to the Club Mediteranée village at Smir in Morocco. This time the accommodation was in a traditional hotel, and I had a great three weeks there. A coach tour to the Roman remains at Volubilis, Tangier town, Fez, Meknes with overnight stops, was very interesting. It gave me a good insight into the lifestyle of the people of the country.

Early in 1972, it became obvious that my lovely Wolseley 1500 was succumbing to a bad attack of rust. The inner wings under the bonnet had rusted through and repair would be uneconomic. I cast around for a replacement and on 18th February, I bought for £730 a russet brown Austin Maxi. This roomy five-door car was very versatile with fully reclining seats and a huge boot capacity. A great feature was the gearbox that had five gears as well as reverse. One of my early outings in May of that year was a trip over to see Taffy Edwards. We toured the Lake District staying at Keswick and York on the way back.

Not long afterwards, I was in my office in Grimsby Police station when we had a visit from our chief constable. Mr. Lawrence Byford was visiting, as he regularly did, and this time he spoke to me. I vividly remember him looking me in the eye, a somewhat unnerving experience, and saying, "I'm moving my best officers down into Lincolnshire, – and you do want to be in my force don't you"? The only reply to this had to be "Yes, Sir," and a short while later I received orders to move to Boston for Town Patrol duties.

The members of staff of the CID Admin office were kind enough to present me with a very nice pair of cufflinks as a goodbye present. I think this was one of the most interesting and happy periods in my police career and I was very sorry to leave the team I'd worked with for nearly four years.

XV Boston & Stamford

On 17th July 1972, I reported once more for duty in Boston. I was on familiar territory, but no one seemed to have got lodgings fixed up for me, so I stayed at the Barge Inn. This was a very old place near the Sluice Bridge in Boston and most of the other guests were labourers or land workers. I was in a shared room and sought new lodgings straight away. Chris Hannath who'd been a cadet with me found me a room at the home of Doris and Alan Bloodworth in Freiston Road. My room was small and at the back of the house. Doris did her best to make a good home for me even though she had a husband and two young children to cope with. Alan was a lorry driver and his tractor unit used to be parked in the yard under my bedroom window. When he set off at 5am in the morning, I got a rude awakening, not only from the diesel engine noise but also from the airbrakes. Getting over this slight annoyance, I was very well fed, and it was a good lodging.

A Policeman's Tale

This was the first time I'd had a section of men to organise, and it was rather different to running an office. The men needed briefing before each shift and their beats determined, together with any additional duties. In the case of probationary constables, - and most of the section were probationers, - extra attention had to be given to ensure they were competent to deal with incidents to which they were sent.

All the reports submitted by my section about offences, road traffic accidents, fires, sudden deaths, and other incidents, I had to check. I had to put my recommendations on the report for consideration by an inspector. There was also the disciplinary side of a supervisory role, and this caused me some problems. One officer was regularly late for duty, and of course, the rest of the section was well aware of this. On courses, you were told that any disciplinary infringement should be reported immediately, but I was also aware that discretion should be in your armoury. A couple of warnings went apparently unheeded, so I determined to put in a report the next time this officer was late. He was about ten minutes late for early turn one morning, but just as I decided I would report him, the inspector turned up also ten minutes late. Of course, I was also very conscious of the very first morning I'd been due on duty for 6am at Boston and the embarrassment of not waking up in time.

Deciding I'd report the offence the next time, I didn't have long to wait. The result was that he was moved to another division very soon afterwards. The sad thing was that he died about six months later from an unexplained cause. This gave me a good deal of heart searching, and I was ever reluctant thereafter to go so far as to put another officer on report.

Later in July, I again went over to see Taffy at his home in Macclesfield and then visited parts of North Wales I'd not seen before. I discovered that you could drive your car onto Black Rock Sands, something not permitted at home in Lincolnshire. The weather was good and great for the beach, or a touch of sunbathing.

In August 1972, I used the Maxi again, travelling with Taffy down to Cornwall staying in Penzance, and then travelling on the 'Scillonian' by sea to Hughtown on the Isles of Scilly. This was a memorable holiday. We even saw Harold Wilson, (prime minister 1964 to 1970), with his dog on one of our boat trips to an outer island. We stayed in Hughtown at a bed and breakfast establishment. Most days we went down to the harbour and chose a boat to a different island each day. I was fascinated to discover that on Tresco there was a place called Old Grimsby. In addition, on Tresco, I enjoyed visiting the sub-tropical gardens where there was a magnificent display of exotic flora. Another trip was out to see the Bishop Rock lighthouse, which was still manned in those days. We took supplies for the lighthouse keepers who hauled them up in a basket from our boat. In the evenings, we found a hostelry for a drink and one evening went to an excellent Gilbert and Sullivan production, of 'HMS Pinafore' by the local amateur operatic society. A lifelong love of G&S works followed from this.

The second half of September saw me attending another refresher course. This time it was held at the Brant

A Policeman's Tale

Broughton College. Once it had been the vicarage, a lovely stone-built house next to the church in extensive grounds. I got a chance to explore the village, which was especially interesting given that it had been my father and mother's home after their marriage before moving to Great Gonerby.

One of the regular Boston happenings at the weekend, as mentioned previously, was the appearance of a star band or performer at the Starlight Rooms in the Gliderdrome. One evening, Saturday, 24th February 1973 the big name was Elton John, and I was on night duty. He was a major attraction and over two thousand fans paid the sum of £1.50 to see him. I was at the back of the Gliderdrome at the end of the entertainment to see the star safely on his way. There was a large gathering around the stage door, and I helped Elton John get to his white Rolls Royce. He wore huge built-up boots and very large spectacles and seemed grateful that someone was keeping the fans at bay for his departure.

In January 1973, I had seen advertised a trip to New York promoted by the International Police Association. I'd joined the association in 1968 while stationed at Cleethorpes and am still a member. The cost was about £72 for one week and this seemed a very good bargain, so I made a booking. The flight was from Manchester Airport on Sunday, 8th April 1973, on a Boeing 707, seating 160 people. We took off at 6.30pm and arrived after a six-hour flight, at John F Kennedy airport New York at 7.30pm New York time.

There were so many memorable things to see and do. The first was getting up at 6.00am to visit Times Square in the early sunshine. I was staying at the Royal Manhattan Hotel on 8th Avenue, 44/45th Streets, on a bed only basis. My first night's sleep was punctuated by the frequent sound of police car sirens on the avenue many floors below my window. Breakfast consisted of crispy bacon and eggs at a breakfast bar on the way to Times Square near Broadway and its theatres. I went up the 1,050 feet high Empire State Building to the 86th floor, saw Chinatown, and visited Wall Street where I saw the almost complete 110 stories, 1,350-foot-tall World Trade Centre under construction. I saw the monuments with the names of the war dead at Battery Park and walked around to the United Nations Buildings with the flags of 132 nations flying outside.

The Circle Line ferry on the Hudson River took me to see the famous passenger liner piers, the Wall Street area, the Verrazano Narrows Bridge, Statten Island and Liberty Island with its great statue by Auguste Bartholdi. The ferry took us around the other side of Manhattan Island seeing the United Nations Buildings from the water and the various notable bridges.

On a trip by coach to Washington, about 250 miles from New York, we travelled under the Hudson River through the Lincoln Tunnel. At the end of the freeway, we entered Washington taking in views of the White House, then over the Potomac River with a view of the Pentagon to Arlington Cemetery to see 150,000 military graves. The Mansion of Robert E. Lee was impressive, and we witnessed the changing of the guard at the tomb of the unknown warrior. Arlington also held the graves of John and Robert Kennedy, both of whom had been assassinated.

A Policeman's Tale

I found Lincoln's Memorial completed in 1922, fascinating, facing as it does the monument to the first president, Washington. After lunch, I saw the Supreme Courts of Justice approaching the Capitol Building. It was awe-inspiring standing under the ornate dome and then being allowed into the congress chamber. The decorations on the corridor walls, consisting of paintings of scenes from early American life were wonderful. After this, it was onto the Smithsonian Institute. There was a spare lunar module on display together with a one-pound sample of lunar surface rock.

Another treat was a night at the Radio City theatre in the Rockefeller Centre. This theatre, seating 6,200 people, was the world's largest with two organs, one either side of the stage, and a huge line up of chorus girls, the Rockettes. We saw their Spring Show. It was truly spectacular.

Especially for the International Police Association members was a tour of New York City Police Headquarters. I found their communications centre fascinating and watched with great interest as they despatched officers in response to 911 emergency calls. They had a computer system up and running long before the Lincolnshire Constabulary – perhaps not surprising given the huge volume of work in New York. It was a privilege to tour the city centre in a police vehicle from the Mid-Town South police division. Various dubious characters were pointed out to me, and this was a real eye-opener to a rural policeman like me.

All too soon, the seven days were over, and we took off over Jamaica Bay on our way back to Manchester, three thousand miles away.

In June 1973, I'd arranged with Taffy Edwards to tour Scotland. Unfortunately, he decided that he couldn't afford a holiday and I set off on my own. I travelled up to Edinburgh, where I took great pleasure in swimming in the magnificent pool built for the Commonwealth Games, and shopping in Princes Street. Next, I went up towards Dundee admiring the magnificent Forth railway bridge. From there, it was across to the West coast, heading up via Ullapool to the very wild country of the Northwest. There seemed to be more water than land and the rocky Stack Polly jutting above the landscape was magnificent. I bed and breakfasted most nights but was unable to find accommodation near the Caves of Smoo, so spent the night in the good old Maxi. It was a bit cold but quite comfortable. The next day I drove east towards Dunnet Head and John o' Groats. At Wick, I visited the glass works, saw craftsmen blowing artistic shapes in molten glass, and bought a lilac-coloured glass display dish as a present for my dear mother. Then I travelled on to Aberdeen, the Granite City, and southwards back to England.

Now back to police work, because I was qualified for promotion to the rank of Inspector, I was invited to attend a selection board chaired by the deputy chief constable. All I remember being asked concerned what I was doing to increase my level of education. In the Autumn of 1973, this spurred me into beginning evening classes at Boston College of Further Education studying for an A Level General Certificate of Education in General Principles of English Law. I discovered that there was much more to the law than police law. Much of our time was devoted to contract law, the principles of equity, and the English system of civil law. I remember discovering that if you find a snail in your bottle of pop, the responsible person is the shopkeeper who sold it to you, and not the manufacturer, because your contract is made with the shopkeeper. We studied numerous cases where ships had run into jetties destroying them or setting them on fire. In particular, the principle of 'res ipsa loquiter' (the thing speaks for itself) stays with me. It was explained that if you were passing a warehouse and a large bag of sugar fell on your head you wouldn't need to prove to the court that someone was negligent because the thing spoke for itself. These, and many more cases had to be committed to memory, together with their names, so you could quote them in the examination.

Back in Cleethorpes, on 18th September 1973 my second niece, Sally Louise Marshall was born.

A couple of months later I was given regular duties as station sergeant at Boston. This meant that I spent my shifts in the station with responsibility for the enquiry office, the communications, and especially the prisoners brought in by arresting officers.

On 1st January 1974, I was posted to Stamford to cover for the absence of an officer on a course. I lodged with Mrs. Pietrzak, (but paid a retaining fee to Doris Bloodworth to keep my Boston digs available for my return). She made me welcome, and I set about my new duties with enthusiasm. I didn't know my way around Stamford and had a new set of street names to learn. It was a complete contrast to Boston, and I found very different people living there. It was also the 'Winter of Discontent' when the government and the trades union were at loggerheads. The result was regular power cuts on a scheduled basis to conserve power station coal. At the police station we had candles, gas, and oil lamps to see us through, as did most of the population.

I had to make regular return trips to Boston for my evening classes and had to attempt to swap duties when I needed time for this.

One interesting case at Stamford related to a burglary where a window had been broken. I went with one of my young constables to investigate and found spots of blood on the edges of the broken glass. There was another spot on the ground, and a couple of yards away yet another. We followed the trail, with some difficulty, but there were enough spots to track the offender down to his home half a mile away. He was wearing a bandage on his wrist, and this seemed very good evidence to us, warranting an arrest.

While at Stamford it soon became apparent that, of the seven or eight men in my section, I was the only one without a moustache. I set about remedying this straight away.

The day of the major changes in local government was approaching. On 1st April 1974, the county of Humberside was created. The three counties of Holland, Kesteven, and Lindsey were abolished, and Lincolnshire County council came into being with authority over the City of Lincoln. Some six hundred Lincolnshire officers were transferred to the new Humberside Police force and the Lincolnshire Constabulary, now 1200 officers strong, became known as Lincolnshire Police.

A Policeman's Tale

Marking the occasion was to be a parade of the old Lincolnshire Constabulary at Lincoln Castle followed by a commemorative service at Lincoln Cathedral. Stamford was by then part of the Grantham Division. We practiced our marching skills at Grantham barracks and on the day, I travelled up with the Grantham divisional contingent to Lincoln for the event. In many ways it was sad to see the end of the force I'd joined with a proud history stretching back to 1857, but progress marches on and us with it.

Yet again, I needed to change my car, but I'd grown fond of my russet brown Austin Maxi and this time I traded it in for another one on 1st April 1974. The replacement was a Maxi 1750cc model in limeflower, which I could never decide whether it was a sort of yellow or a sort of green. It cost £950 and I got a trade in allowance of £550 so only needed to find the £400 difference.

XVI Boston & Skegness

My Stamford attachment came to an end and on 15th April 1974 I was back at Boston. I lodged once again with Doris and Alan Bloodworth and their two children Karen and Robert. However, their old landlord had given them notice to quit, and while I'd been away, they were rehoused by the council at 12 Ingelow Avenue, Boston. This was on the Fenside Estate and quite a number of police customers lived in the area. I was very wary of leaving my nice Maxi in front of my digs and used to keep it near the old folks bungalows a short distance away, as a precautionary measure.

I resumed my regular evening classes studying for my A Level in English Law, but almost immediately received another removal order. This time I was to join the regular summer transfer of officers to Skegness to beef up the strength there. In summertime the town's population swells from about 17,000, to around 100,000 encamped in caravans or at Butlins Ingoldmells site.

A Policeman's Tale

I admit that, heading for Skegness along the A.52 winding road, there was a slight tear in my eye at uprooting myself once again with the prospect of learning yet another set of street names and local knowledge. This was my fourth move in a little under two years and took place on 13th May 1974.

Skegness Police Station was brand new white tower block and I reported in, meeting fellow sergeants. I was sent off to my new lodgings. They were at 93 Sunningdale Drive where Dora and Len Bellamy, a very pleasant couple, took me in. They had a Yorkshire terrier, and Len was a keen gardener.

At work, I soon found my way round the police station and then around the town. As an experienced sergeant, I was often used as the station sergeant with responsibility for the cells and any prisoners. Not long after arriving in Skegness, to be precise on Wednesday, 29th May 1974 at 3.20pm I was dealing with the prisoners in the cells. One of them was Arthur Horace 'Brummy' Mills who needed to be charged and then taken before the magistrates in the court building adjoining the police station.

With Constable Paddock, I went to cell number five. Brummy was wearing only socks, underpants, and a waistcoat. He'd taken off or torn up the rest of his things. He was a local character who regularly walked about the town with a handcart on which was chalked 'As seen on Yorkshire TV'. He refused to leave the cell and eventually we forcibly took him to the charge room. We gave him a pair of WRVS trousers to wear, but he became violent, and the trousers had to be put on him by force. We handcuffed him but he kept trying to push his trousers down, so I sat him down and kept my hand on his shoulder so he couldn't stand and remove his trousers. Eventually he calmed down and I managed to get him charged with the theft of a purse. Unwisely I took my hand off him; he stood and pulled down his trousers. Because he needed to go before the court (with a female magistrate and a female clerk), I knew he needed to wear his trousers. He butted me in the face as I tried to pull them up, resulting in me having a bruised nose, with swelling and considerable pain. His action resulted in my teeth striking together forcibly chipping one of the top front ones. By this time, more officers had arrived and eventually Brummy was got into court and sent off to Lincoln Prison for seven days. He appeared before Skegness magistrates Court on 12th June. He was sentenced to imprisonment for 1 month, suspended for 12 months for the theft of the purse, and to 3 months imprisonment suspended for 12 months for assault occasioning actual bodily harm on me.

There were two sequels to this. I applied to the Criminal Injuries Compensation Board and was awarded £50 for my injuries. The cheque arrived on 13th December 1974 and this useful amount was put towards the diamond engagement ring I was about to buy for Julia. The second consequence affected Brummy Mills when he visited Boston later in 1974 and encountered Sergeant Allan Clifton near the Five Lamps, leaving the sergeant with a broken arm. This time the magistrates sent Brummy to prison for 12 months for the assault on Sergeant Clifton, giving him an extra three months for the assault on me.

Another occasion remembered clearly, was one day

A Policeman's Tale

when I was on a 6pm to 2am shift; I was out in the garden at my lodgings and saw plumes of smoke coming from the north. Setting off to investigate, I discovered there was a fire at Butlins at Ingoldmells. It turned out the deep fat fryer in the Chinese Restaurant (which was part of the Princess Ballroom) had caught fire and this had spread to the rest of the building. The fire was well alight, and I remember hearing loud crackling noises as I saw the roof tiles fracture and fly up into the air. Eventually there were twenty-three fire tenders at the scene. It took quite a long time to bring the fire under control.

When I came on duty, I was sent up to Butlins to spend the evening and night organising the policing at the scene. Very little was left of the structure that was by now a steaming mass of tangled steel girders. This was the first time I'd had close up experience of a major fire. It was very clear to me how a small incident could quickly become a much more major and catastrophic one if correct action is not taken to deal with it speedily.

Earlier in 1974, Taffy had persuaded me that it would be a good idea to take my car on the ferry from Immingham to Amsterdam and travel the continent for a summer holiday. For economy, we could hire a tent and share the cost of petrol and campsites. This sounded a good idea to me, and I set about getting a green insurance card, AA cover for breakdown, booking a tent and ferry crossing. We fixed the dates as 12th to 28th July. Unfortunately, for the second year in succession, Taffy told me he needed to economise and wouldn't be able to make the trip. I decided to go it alone. I went off to Norris the Rubberman in Grimsby for a smaller tent, getting a refund of £5 on the larger one I'd booked, and checked in on the ferry at Immingham at 7.30pm on the 12th of July. Before long, I was across the North Sea and crossing Holland into Germany. My sister had lent me camping gear including a stove and on the morning of 14th, I was boiling an egg for breakfast at the Neiderwaldsee Camp at Gross Gerau.

The spectacular scenery of Austria was next, and I found another splendid campsite there for the night. Next day it was on to Italy through Cortina in the Dolomites, on via Trieste and into Yugoslavia – what is now Croatia. Travelling down into the Istrian Peninsular beside the Adriatic Sea I began looking for likely camping grounds. A huge sculpture beside the road indicated the entrance to Solaris Auto camp at Lanterna. Turning in, I paid the camping fee at the kiosk. I began looking for a place to put my tent, hoping to be as near the sea as possible. It was then I noticed that the campers revelling in the waves were not wearing swimsuits. It took me no time to work out that I'd stumbled on a naturist site. I had paid my money and I pitched my tent. Christina and Deitrich, in the next tent, had their clothes on so I was reassured and before long we were making a meal gathered by their campfire,

An invitation to badminton from a nearby group was accepted, but now I was the only one in clothes, and not wanting to be the odd one out, joined in as nature intended. It was the same in the restaurant and at the small supermarket and I quickly forgot that no one was wearing a swimsuit or anything else for that matter. The only drawback was the lack of pockets for your money when

A Policeman's Tale

buying drinks or shopping.

I toured the area visiting the Roman Amphitheatre at Pula and exploring the ancient town of Rovinj. Poreč was interesting with its old Roman main street, and I visited the harbour at Vsar and the interesting scenery around the Limski Canal, which is a five-mile-long sort of fjord. Another trip was to the resort of Opatija. With my neighbours, Christina and Deitrich, I went to see the underground wonders of a cave system in the limestone hills. These were the Slovenian Postojna Grottoes and we each paid our thirty-four dinars (about one pound) for a two-kilometre underground train ride and tour of the caves.

The week at Lanterna passed quickly. The sun was hot, and the sea quite cool. Sunbathing could be followed by a cooling dip from the rocky beaches in the Adriatic.

Heading back, I travelled towards Italy on 24th July, and found a campsite near Venice. I took a vaporetto (small motorboat) across the lagoon and spent a wonderful time looking around St. Mark's Square, the Bridge of Sighs, the Doges Palace and the various canals and bridges. From Venice, I headed towards Lake Como, and then into Switzerland via the St Gothard Pass. Snow was near the summit at 6,860 feet. My route took me around Lake Lucerne and into France where I camped at Saint Dié.

Next, it was onto Luxembourg, passing the Grand Duke's Palace and visiting the studios of Radio Luxembourg set in beautiful parkland. Then on through Belgium back to Amsterdam for the journey by ferry home to England. A grand total of 2000 miles was covered with no problems from my Maxi. I was able to return the AA spares kit I'd hired from them unopened.

Back at Skegness, I got the result of my A Level examination. Despite all the difficulties in getting to evening classes because of all the moving about, I just managed to pass the examination gaining a grade D. I was quite pleased with this and was ready to mention it at all subsequent promotion boards. Disappointingly, I was never asked again, what I'd been doing to further my education!

I continued working at Skegness, returning home to Cleethorpes on rest days, and going out with Julia whenever possible. It was force policy to give sergeants experience of prosecuting in court, although this was normally an inspector's duty. One day I was sitting in Skegness Magistrates' Court, next to the Inspector, so I could learn the ropes, when he was called away to an incident. He pushed the heap of files towards me and said, 'Do the best you can'. This heap of unread files was a worrying sight, especially when the clerk leaned forward as I floundered over one case, and whispered, 'It's not as easy as you think, is it?' Somehow, I managed to hold the fort with a few simple cases until mercifully the inspector returned to carry on.

In the Autumn I managed to get over to Wales to see Taffy again, staying for a week at 'Swn-y-Mor' (Sound of the Sea), a cottage belonging to the parents of one of Taffy's friends. This cottage near Abersoch on a huge sweeping, wild bay, called Porth Neigwl (Hell's Mouth), was a good base for touring the tip of the Lleyn Peninsular. I practiced belly boarding in a borrowed wet suit and went for a few early morning runs, picking mushrooms for breakfast on my way.

The end of the Skegness season came towards the end of October and all the officers on temporary summertime postings were sent back to inland stations. I returned to Boston on 23rd October 1974 for my fourth spell of duty there. Fortunately, I was again able to lodge with the Bloodworth family in Ingelow Avenue.

From 25th to 29th November, I was sent off to Brant Broughton College for a Home Defence Instructors Course. The food at the college was excellent as ever, and I looked forward to the course. Regularly, while I'd been a police officer, we'd had instruction in War Duties. Now it was to be my turn to be the one giving the lessons. I had to set about learning all the information so that I could do this. I qualified as a Police Instructor in Home Defence and War Duties following this course and was given a certificate to prove it.

Christmas was approaching, and Julia and I decided the time had come to announce our engagement. On 21st December 1974, we went off to Victoria Street in Grimsby and at Palethorpe's the jewellers we found a very pretty engagement ring for Julia, while she found a Rotary wristwatch for me. We dined out at the Lifeboat Inn on the Kingsway at Cleethorpes that evening. The following day we had a party at 'Avonlea', Lyndon Crescent, Louth, hosted by Julia's mother and father, Eve and Jack. My parents, Susan, David, Anne, and Arthur Platts (Julia's sister and brother-in-law) also attended. The wedding was fixed for 14th June 1975 and preparations began.

Back at the police station, I continued work as usual and in addition went about reporting details of my wife to be and seeking approval to be put on the married strength of the force. A house was top priority and I wondered if we could afford to buy one or whether we should ask for a police property. In Boston there were some good looking four bed-roomed houses on the market for around £10,000. This was at a time when my net annual income was around £2,400, and petrol was still only a little over five shillings (25p) a gallon – less than 6 pence a litre.

My ponderings on this subject were greatly affected when Chief Superintendent Bulman called me into his office and said I was to be posted shortly and could choose either to go to Gainsborough or Market Rasen. He said that if I chose Market Rasen I could live in the former beat police station at Tealby. Julia was consulted, and we chose Market Rasen for my next posting, which took place on 3rd March 1975.

XVII Market Rasen

The posting to Market Rasen gave me the role and title of Rural Sergeant. I was one of three sergeants for the Market Rasen rural section. Sergeant Bill Fidler was based at Caistor and Sergeant Alistair Miller at Wragby. We were under the command of two inspectors who were in charge of all the Lincoln Rural sections, and they were based at the Divisional headquarters at the Sessions House in Lincoln. This posting to Lincoln Division meant that within twelve months I'd served in all four divisions of the force, and I felt this must be a record. One obvious thing to me was that, despite pronouncements to the effect that procedures were to be standardised across the force, this had not yet been achieved. For instance, a perfectly good accident file submitted and accepted in Boston Division, would be rejected in Grantham Division, because they liked the papers presented in a different order. Some frustration accompanied this discovery, but I was getting used to these discrepancies.

We shared our shifts to cover as much of the twenty-four hours as possible. We had two area cars with five officers allocated to each. One of the cars was based at Market Rasen and the other worked from the North Box, on Nettleham Road, in Lincoln. Additionally, there were a small number of officers for Market Rasen town patrol, and more officers for each of the rural beats, making about twenty in total. A CID officer was based at Market Rasen, and regular calls by the traffic patrol cars meant there was plenty of activity at the police station. One officer manned our enquiry office from 9am to 5pm, and court days were held every other week in the adjoining Magistrates Court. Alternate weeks saw the court held at Caistor.

My home, for it was my first, was in the former police station at 11 Cow Lane, Tealby. The beat had been amalgamated with another one and the police station was now serving as a police house. However, the office with the property was very useful. Eventually it housed Julia's piano, becoming a music room, study, and store. The kindness of parents and relatives enabled me to set up a bed and enough furniture to get by, and as our wedding day approached, we gradually carpeted, and decorated the house. There was also a garden to attend with lawn to mow and I set about getting it in order. The house was relatively new, and had oil-fired central heating, although this was only downstairs. We had a huge black oil-tank in the garden. It seemed necessary to spend a fortune to fill when we arranged for a call by the Newlin Oil Company oil tanker based in Louth.

I managed to obtain a black and white television,

A Policeman's Tale

second-hand, arranging insurance for the television aerial to comply with force orders, house contents insurance, and what seemed a myriad of new responsibilities as a householder. A new Qualcast Astronaut lawnmower was purchased together with a Hoover vacuum cleaner, and Hoover washing machine. An important outing was to visit Hewitt's the jewellers to purchase Julia's wedding ring, which we did on 26th April 1975. Other plans for the wedding were made and I made bookings for the honeymoon. Julia's parents in consultation with her were meanwhile busy with the arrangements for the wedding itself and the reception at Darley's Hotel afterwards. My mother and Susan set about fixing the flowers for the occasion.

The Chief Constable, Mr. Byford, asked me to go and see him at Headquarters on 7th May 1975, and I duly appeared at his office. He told me that he wanted me to have experience as an inspector and had been minded to send me to Skegness for the summer as an acting inspector. He said that he realised however that being newly married I'd be unlikely to welcome being posted away from home as soon as I began life with a wife. He'd decided to postpone my trial in the acting rank, but it was clear that this might take place the following year. Before Julia had accepted my proposal of marriage, I'd told her that a policeman's life involved having to move about as the police force required and asked if she could cope with this. She'd said it would be fine – no problem – but I still don't think she knew quite what might be in store for her as a policeman's wife.

The wedding took place as planned on at 11.30am, on

Saturday 14th June 1975 at Wellington Street Methodist Church, Grimsby. Colin 'Taffy' Edwards was my best man. Julia's bridesmaids were nieces, Deborah Platts, and Bridget Marshall. This was the church where Julia's parents, Eve and Jack, had married. It was a fine, though windy day, and from the church, we went on to the reception at Darley's Hotel in Cleethorpes.

After being sprinkled with traditional confetti, Julia and I were taken by brother-in-law, David, to our hidden car (to avoid old boots and tin cans tied to the back). We set off down to Windsor where we stayed the night at the White Hart Hotel close to the castle. Next morning after breakfast, we had a look round the castle and then travelled on to Heathrow Airport for our flight to Minorca.

Staying at the Topacio Hotel was a wonderful experience. It was situated on a superb horseshoe shaped bay at Arenal d'en Castel on the north coast of the island. While the hotel pool was good, it was great to walk over to the nearby beach. The sea was warm and the soft golden sand excellent. We made friends with other holidaymakers and enjoyed touring the island on a red motor scooter we christened 'El Torra Roza'. One highlight was visiting the old capital, Cuidadela, where celebrations for St. John the Baptist's day were in progress. This involved horsemen and their ladies, trying to keep their seats while the crowd threw hazelnuts under the horses' hooves. We also pushed the scooter hard going up the hairpin bends to the monastery on Mount Torro.

One attempt to do a good turn had an unfortunate outcome. We'd met a lady who'd invited us for refreshments to her villa, which was up a steep hill on the south side of the island. As she seemed quiet elderly and a little infirm, I offered to run her up on the back of the scooter, while Julia walked up. She accepted a little hesitantly and clung on tightly with her arms round my waist. I hadn't practiced starting the scooter on a hill, my clutch control was not very good, and I set off with a quite a jerk. She tumbled off the back of the scooter rolling backwards to Julia's feet. She decided it was better to walk up after that. Nevertheless, she treated us to some cool orange juice in her villa.

We returned home to Tealby on 29th June 1975 and began married life. One pleasant thing that happened early on was a knock on the door from our neighbour Mr. Bell who ran the Barn Restaurant opposite our house. He had a huge vase of flowers to welcome us home. This was a good start for us both.

In no time at all, we set about securing home comforts for ourselves. I planted vegetable seeds in the garden and Julia practised cooking great meals and especially good puddings. We made sure we always had a chocolate digestive biscuit with our cup of tea and in no time at all, found we were starting to put on weight. Perhaps married life was proving too comfortable.

Julia had given up her job as an architectural assistant when we married and now devoted herself full time to the role of housewife. She was almost immediately signed up as a member of Tealby Women's Institute, while I joined the garden society.

At work, I found the new duties a great change from my

days on town patrol or as station sergeant. I had much more discretion over my hours and sometimes worked in the morning, had an afternoon break and then went out again in the evening. Market Rasen is famous for its racecourse, which attracts a great following of racegoers. Policing the racecourse was a regular task, which I found very interesting. From my vantage point on the side-lines, I felt betting on horse races always seemed to favour the bookmakers rather than the punters.

Because of my interest in photography and tape recording, which had come to the ears of the training superintendent, Steve Vessey, I had got involved in the police television unit. This had been set up by the training department, primarily as an aid to training. I found myself called away from Market Rasen for a week at a time to help produce training videos, recorded at that time on reel-to-reel tape, about issues such as dealing with drivers under the influence of drink. We made this one on the redundant main road at Nettleham near the Brown Cow Inn. Another one was about the importance of correct procedures when dealing with drivers following a chase. I had an exciting time as cameraman in the back of a patrol car tearing through red traffic lights in Lincoln following an errant driver. Fortunately, we'd taken the precaution of hiding an officer out of sight to stop the traffic to prevent an accident. As a sergeant, I was given responsibility for organising this unit, although one of the constables in it was the technical expert.

We had a good summer that year at Tealby. The weather was kind, and we had several lots of visitors, including the

A Policeman's Tale

Bloodworth family and Taffy.

The force television unit was called upon to record the opening of the new Divisional Headquarters for Lincoln Division on West Parade, Lincoln on 1st October 1975. I was stationed with a large camera on a tripod in the foyer of the new station as Her Royal Highness the Duchess of Kent unveiled the plaque commemorating the event.

At work, another development was to have repercussions in my future career. This was the finding of a man's body in a cornfield at Bigby Top at Somerby a few miles south of Brigg. This location was in the far north of the territory I covered, almost at the Humberside border. The body had strange grooves in the skull. It turned out that the dead man was a Yugoslavian national, Major Charlie Spasic. He was the warden of Pingley Camp, an old prisoner of war camp just outside Brigg – about one hundred yards into Lincolnshire. He had been in dispute with two of the landworkers he employed over money and about who should rightfully rule in his homeland, (then under Tito's communist dictatorship). They had killed him by striking him over the head with a Bullworker. This was a chest exercise device and the grooves in his head had been caused by the finger grips on the handles. A Murder Incident room was set up at Grasby village hall. I was called on to work in it. This situation was similar to the one at Moulton Chapel where I'd also worked in the murder room. To cut a very long story short the two killers were arrested in Yugoslavia, we sent over the evidence with our detective superintendent John Standish, and they were convicted and imprisoned over there. As was to become a tradition the officers involved in the investigation were able to obtain a memento in the form of a tie. This one was in the Yugoslavian colours of red, white, and blue with royal crowns representing the victim and red communist stars representing the offenders.

In November 1975, our television unit was showcased at the Bishop Grossteste College in Lincoln. A cutting from the Lincolnshire Echo pictured the event and gives an outline of its purpose.

The winter brought heavy snowfall and while this made the picturesque village of Tealby look even more attractive than usual, it created significant problems on the roads heading east out of Market Rasen over the Lincolnshire Wolds. I spent most of one morning on Willingham Hill on the Louth Road dealing with lorries that couldn't get sufficient grip to go up it. We found that just a gentle push on some of them got them going and we were able to clear the road. I was glad I had stout boots with a fleece lining to keep out the cold.

On 27th January 1976, I was again called to see Mr. Byford at the Chief Constable's Office in Church Lane at Lincoln. He talked to me at some length and discovered that I had joined a gym club, Gateway to Health, at Grimsby. This had been an attempt to cope with the weight increase mentioned earlier. I think the chief constable got the impression that I was a much sportier person that I thought I was. This was to have a bearing on later developments. He said he would be posting me to Skegness for the summer season in May so that I could be assessed in the inspector's rank. I went home and broke the news to

A Policeman's Tale

Julia that I was to be an acting inspector.

The house at Tealby had been furnished a little sparsely because of lack of funds leaving the small box bedroom empty. This had enabled me to set up my old Triang 00 train set for the first time for years. My old enthusiasm came back, and I began to buy track and rolling stock bringing my layout up to date. A baseboard using timber and fibreboard was constructed, and I had great fun setting up the trains and running them.

Some of the people in Tealby regarded me as their police officer and, since the telephone number of the house was still Tealby 222, the same as when still a police station, Julia and I often used to get calls about police matters. One of these was from Miss Fytch, who was the elderly sister of the vicar, living in the rambling large rectory on the main road next to the church. She wanted to know what I was going to do about the paperboy who constantly left her front gate ajar. She was most concerned as this meant that the hedgehogs in the garden got out onto the road and were in great danger of being flattened. Indeed, several had suffered this fate. I reassured her that I would look into this matter and see that her paperboy was suitably advised.

In my days at Grimsby, Tealby was in the Grimsby Division, and when the powers that be were casting about for economies, they looked at the workload of each beat with a view to amalgamating the least busy ones. I'd been asked to point out which beat had the lowest crime rate in the division. My statistics showed that Tealby beat had very little crime and I'd supplied the relevant figures. Very shortly afterwards the beat officer was moved away, and the beat amalgamated. I always felt guilty it was Tealby that had been closed. It lost its dedicated officer, and Julia and I benefited by having the chance to live in this beautiful village.

As a member of the International Police Association, I heard about a trip being run jointly by the Lincolnshire and Humberside branches to Paris. Julia and I booked for 30th April to 3rd May 1976, being picked up by a bus and travelling down to Dover for the crossing to Calais. This was followed by a great time in this most glorious city, seeing the sights and enjoying the May Day celebrations around the Arc de Triomph. The visit to the Louvre was a highlight especially seeing the Mona Lisa and the Venus de Milo. Going up the Eiffel tower was a must and Julia, and all the ladies, were presented with a bunch of fleurs de lys, the national flower, as it was May Day. We travelled out to the palace at Versailles and by the time we got home felt we'd done Paris very well. Unfortunately, the bus journey was not kind to Julia's back, and we decided long bus trips were not for us in future.

On the afternoon of 13th May 1976, I reported to Laundry House in Church Lane at Lincoln – the uniform stores and saw Harold the force tailor. He fixed me up with an inspector's uniform for my forthcoming summertime duties in Skegness. Inspectors had patch pockets on their tunics, brown gloves, and raised seams on their trousers. Harold told me I'd have to make do without the raised seams and stick to my own sergeant's trousers, but I got the white shirts and other gear including a single bath star for each shoulder. The other item was a hat with a black braid

A Policeman's Tale

on the peak. Trying this gear on was great – here was my chance to play the senior officer.

I went home to Julia and showed off my gear. There were just two more days of duty at Market Rasen before I'd be leaving her for lodgings at Skegness.

XVIII Skegness

Back at Skegness on 15th May 1976, I was pleased to find myself in lodgings with Len and Dora Bellamy once more at their home in Sunningdale Drive. We didn't realise it then, but we were about to have one of the hottest summers of the century. The first sign was a huge increase in the number of ladybirds everywhere. The resort was also very crowded as the sunshine attracted huge numbers of visitors.

When not on duty it was a pleasure to cool off in the sea, which was only a short walk from my lodgings. The beach, as the season progressed, became covered in ladybirds, and it was difficult not to tread on them as you walked over the now red sands to the water.

I found the extra responsibility of my acting rank interesting and fortunately, my experience over the years as a sergeant doing many different things helped me when difficult decisions were needed. There was plenty of help and support from the Divisional commander and his deputy and from my fellow inspectors. The main task was to

A Policeman's Tale

supervise and support the sergeants in their duties, to ensure the control room was running smoothly and to see that the charge room and cells were properly controlled. Additionally, there was the paperwork from all the sections that needed checking and recommendations made about prosecutions or otherwise.

There was still time to get out into Skegness and sometimes when their own inspectors were away, up to Louth, Horncastle, or Mablethorpe, which were also part of Skegness division.

In September, Julia and I took a break in North Wales, staying at Swn-y-Mor. We arrived after a heavy storm to find flooding inside the kitchen of the cottage. However, we soon managed to clear this up and enjoyed ourselves touring. Enjoyable visits included a run over the Ffestiniog Railway, wandering around the extraordinary Italianate village of Portmeirion, and some pleasant time on quiet beaches.

On our return, we attended the celebrations for my parents' ruby, wedding anniversary on 19th September 1976 celebrating the forty years since their marriage at Stickney. There was a family gathering at 43 Lindum Road, Cleethorpes.

On 23rd September 1976, I was again asked to see the Chief Constable. Mr Byford seemed pleased with my efforts at Skegness. He talked about the need to replace the current inspector in charge of cadet training. He needed someone who would be responsible for the one-year initial residential course cadets undertook. This involved college courses, police law lessons, outdoor activities, such as rock-climbing, canoeing, and lifesaving. He felt I was the right person for this post and proposed to promote me to the rank of inspector on 27th September 1976 from which date I'd move to the Headquarters Training Department at Lincoln. I didn't say that I knew nothing of rock-climbing or canoeing, and of course, I accepted his proposition with alacrity.

I rushed home to break the news to Julia. She was about to experience the first move of our married life.

A Policeman's Tale

XIX Headquarters Training

Headquarters had grown over the years and now occupied around five different sites in uphill Lincoln. Training and Traffic Departments were in temporary offices behind the Territorial Army drill hall in Newport at Lincoln. The cadet training section had a couple of offices and a storeroom in one building and several classrooms shared with the rest of the training department in another block of offices. The residential cadets had rooms at Lincoln Divisional Headquarters on West Parade, with a gymnasium there for physical education.

My staff consisted of two sergeants, a constable, and a clerk. Additionally, I was able to call on the services of the Underwater Search Unit sergeant for outdoor activities, and a few other officers with specialist skills as needed. One of the sergeants, Edward McQuat was in residence with the cadets at the West Parade station.

The first job I had to do was to obtain the extra stars so

that I was properly turned out with a full inspector's set of two bath stars on each shoulder. Next was a visit to the police housing office. They had a police house becoming vacant in Lincoln at Broadway, just off Newport, which Ken Mott and his wife had been living in. This sounded very good, and a brief inspection confirmed that it looked a good prospect for Julia and I to occupy.

A benefit of my new post was that mileage would be paid for police journeys in my own car. As my limeflower Maxi, AFU 65K, bought second-hand in 1974, had begun to cost an excessive amount to keep in running order; we decided to go for a brand-new Maxi. It was to be russet green, and we took delivery early in November. The registered number was SFW 208R. Soon after it arrived, we played host to a visit by best man, Taffy, and had the pleasure of gently running in the Maxi, with trips in the winter sunshine.

I started work finding out about the cadets' residential course, so I knew what they did and attending some of the sessions. One of the objects of their outdoor activities was to prepare them for their camp in Wales when they would be tested on an expedition similar to those of the Outward-Bound Association. I went to their swimming sessions at RAF Scampton, where the pool was used to practice lifesaving, and some of their physical training and sports sessions.

Taking Julia with me, we went to look at the house offered us, in Broadway. The owner of a plumbing firm had built it in the nineteen-fifties. There were three good-sized bedrooms, a sitting room, a dining room, and a rather small kitchen. It was centrally heated, and a new gas boiler had

A Policeman's Tale

been installed. To my delight, there was a splendid brick and wood greenhouse and a decent garage. Julia was very pleased with the exotic pink and black fittings and tiles in the bathroom. It seemed to have been built with no expense spared. We decided this was the place for us and set about fixing up our removal from Tealby.

Because Police Regulations require officers to live where directed by the Chief Constable, there is also provision for the payment of removal expenses including the cost of replacing (within limits) curtains and carpets. We set about providing a comfortable home in Broadway and carpeting the rooms where this was needed. We moved in on Thursday 18th November 1976.

Soon after arriving our neighbours from the house next-door-but-one, number 41, Olga Yeates and Ruth Morris introduced themselves to us. They thought we'd been long married – not just the eighteen months that was actually the case. Both of them turned out to be excellent friends eventually becoming godparents to one of our children - but that is a story for later. While we lived in Broadway, they were kind enough to introduce us to their established circle of friends. They included us in parties at their house and often invited us to take afternoon tea on sunny days in their garden. This was always a welcome break from our enthusiastic gardening sessions.

As a member of the Training Department, I soon found that I was expected to do far more than look after the cadets. It appeared that I was to be the treasurer of the Headquarters Sports and Social Club since my predecessor had held this post, I was the natural successor. Rapidly I learned how to manage income and expenditure of the club. Eventually I improved some of the systems so that funds earned interest when they were not needed immediately.

One of the other tasks assigned to me was that of police representative on the board of the Lincolnshire branch of the Outward-Bound Association. Regular interesting meetings were held at the Morning Star public house on Eastgate in Lincoln.

On Monday 22nd November, having just moved into the new home at 45 Broadway, I went off to Horncastle to assist in the running of a Constables Senior Development Course for a fortnight. I spent two weeks doing this, but as I'd never had any formal Instructors Course, had to very much feel my way. When they told me that the inspector always gave the lesson about the law on explosives, I felt inadequate, since I knew little about the subject. I studied rapidly until I hoped I knew just a little more than my students.

Being in our new home, we found our relations were keen to visit us and we were pleased to entertain them. We even had a visit from Julia's Aunt Christine and Uncle Lesley (brother of her mother, Evelyn), who'd travelled over from Canada.

After Christmas, I was again off to Horncastle, this time for a War Duties Course. I seemed to be spending very little time with Julia and I was soon off on another course from 2nd to 6th May at Brant Broughton College. A solution was found to this next time it was proposed I go off somewhere else. Still involved with the television production unit, I was offered the chance to attend a production course at

A Policeman's Tale

Plymouth Polytechnic College for two weeks, 15th to 27th May 1977. This seemed a great idea and I suggested that Julia could come down with me for the two weeks. There was no objection to this, providing I paid for her accommodation. We stayed at the Mirrelees Hotel on the Hoe at Plymouth.

Two good weeks were had in Plymouth, and I found the course very interesting. Julia was able to use the Maxi to explore the surrounding countryside. In the evenings and at the weekend we were both able to take advantage of the time to visit an old friend from Cleethorpes, John Carter, the editor of the Western Morning Post. He was kind enough to give me a review copy of a book about Arthur Ransome, author of 'Swallows and Amazons'.

The next duty, which called me away, was for the annual camp in Snowdonia held for the residential course cadets. We stayed at 'Jessie James Bunkhouse' near Llanberis and Sergeants McQuat and Simmons assisted by Constable Maybelle McCann put them through their paces. I tried my hand at some of the activities, including abseiling and walking up Snowdon in thick mist using the Pyg track, which I found quite difficult.

During the period of the camp Mr. Byford visited us. In my Maxi, I drove him around Snowdonia showing him the cadets activity groups. He was invited to have a go in a canoe in the sea at Conway but declined.

The fortnight culminated with the cadets' trekking expedition over three nights, when they had to fend for themselves. All of them managed to complete this successfully and were almost ready for their passing out parade followed by posting to divisions.

Soon after returning from Wales, it was time to set up the summertime lifesaving posts at Ingoldmells and Chapel St. Leonard's. Each year cadets manned these posts keeping an eye on holidaymakers, some of whom were prone to getting into difficulties in the sea. The cadets were selected from all the county's cadets and spent a period on this duty, providing they had properly qualified in Royal Lifesaving Society examinations. Edwina Tarpley for Yorkshire Television News interviewed me in front of the post at Chapel St. Leonard's, about the work of our cadets.

I paid several visits to the lifeguard posts over the summer to support the youngsters in their work and check that all was going well. The cadets used an inflatable launch for patrol and rescue. Taking the precaution of wearing a wet suit because of the cold water-temperature, I was able to join them on patrol.

The passing out parade for the residential course was held on 4th August 1977 at Lincoln Divisional Headquarters. The Chief Constable, Mr. Byford, who was accompanied by the Deputy Chief Constable, Mr. Kerr, inspected the smart cadets, as proud parents watched. There was a display in the gymnasium of self-defence and physical education. A slide show of the year was given for the benefit of the parents and then awards for first aid, and lifesaving were presented. Prizes were awarded to the best cadets for their achievements. Cadets Wheeler and Kemp were two of those to receive prizes.

Through the advice of Ian Symmonds, Julia and I decided to try Scotland for a holiday, and we went up to the

A Policeman's Tale

border area. We took bed and breakfast accommodation in a wonderful little Scottish cottage at Gatehouse of Fleet. We explored the Galloway countryside and found the area delightful. Ayr and Dumfries were interesting places to visit. Wonderful, out of the way spots were found for picnics beside burns, and I picked wild raspberries in the woods. We drove up to Port Patrick and enjoyed an afternoon on the beach. It was good to relax after a hectic year at work.

Of course, I was soon back to work routine, and one of my tasks was interviewing prospective cadets for the next residential course. The aim was to find about twenty youngsters aged sixteen with the potential to become good police officers and if possible, with the further potential for promotion to higher rank.

Our social life was enhanced by attending concerts whenever possible and one highlight always was hearing the Hallé Orchestra perform in the cathedral on their annual visit. Another social function we enjoyed was membership of the officers' mess. The mess arranged dinners on a regular basis and ladies' nights. Julia and I went along for a pleasant evening with good company.

On 3rd October 1977, I was sent off to Brant Broughton in charge of a Junior Development Course for constables. This occupied two weeks. Immediately on my return, on 16th October, I was off again to Symmonds Yat on the River Wye as a delegate on a leadership course run by the Leadership Trust. I didn't realise it at the time but there was a plan to cultivate me as the person to run leadership training in the Lincolnshire Police. The course was a wonderful introduction to leadership theory and practice. I learned a great deal. The course was very practical with lots of exercises. These usually involved a team trying to achieve the crossing of an obstacle with limited resources

During the course, the delegates learned a number of useful skills, such as constructing an 'A' frame, using a two-rope pulley system to cross the wide River Wye, raft construction, and many aspects of problem solving. One exercise called 'Mirror' was devoted to getting the team to indulge in teasing out the strengths and weaknesses of each individual. There was a good deal of physical effort involved as well as fun. We all had to climb the vertical pillar known as the Yat Rock. Fortunately, I'd had a little rock-climbing practice in Snowdonia with the cadets. If you managed to reach the top, to mark your achievement, there was a little box with a notepad inside where you could write your name. I hope my signature is still there.

On one occasion, at about seven in the morning, I'd successfully retrieved a piece of paper, bearing an important clue, from the far side of the river Wye, and was on my way back when I fell out of the boat. As I descended the six or seven feet to the bottom of the river, I looked up and saw my hand clutching this now very wet piece of paper. I thought I must keep enough presence of mind not to lose it, while I swam to the surface, and struck out for the riverbank. I'm pleased to say I did manage this. Dripping wet I ran back to the team base with the vital information needed to complete the exercise, feeling quite heroic!

The course was rounded off with an evening of fun and games when each team presented a playlet on the theme of leadership training. Several of them included our version of the course director, ex SAS officer, Mr. David Gilbert-Smith, MC., who was never seen out of his climbing boots ready for action.

On returning to Lincoln, I was straight away into a new activity called an Action Learning Project. This was designed to run for six months and took six middle managers giving them a task to complete. Ours was to improve the interface between schools and industry. We had the benefit of Geoff Gaines who worked for GEC. He was assigned to us as a facilitator and external sct adviser.

One of his first actions was to send us off on 6th November 1977, to GEC's Management College at Dunchurch near Rugby. It was a short course on techniques designed to encourage positive interaction among us. I remember one of the first sessions encouraged us to talk about a set topic in a large group. Only one member of the group was allowed to talk at a time, and this could only happen if you held a roll of sticky tape. After a while, the group was split in half and the process repeated. This happened again so that we became four groups. There was no explanation given of how group membership had been decided, but eventually I asked our tutor. He said he'd counted how often each person spoke and for how long. He'd then split the group each time so that the ones who spoke the most were in one group and those who spoke the least in the other. This meant, he said, that group members ended up with a fair chance of airing their views in their group. I asked which group I'd been assigned to, and it turned out I was in the noisiest group – another lesson learned.

Back home in Lincoln, on Tuesday, 13th December 1977, I was awoken by what sounded like breaking glass. It was still dark, and I thought the milkman must have had an accident with a milk bottle. Opening my eyes, I saw something strange. The bedroom window on the east side of the room, which overlooked our neighbour's house at number 43, was glowing through the curtains with an orange light. Immediately I got up and looked out of this window to see smoke and flames billowing up from the lounge at the back of our neighbour's house. Our neighbour was the headmaster of the secondary school at Branston, Gerald Roussell. He had been ill recently, and he slept in the downstairs lounge, from where the flames were coming.

I shouted to Julia, who was still in bed, 'Fire, Fire! Ring 999' and rushed to the bathroom where there were two full buckets of water. These had been placed there as a fire precaution, because at that time the fire brigade was on strike. In my pyjamas, I rushed out of the house with my buckets and entered the front garden of number 41. The front door was open and thick black smoke was pouring out of it. Approaching the door, I could see little inside. I was contemplating entering to look for Gerald, when mercifully Olga Yeates appeared from next door and told me Gerald had taken refuge in their house. A few minutes later a Green Goddess fire engine, crewed by police officers and the army arrived to begin squirting water into the inferno. Shortly flames were issuing from the front of the house, and I feared my garage, with my precious Maxi inside would catch fire.

A Policeman's Tale

Rapidly I moved Julia's car and my car away from the fire. One of the officers manning the fire engine and the hose was Constable Les Rush, who'd been a cadet when I was at Boston. They were making little impact on the fire and soon a very large fire engine from RAF Scampton arrived to give extra help.

When the fire was quelled, the house was completely gutted. It was many months before builders made it habitable again. In the meantime, the house stood empty, and the garden at the back became something of a wild prairie. It turned out that Gerald Roussell had plugged seven appliances into a single thirteen-amp plug in his lounge. When he switched on the kettle to make an early morning cup of tea the overloaded circuit had set fire to the heavy velvet curtains and quickly spread. I asked why the fuse hadn't blown and was told he'd got tired of the fuse blowing and had replaced the fuse wire with a nail! This was clearly a lesson for him, but not one I needed to learn, fortunately.

After the fire, I got on with another day at work. A lecture on home defence at Lincoln in the morning and interviewing one of my cadets in the afternoon was on the programme for the day. That evening was part of the action-learning course and meant a visit to AEI Semiconductor's works in Lincoln for a meeting. The following day I began another course at Bishop King House in Lincoln, by the cathedral. It was a two-day session on effective speaking, and I think this was very beneficial. I gave a talk about making wine at home, which was one of my current hobbies.

In April 1978, the six members of the Lincoln Regional Action Learning Set gave a presentation to the managing directors and senior officers who'd nominated us. The presentation took place in Lindum House in Lincoln, and I was responsible for the introduction. Our study had been aimed at initiating action to secure a radical and ongoing improvement in the two-way interface between businesses and the educational system. We hoped the proposals we made, which called for exchanges of staff between industry and schools, would promote greater understanding of each other's problems and needs, between those in industry, and those in education.

In May 1978, I was asked to act as deputy director of the Lincolnshire Police Leadership course held at Harlaxton Manor. This nineteenth century edifice served as the overseas campus of Jacksonville University in the United States of America. While in the training department I'd visited it to lecture students on English Law. Now I was to assist Chief Inspector Sid Tomlinson run a course for sergeants from our force and middle managers from industry. The course was very similar to the Leadership Trust courses at Symmonds Yat. We used tutors who also tutored for the trust. By now, I'd become a trust tutor and was used several times by them in this role.

After this course, I was sent on the first part of the national inspectors' course. This consisted of a five-week spell at a regional centre, in this case Derbyshire Police Headquarters at Ripley, and then three months at the police college, Bramshill near Hartley Wintney. The course at Ripley began on 22nd May 1978. I soon found I needed to

A Policeman's Tale

brush up my typing skills, as I had to produce an essay on vandalism and then give a presentation on the subject. This was to be the first of many essays on a wide variety of subjects, not all of them directly related to police work.

The course aimed to cover the duties of inspectors with their increased responsibilities. For instance, we had a good deal on explosives, including a visit to an explosives factory. The nitro-glycerine plant looked to me like a dry-cleaning plant for clothes. It had a stainless-steel casing, windows, dials and levers, and looked very interesting. It impressed me very much. All the workers wore wooden shoes, used wooden implements, and we were issued with rubber overshoes. The explosive making was carried out in separate huts. We walked around these peering into each of them. We were warned the fumes given off by the chemicals used could give us a bad headache. Where one of the huts should have been, was a charred patch of ground, which our guide informed us, was the result of an unfortunate accident. Our visit culminated with a demonstration, when a sack full of explosives was detonated in a pond. The bang and waterspout were considerable and ended a very memorable day out. We all managed to get back to Ripley in one piece.

After this course, we moved on to the Police College at Bramshill in Hampshire, on 3rd July 1978. This splendid place is based around the wonderful Jacobean house, which housed the library and several grand meeting rooms. The rest of the college was of twentieth century design. Bedroom accommodation was in basic blocks, with further blocks of classrooms, and a splendid Nuffield dining hall built with funds from the Nuffield Trust. The extensive grounds with a large lake, kitchen gardens, plenty of sporting facilities, and a deer park, with white deer were impressive.

We were grouped in syndicates for the duration of the course. We were expected to do considerable amounts of research using the extensive library. An interesting aspect was the course of study on Irish history. I was set the task of researching and writing up Theobald Wolf Tone. We each did a presentation on our research to the rest of the syndicate. Another course of study related to economics, which our tutor called 'the gloomy science'. My task was reading Keynes Monetary Tract, written in 1923, about the gold standard and the effects of inflation. Then I wrote several thousand words on the subject and spent a considerable amount of time bashing my typewriter. The tutor was complimentary about my efforts, and this encouraged me since I had several such studies to do.

Time was set aside for sports and volleyball was a favourite of mine. Each syndicate had a team, and we played many inter-syndicate games aiming to win the championship. There was an excellent gymnasium although five-a-side football was not my cup of tea. I used the swimming facilities at the Blackwater army barracks a short drive away. I also went into Basingstoke occasionally for a swim in the public underground pool there. We were expected to keep fit and jogging around the college lake was one way of trying to achieve this. Certainly, after eating some of the Kromeskis, provided by the college cook, you needed to find a way to exercise off the weight gained. Miss

A Policeman's Tale

Dunlop was famous for her Kromeskis, which were a sort of rissole, and the college students used to imagine the ingredients used to make them.

Another fine event was the college mess night when wives were invited up. Some wives stayed locally at bed and breakfast accommodation. Often the alternative was to squash together in the single bed in your room at the college. Julia tried this once, but the next time decided we needed to pay for a proper room in the village nearby. Mess night saw everyone dressed in best uniform with the ladies beautifully attired. The meals were always special and surreptitious bets were taken on the time the toast to the health of Her Majesty would be proposed.

I didn't make the long journey home to Lincoln from Hampshire every weekend, but when I did, it was great to enjoy our garden in the sunshine. Having a greenhouse meant that I could produce half-hardy plants for bedding out in the garden. Julia and I enjoyed spending time after our labours there, especially when our parents came to visit, and we could all sit on the patio enjoying a cup of tea.

Sometimes Julia and I would take a break from gardening and cross the 'prairie', which was the garden of the empty house at number 43 and respond to an invitation to join Ruth and Olga for light refreshments on their terrace. Maybe this sounds a little posh, but it was always pleasant.

The college took a summer break in August. Julia and I decided to visit Norfolk travelling down on 6th August and staying at the Wentworth Hotel in Aldeburgh. We were interested in seeing the concert hall, Snape Maltings, associated with Benjamin Britten. We travelled across the ferry at Walberswick and travelled down to the lovely village of Kersey in Suffolk. The old town of Dunwich, which is, now mostly under the waves of the North Sea was a fascinating place to visit. We sat on the shingle beach where once a thriving town had existed.

After this relaxing break, it was back to Bramshill where my course continued until 29th October 1978, when I returned home to be posted to Headquarters Operations Room.

XX Headquarters Operations Room

On 2nd October 1978, I was back at Headquarters working once more in Church Lane. Since I'd last worked in the old Information Room it had not only been renamed but had moved eastwards into the old schoolroom, where I'd reported aged sixteen just twenty years before as a prospective cadet. This time however, the old trestle tables had gone to be replaced with two rows of consoles on which were numerous illuminated push button switches for various radio channels and telephone networks. My role was to be shift inspector and once more, I was on around the clock shifts, beginning at 6am.

My sergeant was Peter Wilkinson who I'd known for many years and who had great experience in operations room work. The other staff members were constables and civilians who acted as radio or telex and teleprinter operators.

I enjoyed the work and found that the frequent moves around the county, which had been part of my police life, had given me an excellent knowledge of many different localities. This helped considerably when incidents occurred out in the countryside. The local divisional control room usually controlled incidents in towns because they had local radio schemes, but in general, these didn't work beyond the towns. A radio car despatched by Operations Room to attend incidents in the countryside, and our role was to control the incident if necessary, and deploy resources as needed.

We had links with surrounding counties and other emergency services. We were well equipped to deal with border matters or incidents that moved from one area to another. A large proportion of the work related to traffic matters, either accidents or hold ups caused by road works or abnormal loads.

Our headquarters location also meant that we monitored any serious incident and where necessary senior duty officers contacted to take charge if necessary. Firearms incidents always needed authorisation from a chief officer. There were a number of plans kept in sealed envelopes in the safe available for certain unusual events, such as a radioactive leak, a military aircraft crash or serious public disorder. The Operations Room Inspector would usually be the most senior officer on duty in the whole force area, after 2am, with the exception of Lincoln Division. They operated with twenty-four-hour inspector cover.

My first task on arriving for a shift was to receive a briefing from the inspector on the previous shift before he

A Policeman's Tale

went off duty. Then I'd read up the message sheets detailing activity since I'd last been on duty. Any running sheets needed to be looked at and if necessary progressed. After checking all my staff was present and up to date with current events, I'd monitor activity over the various radio channels. This could all be done from my console, but a certain amount of walking around talking to staff helped maintain good contact and ensure everyone was doing their proper jobs.

We had an anteroom where the noisy teleprinters and telex machines functioned. Most of the incoming and outgoing messages, within the force, and to other forces, went through these machines that produced paper printouts. Constant monitoring of these was needed so that details of incoming stolen vehicles, missing persons, or criminal activity could be passed on to divisions or to patrol vehicles.

This was the first time for several years that I'd been doing 24-hour shift work and for Julia it was her first experience. At that time, it was normal to work seven shifts of nights (10pm to 6am), have two days off, then seven late turns (2pm to 10pm), two more days off, then finish the months with seven early turns (6am to 2pm) and have three days off. This gave a nice long weekend because you finished work at 2pm on a Friday, and next worked at 10pm on the following Monday.

I had been happily working in the Operations room for a couple of months when arriving at 9.45pm one evening for night shift I was greeted with, "How do you like the idea of working down in the city?"

One of the members of the previous shift had been up to the admin office upstairs during the evening and seen my name in the removals book. They said there was no point in being at headquarters if you didn't get to know everything early, and clearly perusing the removals book was one way to do this.

It seemed it had been decided to move me down to Lincoln as shift inspector in the New Year, and this was confirmed when I was called to the Superintendent's Office to be officially told the (old) news.

XXI Lincoln Swift Inspector

My move down to Lincoln Divisional Headquarters for duty was with effect from 3rd January 1979. You'll remember that I'd been a regular visitor to this building, usually because the residential cadets lived there and used the gymnasium. The building's nickname was Ryvita House, because of its strong resemblance to a pack of the popular crisp bread biscuits standing on edge. Its construction was of concrete, the edges of which were deliberately chipped to give the resulting appearance.

Five inspectors occupied the office next to the foyer. There was one inspector for each of the four shifts, and one reserve that filled in and had several functions not assigned to the others. He did tasks such as ensuring duty sheets were completed and published, and that operational orders for coming events were prepared.

My shift was red shift. I took over from Les Duke, who had been a Lincoln City officer and who was retiring. His son eventually inherited my old number 54 as his collar number. He kindly left me his city inspector's silver knobbed cane in my wardrobe, although I never took it on patrol with me. In due course, it was handed on to my successor.

There were three patrol sergeants assigned to my shift and a station sergeant. It was my job to see that proper briefing took place at the beginning of the shift, and that all officers were assigned to beats or other duties. Anything happening during the shift I kept an eye on. If extra attention or resources were needed, and depending on the scale or importance, I'd see that a sergeant or I got involved.

Staff problems seemed to take up more time in this post than in any previous one. There were several officers with domestic difficulties or who for one reason or another needed to be carefully watched. Two of my sergeants, Dave Broom and Dave Sandy I found were very good at dealing with some of these things, although sometimes I needed to get involved too.

Something I soon discovered about Lincoln was that we spent a disproportionate amount of time in the Monks Road area dealing with people of Irish descent. These incidents were usually drunkenness, domestic disturbances, and sometimes crime. Another heavy commitment was to Lincoln City football matches at their ground Sincil Bank and the ground approaches. Influxes of away fans often meant trouble, and this needed police action, especially if disruption to Saturday shoppers in the High Street threatened.

When I'd first come to Lincoln as a sixteen-year-old

A Policeman's Tale

cadet I'd been struck by the frequent sight of what seemed to me elderly police officers with greying hair, whenever I went into the city centre. There always seemed to be several in the High Street, especially near the Stonebow. After the amalgamation, I noticed a lack of police officers in the High Street, and I knew that the public felt this too. This was the early days, when the public demand for visible policing, was first beginning to be recognized.

Trying to resolve this, as a city inspector, I'd always station a couple of officers near the Stonebow when my shift came on duty. I tried very hard to achieve this. At 2pm, I'd send my officers to the High Street, but within half an hour, they would have arrested a shoplifter or be dealing with an incident. Therefore, they were soon back at the police station with prisoners. My ambition to keep officers visible in the High Street was rarely achieved.

Another scheme, which was instigated by the city Chief Inspector Mike Baumber, also ran into problems. He had a traffic policing background and he lived out at Branston. Every day on his way to work, he got stuck in traffic queues and he determined to sort out Lincoln's traffic flow. We inspectors were instructed to assign officers to the main road through the city centre, especially Broadgate and Lindum Hill. Any hold-ups were to be sorted out immediately and broken down or parked vehicles were to be moved expeditiously. We did our best and made some improvement to the speed of traffic. Just as with my scheme in the High Street, it was almost certain that officers dedicated to promoting traffic flow would be called away to deal with other pressing matters, leaving the traffic to flow as best it could.

With theoretical shift strength around twenty-five constables, I found that the demands of policing a busy city, as well as the outlying Hykeham, Boultham, Birchwood, St. Giles, and Ermine Estate areas meant that officers, once deployed, were thinly spread. Often several incidents queued up for an officer to deal with them.

My membership of the Officers Mess was ongoing, and in 1979, I was voted in as Mess President for the year. This meant I presided over mess functions, welcoming guests, and ensuring that grace, toasts, and speeches progressed according to plan. Julia remembers particularly one ladies night when she and I sat opposite Mr. Byford and his wife. He was visible through the tall flickering candles in the candelabrum on the table. He tended to whistle through his false teeth when he spoke leading to an odd conversational mode. She also recalls that, when I called for silence, I lifted the cut glass ashtray and started banging it on the tabletop, which rather alarmed her, as she feared I would break it. (She knew that I had form for this as I had previously broken her mother's glass cake stand during the cutting of the cake at our engagement party). We all felt terribly smart. Men were wearing black tie and ladies were in long dresses ready to enjoy the meal at Elsoms Restaurant at Horncastle.

During March and again in April I went down to Symmonds Yat to act as tutor for the Leadership Trust. In May, from 12th to 18th, I was a tutor on the Lincolnshire Police version of a Leadership Course for a mixed set of delegates. These were line managers picked from industry, the county council, and police sergeants. The course went

A Policeman's Tale

well, especially as the other tutors were very good at their work.

Back at work, a new shift system had been introduced. Instead of doing the same shift for seven days, we now always started our seven shifts with two-night shifts, then two or three late shifts, then two early shifts. This meant longer rests between sets of shifts, but two very quick turn rounds during the week. This rota I found quite punishing to my system. I like plenty of sleep, and by the time rest days arrived, I felt whacked.

Early in 1979, Julia and I decided to take our holiday in Portugal with the firm Page and Moy. Two weeks were booked at the Miramonte Hotel from 29th May to 12th June 1979, flying from Heathrow to Lisbon. The hotel was at Pinal, near Colares not far from the coast and Sintra. Byron called Sintra 'this glorious Eden'. It was in this town the old kings of Portugal used to spend hot summers, away from the heat of Lisbon in the palaces they built there. Julia and I enjoyed the excellent beaches, and visiting the sights in Sintra, Lisbon, and Estoril. We hired a car for a few days, and used the buses, trains, and trams in Lisbon.

The hotel was good and one feature we particularly liked was the 'lavendaria'. Putting our clothes out for collection resulted in them being beautifully laundered. We also enjoyed the maid service, each evening finding our beds turned down and our nightclothes laid out ready for us. There was a super swimming pool, which we both enjoyed. It was a good walk to the beaches, but reaching them was well worthwhile, as they had wonderful sand. Although the water was cool, it was beautifully clear and blue.

A memorable trip in our hired car took us over the wonderful suspension bridge over the River Tagus to Setubal. We found a restaurant by the harbour serving the locally caught fish. The restaurant constructed of corrugated iron sheets, and clearly was designed to serve the dockworkers and fishermen. We dined on thick fillets of freshly caught Atlantic cod. On returning over the bridge, I mistakenly took a wrong turning, and we did a return crossing of the bridge – still the views were magnificent.

An evening trip found us at a more conventional restaurant. No one spoke English and our Portuguese was almost non-existent. We ended up being served a thin soup on top of which floated a fried egg!

We wouldn't have wanted to miss these adventures. The holiday had been thoroughly enjoyable and relaxing, and we were sorry when, after fifteen days, it was time to fly home to England.

Around this time, Julia had become pregnant. This was confirmed early in July at St. George's Hospital in Lincoln when she had tests and a scan. She was admitted to the hospital a few days later for a one-week stay, leaving on 24th July. Unhappily, on 5th August 1979, the baby miscarried, and Julia was readmitted to hospital for another stay of six days. Since both of us had hoped to begin a family, we were both upset and sad at this turn of events.

Only a few weeks later a small pimple began to show on my right cheek. It began to grow until it was the size of a broad bean. Consultation with the doctor resulted in a referral to hospital at the end of September, where a biopsy was taken. This indicated a non-malignant growth called a

A Policeman's Tale

Pileomatrixoma (Latin for 'a hairy gathering'). Julia and I drove down to a hospital in Leicester on 16th October, where an operation to remove the growth was performed. I was conscious during the operation, the only discomfort being cold feet, soon remedied by a kind nurse pulling a blanket over them. Having been neatly stitched up by the plastic surgeon with thirty-two tiny stiches, I drove home to Lincoln, hoping the scar wouldn't be too noticeable.

I carried on working my shifts in Lincoln. One of my duties as shift inspector was to consider the office 'In Tray'. Allocating the files to the inspector in charge of the shift to which the officer submitting the work belonged could usually reduce the heap. Other files just had to be dealt with. Among these were letters and notes from people who'd been reported for parking or more serious offences asking to be let off. One day I got a letter from Mr. Owen Roberts, with a Cleethorpes address, who had been driving on Lindum Road, which is the hill bringing main road traffic into Lincoln. On the sharp bend at the top, he'd been caught crossing the double white lines and a file for prosecution had been submitted. My job was to recommend whether he be cautioned, prosecuted or no further action taken. This type of recommendation was a regular part of the decision-making process which inspectors were involved in.

The problem for me was that I realised the offender was my old PE master from Clee Grammar School. As a rule, when you knew someone, you still considered the file, and made your recommendation based on policy and the facts. This is because you often knew the people involved, especially if they were local, or even regular offenders. On the face of it, crossing double white lines was regarded as a serious offence, which should go before the court, resulting usually in a fine and penalty points. Mr. Roberts had made several good points that merited possibly not taking him to court. I remembered his kind visit to see me after I'd broken my arm in the gym and the concern he had shown. On the other hand, I recalled how a form mate had suffered for breaking the rules. He had worn underpants beneath his gym shorts. In the changing room, Owen Roberts had spotted this, and impressed on us all the need to abide by the rules. Then, while we watched, he'd whacked the poor lad's behind, minus shorts and underpants, with a plimsoll, as a lesson to us all.

How times have changed. Completely opposite attitudes seem to apply today. Schoolteachers fear any physical contact with a pupil. They are left in no doubt the lawyers will soon be upon them if they touch a child, even if it is intended for their good and meant to teach them how to behave.

On balance I decided that Mr. Roberts had always been keen to see rules were kept, and I should do the same, so I recommended a prosecution. I wonder if I was right, especially as Mr. Roberts has now passed on, and I still remember the lessons he taught.

In October 1979, I was called up to see the Chief Superintendent. He told me that consideration was being given to moving me to Horncastle as Rural Inspector in charge of the section. When he asked whether I would be interested in such a move – I leapt at the opportunity and didn't hesitate to tell him that indeed I would.

My move was fixed for 12th November 1979. Meanwhile Julia was back in hospital from 7th to 25th November. (Incidentally, you may wonder how dates such as these can be included in this tale with accuracy after all these years. Like Samuel Pepys, Julia and I kept diaries, many of which we still have, and these reveal the details). Julia's gynaecologist, Miss E. Helen Walker, had decided that she should have a major operation to sort out the problems that had become apparent. Therefore, while Julia was hospitalised, I had to carry on working, and begin travelling over to Horncastle.

XXII Horncastle Rural Inspector

My first day at Horncastle coincided with an inspection by Her Majesty's Inspector of Constabulary. A few hours after my arrival, this important person, the chief constable, and a couple of members of the police authority were sitting in my ancient office quizzing me about the conduct of policing in Horncastle Section. Suffice it to say that some of my answers were a little vague. One of the police authority members commented that at least I could have taken a little time to mug up on my new posting. It didn't seem appropriate to give him details of my recent doings in Lincoln, which had been to say the least hectic.

Horncastle Police Station had been built in 1853, several years before the formation of the Lincolnshire Constabulary in 1857. The Lindsey Justices of the Peace built it on The Wong (a Scandinavian name for a wet place). The building then contained three cells and an exercise yard with an office for the Superintendent, who was Thomas Copperthwaite.

A Policeman's Tale

In 1881, two cottages were built adjoining the police station to house the superintendent and to provide a stable and coach house for his horse and trap.

When I arrived at Horncastle very little had changed except that the superintendent's house had become offices, while the constable's cottage next door was rented out. A new house for the inspector was built in the 1950s on the old horse paddock at the back of the police station.

Horncastle police section was in the Louth Sub-Division of the Skegness Division. There were three beats centred on Horncastle, Scamblesby, and Woodhall Spa, covering fifty-five parishes. The establishment when I arrived was one inspector, two sergeants, one detective constable, and thirteen constables. Five of the constables were on Horncastle town beat duty, five patrolled the surrounding countryside in a car, two constables policed Woodhall Spa, and one officer covered the Scamblesby beat. A civilian clerk, Olga Mann, manned the police station in the daytime. Visitors out of hours were expected to use a phone box on the wall of the police station to call Louth Police Station.

A little further along the Wong was the Magistrates' Court, built in 1912. The clerk to the justices, used to call at the police station on Tuesday mornings before court began at 10am for a cup of tea, and I soon found this a very welcome routine. His long experience both as a solicitor and as a magistrate's clerk was very helpful to me. Additionally, he was Her Majesty's Coroner for the district. My role was sometimes to act as prosecutor in court if the prosecutions inspector at Skegness was not available. I'd be told a couple of days in advance, and on Monday a huge file of court papers would arrive from the Prosecutions Office at Skegness for me to read, enabling me to take the cases before the justices on Tuesday morning.

Sergeant Corby, one of my two sergeants, who occupied the house built for the inspector, was looking towards his retirement. He'd decided to buy his own house in the town and was vacating the police house. I was conscious that buying your own house was probably a wise thing to do financially, and the attitude of the force towards this had shifted considerably since amalgamation with Grimsby and Lincoln, where most officers lived in their own houses. Discreet enquiries resulted in me being told that it was not a good idea for me to buy my own house, but that the one being vacated in Cagthorpe would be ideal for Julia and me.

Meanwhile back at our Broadway house in Lincoln, having been discharged from hospital, Julia needed time to recuperate after her operation. Over Christmas Jack and Eve, her parents came to stay, and help with cooking lunch on Christmas Day. Our celebrations on Eve's birthday on Boxing Day were helped by invitations to visit our neighbour Aubrey Rayne's house in the morning and Olga and Ruth's home in the afternoon. The following day I proposed that we all trek to Horncastle to view the police house in Cagthorpe.

Our inspection revealed that there would be a considerable amount of decorating and cleaning to be done on moving in. The garden was huge and would be a test of my gardening talents, but we decided that with limited options this was to be our home for the time being.

In Lincoln, on New Year's Day 1980, Julia and I drove

A Policeman's Tale

round to R.M. Wright's showroom to collect the new Maxi, which I'd ordered. We traded in the green for a brown one and drove round to Angela and David Pengilley's house in Orchard Close at Welton for a celebratory New Year's Day party. It was great when we were asked how long we'd had the Maxi and I was able to say, 'about half an hour'.

My early days at Horncastle, before we moved there, meant a twenty-mile drive each way, and lunches at the Rodney Hotel in Horncastle. This was quite a pleasant experience, as a number of businessmen, and Mr. Mitchell-Smith, the magistrates' clerk used to have lunch there too.

Meanwhile Julia gathered friends and relations to travel with her to Horncastle to begin a clean-up operation at what was to be our home in Cagthorpe. Much help was given and scrubbing, and polishing was undertaken. Decorating began and gradually the place was brought around to the style we wanted. Both of us seemed to find everything a bit much at this time. I suffered boils and Julia had bad nerves. We both had to visit the doctor to help us through a bad patch; you might say we were 'run down'. Even so there was a good deal of social life, with a Horncastle Police Ball at the Town Hall on 16th February 1980, and visits and visitors to cope with.

We were due to move in on Tuesday 18th March 1980. The day before it snowed all day, and on removal day, it was cold and rainy. We sadly said goodbye to our house in Broadway at Lincoln where we'd had some happy times and hoped our new residence would be as comfortable.

On 22nd March, we attended the Woodhall Spa Police Ball at the Golf Hotel, and the following day, Julia's birthday, entertained eight members of Julia's family for tea. A few weeks later, we went to the Rotary Ball in Louth with Anne and Arthur Platts. In May, we travelled down to London with Ruth and Olga. We stayed at the Soroptomist's Club, where Olga was a member, and enjoyed a performance of Die Fledermaus at the London Coliseum, by English National Opera

Around this time, Julia's mother had given up her car. We proposed that in view of this we should holiday together. Jack and Eve seemed pleased with this proposal. We found a cottage to let in Helston in Cornwall and booked from 21st June to 5th July 1980. Travelling down in my Maxi, we found the cottage to be comfortable and a good place to stay. Helston itself is an interesting small town where the old and the new were well blended. It was not far from the coast.

We visited wonderful beaches, harbours and villages in the vicinity of Helston, and enjoyed exploring the Lizard Peninsular. We had some great meals out and tried to have as many cream teas as possible. Some of the places we visited were Porthleven, Marazion, Mevagissy, Lands' End, Mullion, Poldhu Cove, Kynance Cove, and St. Mawes. A favourite spot was St Just in Roseland where we looked round the lovely old church and enjoyed the pleasant landscape by the river.

Travelling to the Royal Naval Air Station at Culdrose one evening we arrived for the ceremony of beating the retreat. The base was the centre for the helicopters used for air sea rescue, which we often saw on practice runs as we enjoyed the beaches nearby. A demonstration of the

A Policeman's Tale

capabilities of the helicopters and their crews was given. Watching the band of the Royal Marines go through the ancient ceremonial associated with the end of the day and the lowering of the ensign at sunset was a moving and interesting experience.

All too soon, our break in the far west of England was over and it was time to return to Lincolnshire. Our summer was not over though, and we soon had a visit from Taffy, while in August Ruth and Olga came to stay for a couple of nights. Then we went up to York for an overnight stay at the Jorvic Hotel. I especially enjoyed a visit to the railway museum – an interesting place even for non-railway enthusiasts.

Our visitors were many and while the family usually appeared at the back door (which perversely was at the front) friends usually came to the front door, which was at the side of the house – all very confusing. On 1st September, just after returning from York, we'd had lunch, which was curry, on that particular day. We were in the sitting room and were about to experience one more of the little embarrassments that life throws at us. Having asked Julia to carry out a small repair to my trousers, I had removed them so she could sew them. Suddenly there was a tap on the front door. Then immediately afterwards, at the sitting room window just to the left of the front door appeared three elderly female faces looking in on us. It was Hermione, Frederica, and their friend, who'd decided to call on us having had a run out from Lincoln. Hermione and Frederica had often been at parties hosted by Ruth and Olga, and we'd become friends. Quickly I took my trousers from Julia and put them back on. We invited them in for a cup of tea, hoping the smell of curry from lunch, and the sight of my bare legs wouldn't prove too much for them.

At work, I'd found that weekends were usually quite enjoyable. Generally, I had to cover the whole Louth subdivision. Louth had a chief inspector and two inspectors, but at weekends, we all shared the duties. I used to go up to Louth in my car and check on activity at the police station there. Sometimes there were prisoners to deal with or cautions to be administered. It made a change from Horncastle. I always enjoyed the ride over the Lincolnshire Wolds, especially Cawkwell Hill, and the area round Cadwell Park, which is Lincolnshire's circuit for motorcycle and car racing.

Having enjoyed our previous outing with Ruth and Olga to London and we planned another trip there, going down on 20th November 1980. The events we enjoyed were a concert at the Royal Festival Hall with Daniel Barenboim and the English Chamber Orchestra, and then a night at the theatre with Hinge and Bracket who were exceptionally funny. Another treat was a trip around the newly renovated Covent Garden Market area. Our first night at our hotel was a little alarming. Around midnight we heard banging from above our heads. We were on the top floor. It was confirmed that the noises were workmen in the roof, and a little later, the fire alarm went off. We got up and went into the corridor in our nightclothes just as everyone else was doing and saw thin smoke in the air. Workmen had set light to something in the roof. Fortunately, whatever it was extinguished. I complained about the noises above and Julia

A Policeman's Tale

and I were sent down (still in our nightclothes) to a lower room for the night, where it was a little more peaceful.

On 24th November, another new experience came my way. Blackpool beckoned. I was sent off to join the Police Promotion Examination marking panel. My time in the training department seemed to have qualified me for this task, and I found myself in a large hotel room with lots of other inspectors, marking the recent examination papers for promotion to sergeant. We all marked a sample paper, then compared notes, and received guidance designed to achieve a standard of marking. Then we were given a great stack of papers that were to be marked.

There were quite a number of old hands on the marking panel that knew the tricks of the trade. We all agreed however that two hours of marking at a time was quite sufficient as little red numbers began to dance in front of your eyes. At this point, a bracing walk in the late autumn sunshine was called for. I enjoyed exploring Blackpool. One evening I went to the theatre to see the late, great Les Dawson and the Roly Polys in a show. The marking panel lasted for a month. During the time we were there, we had a civic reception at the town hall given by the mayor of Blackpool. I also found time to explore Fleetwood and St. Anne's.

As a break from marking, several of us visited local hotel swimming pools. One morning with a couple of other inspectors I drove up to the Norbreck Castle Hotel which had a very large indoor pool. Near the entrance to the pool, a sign advertised Swedish massage. On the way to the changing rooms, we passed the massage room with its couch also seeing a lady in a white coat who appeared to be the masseuse. We had a great swim, and returning to the men's changing room afterwards, took advantage of the communal showers. We'd stripped and were applying shampoo when the lady in the white coat appeared. She gazed at the three of us, wearing only soapsuds, enquiring whether we wished to take advantage of her skills in Swedish massage. She didn't seem in the least embarrassed, but I know I was. As nonchalantly as possible, we declined her kind offer.

The marking panel completed its work, and it was back to Horncastle on 19th December 1980. We celebrated Christmas, Eve's birthday, my 39th birthday, and the New Year.

By now we'd become tired of all our mail being addressed to The Police House, Cagthorpe, and had rechristened the house number 19. Shortly afterwards plans emerged to improve the road outside our house and we learned that part of our garden would disappear together with our flowering cherry tree. It was a shame, but the improvement turned out to be very good and so we were happy to lose the tree in return for the better road.

The next year at Horncastle, 1981, turned out to be a momentous year, almost turning our lives upside down. It started routinely for me continuing my inspector's duties in the Horncastle section. Julia got back into her routine with Lincoln Symphony Orchestra rehearsals where she played 'cello. We paid the usual visits to family and friends and had them to stay overnight.

On 3rd and 4th February, I went down to Symmonds

A Policeman's Tale

Yat with Alan Clarke, another inspector, to the Leadership Trust.

One problem had surfaced in September 1980. Following Julia's operation Helen Walker, her gynaecologist, had arranged tests on both of us. A little later, a letter arrived from her, informing Julia that it was unlikely she would conceive a child. We talked about this and considered adoption and sought advice from our parents. My mother gave some advice to Julia she'd read in her copy of Woman's Own. We arranged to see the local social services people to talk about adoption. They said we were on the old side for adoption and that we would only be considered for an older child. Therefore, we stood at a crossroads so far as beginning a family was concerned.

On 9th February, the road workers chopped down our cherry tree. Later that week we began more decorating of the house. This time it was to be the sitting room, preparing to paper the walls. On Friday 13th February, I was up a pair of steps hanging a strip of wallpaper. Julia was pasting the next one when she announced that she would have to take a break. Somewhat annoyed, because I was keen to motor on, I enquired why this was and she said that she felt pregnant. I thought she must be mistaken and suggested she get on with the job in hand. This didn't go down very well with her. However, that evening we attended the Horncastle Police Ball, and the next night went out with Anne and Arthur to the Woodpecker Restaurant at West Ashby for a meal followed by a dance.

On 3rd March, I went off to Lincoln for Police Support Unit duty for the day. For several years, I'd been involved in training for these duties. Police Support Units were groups of thirty constables, three sergeants, and one inspector who trained together for emergencies. They had been developed partly in response to the riots, which had taken place in Brixton and other cities, and our training included dealing with rioting. Mostly we went off to old RAF camps using the buildings and open areas to practice our techniques.

The Police Ball at Woodhall Spa was held on 21st March at the Golf Hotel, and we had a lovely night. Then on 24th March, I had another day of Police Support Unit training at Lincoln. Meanwhile Julia had a busy week with her birthday on 23rd, a decorator working on our hall, stairs and landing, and a trip to see her sister, Anne, for lunch. Ruth and Olga visited us for lunch on 26th. There was a visit to Cleethorpes on Friday 27th, and she saw Doctor Wallis on Saturday 28th. Doctor Wallis had news for her – she was pregnant. This was wonderful and completely unexpected news in the circumstances previously explained. It seems that the advice my mother had gleaned from Woman's Own had paid off.

The next day I was off to Symmonds Yat, tutoring for the Leadership Trust, for a week. The following week saw me travelling to Sheffield for a briefing in preparation for the forthcoming Football Association Cup semi-final to be held at the Hillsborough Stadium. On Saturday 11th April 1981, I took my bus full of Police Support Unit officers to Sheffield where we deployed on crowd control duties. All was going well until I parked my PSU behind a grandstand while I reconnoitred round the corner. When I returned

A Policeman's Tale

another officer was marching my men off in the other direction and I had a quick gallop to get them back so that they could line the touchline prior to full-time. This was quite unpleasant, as those spectators at ground level objected to having, we large policemen obscuring their view. Some of those in the stands above decided to hurl seat cushions and coins at us. I've rarely found football duty pleasant, and this definitely was not.

On 14th April, there was to be more PSU training and at 7.15am, I joined the Skegness PSU in their bus on the way to RAF Newton where we spent the day practicing manoeuvres. The most interesting involved opening our ranks so that police horses could be ridden through towards trouble. The training for these police support units became more intensive as riots erupted during hot summers in cities like Nottingham. Our units were called to stand by to assist local police deal with fire bombings, and brick throwing. Our practices became more realistic. We were issued with polycarbonate plastic shields. These full-length shields were meant to protect us. In training, we advanced under a hail of wooden blocks to simulate bricks being thrown at us. The second rank would hold their shield aloft to protect our heads. Initially we had helmets with heavy straps to protect our head. These looked like the traditional ones, but they were soon found inadequate against bricks and firebombs. We were given encompassing helmets with visors to wear, and woollen fireproof overalls. Because we were now almost unrecognizable as individuals, we had our ranks painted on the back of the helmets so our men could find their leaders. I was issued with steel capped boots, shin pads, a plastic cricket box, and jockstrap together with a large blue holdall to store and transport all this gear. Things were clearly becoming more serious and seemed a far cry from the days when I'd joined the Lincolnshire Constabulary and riots were almost unheard of.

Horncastle is susceptible to flooding sitting in a valley at the confluence of two rivers, The Bain and The Waring. You may remember my reference to severe flooding there in 1960. After those floods, considerable work was done to heighten and strengthen the banks of the rivers and improve their flow through the town. During the last weekend in April 1981, heavy rain totalling four inches fell, leading to the two rivers breaching their banks. Soon shallow floodwaters were beginning to cover Cagthorpe. Our neighbours, the Evisons, helped Julia, while I was working, by sandbagging our French windows and doors. Meanwhile I had deployed Sergeant Bill Anderson and other officers into the town to help move people out, while I ensured communications at the police station were maintained. A farmer leant us his four-wheel drive Range Rover for the duration of the flooding, but even it was unable to go through the waters, which were nearly five feet deep near the Market Place.

By 3pm on Sunday 26th April, the river Bain had broken its banks at Kirkby as well as Horncastle, and evacuees were moved to Horncastle Town Hall, which was used as a reception centre. I worked from 8am to midnight that day dealing with the 180 flooded homes, and three hundred people evacuated.

Fortunately, our house was about one hundred yards

A Policeman's Tale

from the river Waring and with the sandbagging and slight rise to Cagthorpe, this prevented water getting into our house.

A couple of weeks later from 10th to 17th May, I was back in the thick of the fifth Lincolnshire Police Leadership Course at the 19th century Harlaxton Manor with the kind permission of the University of Evansville. This time I was the course director and very quickly the countryside around Harlaxton seemed full of people rafting, crossing rivers on ropes, cycling, and abseiling off railway bridges. The benefits of all this are not always immediately apparent to those involved but over time the lessons learnt are usually much appreciated. The course participants included ten Lincolnshire Police sergeants, and one from Warwickshire. There was also a social worker, education officer, water engineer, security officer, a works convenor, and a shift foreman on a mint sauce production line. This mixture helps show how individual skills can be of use to a team and its leader. Each day started at 6am and usually finished around 11pm. I followed the example of David Gilbert-Smith by dressing ready for action at any time.

It seemed to me that the course went well, and the week rushed by very quickly. Then it was back to Horncastle catching up with a couple of back rest days, a couple of days duties in the section, and then a three-day stint for the bank holiday at Skegness.

Bank Holiday crowds were huge at the coast, and trains bringing up to six hundred holidaymakers from the midlands queued up to enter Skegness station. Some of the trains were filled almost entirely with youths with painted heads, usually red or blue signalling their devotion to particular football teams. Seeing that all these got from the station to the promenade and beach was a considerable task for the police. The most important part was trying to ensure that rival sets of six hundred youths supporting different teams didn't meet and do battle.

On Monday 25th May 1981, I was on my third day of duty, and was observing the crowds near the Clocktower when my personal radio crackled into life, with a message to contact my station at Horncastle urgently. When I did this, I learned that Julia had been taken to hospital at Lincoln on the advice of Doctor Hovendon. Julia had feared another miscarriage and an ambulance took her to the maternity wing of the County Hospital. I was released from duty to return home and then on to the hospital.

After a couple of days of total bed rest, she was given a scan and when I got to the hospital to visit her on Wednesday 27th she told me to sit down when I got to her bed. She announced the scan result had shown that she was expecting triplets. I was highly delighted to hear this, but Julia was a little more tentative. I was keen to pass on the news to our parents. Travelling up to Louth for tea, I broke the news to Jack and Eve. Eve seemed stressed on hearing the news, as I think she could see all the implications that I could not. I travelled up to Cleethorpes to see my parents in Lindum Road. My father was keen to tell me all his news, but eventually I was able to relate the news of the forthcoming triplets.

Later I called on Olga and Ruth telling them the good news. A little inadvisably, as we talked about the matter and

A Policeman's Tale

discussed how it could be triplets were expected, when there were no twins or triplets in the family, I suggested to Ruth that it was the result of a good shot. She delighted in reminding me of this comment for many years afterwards.

Julia was released from hospital on 9th June with strict instructions to have total rest and be very careful. Not surprisingly, relatives and friends visited us almost every day, but we instituted a regime of dining out or having fish and chips brought into spare Julia from having to do the preparation. After a little while we engaged a home help for a couple of hours a day.

The summer weather was good, and Julia was able to spend a good deal of time in the garden resting. I'd devoted a great deal of time to gardening and had a good vegetable plot, and pretty flowerbeds. We liked to entertain in the pleasant surroundings.

We'd booked a holiday in Ibiza earlier that year; however, the news of the triplets was accompanied by advice not to take air journeys, so we had to cancel our booking. We consoled ourselves by getting as much sun as possible in Horncastle.

Horncastle section was good at organising social events and on 10th July, Julia and I went to a fancy dress social at the Bull Hotel. Julia regaled herself as a gypsy and I went as an Egyptian.

Something that affected Julia more than me was the fixation developed by Mrs. Bryant, an elderly resident of Horncastle. She visited me to tell me that before the war the chief constable had promised her father, who was then the Horncastle Superintendent that a new police station would be built. She had been in touch with the present chief constable and couldn't get any indication that this promise would be fulfilled. She took to ringing Julia at regular intervals, and calling for tea to further her mission, much to Julia's alarm. One day she rang the police station while I was away, and Inspector Pat Munn was standing in. She talked to him, and he got little further than saying 'Pat Munn'. Mrs Bryant had then retorted with 'What sort of name is that?' A little while later, Julia, and her mother went round to Mrs. Bryant's house for tea at her invitation, so perhaps we managed to mollify her a little.

Julia followed instructions over the summer. She was careful to rest as much as possible, especially in the afternoons. Julia later reflected that it would have been much more of a trial if there had been other children. We began to look at what would be needed for three new babies. We cast around for the loan of cots and other gear and were promised help by kind friends and relatives. Helen Walker arranged that Julia should enter the maternity wing of Lincoln County Hospital on 1st September, so that she could have complete bed rest and attention before the birth of the babies, due towards the end of November. She even arranged that Julia had a private room, which was mostly very peaceful. I visited every day bringing new maternity nightgowns and other needs as required.

In Horncastle, I began decorating what was to be the nursery, and preparing for the happy event, while continuing to appear at my office when required.

After over seven weeks in the maternity ward, Julia eventually decided the time had come to bear the triplets

A Policeman's Tale

and her size was quite remarkable. Pleadingly she spoke to Helen Walker asking her to do something! She obliged and the event was fixed a month early for Monday 26th October 1981. She went to the theatre at 2pm for a caesarean section, and at 2.29pm, John Carl was born. Giles Patrick followed at 2.30pm with Peter Francis appearing at 2.31pm. As I waited with other fathers in the waiting room, it was wonderful when a procession of nurses appeared each bearing a bundle wrapped in green sheets to show me my three sons. I was delighted, while the other fathers seemed somewhat bemused. I was allowed to see Julia shortly afterwards. She seemed reluctant to open her eyes, but did with a little persuasion, enabling me to blurt out joyfully 'Its three boys, its three boys!'

After a little while talking to Julia and Helen Walker I was tactfully ushered out of the delivery room and went off to telephone the great news to family and friends. Back at Horncastle, I was soon in demand by the press for photographs, as was Julia in the hospital.

Julia remained in hospital for a while before coming home with Peter, the heaviest and strongest of our three new arrivals on Friday 13th November 1981. On that day, I went to the hospital ready to take Peter and Julia home by me to settle into a new life. The staff seemed sad to see Julia go after her prolonged stay. Giles came home a week later, and John was picked up and brought home on 20th November. Now we were a family of five with a new routine to get used to. The first job for me was to make sufficient baby milk for twenty-one bottles each day – filling much of our fridge. The next job was to learn nappy changing – a task at which I soon became very proficient.

Every two weeks I went round to the back of Boots the Chemists and met one of their staff at the stockroom. I loaded up the Maxi with a gross of disposable nappies, called 'Three in One', which would last for the next fourteen days. They always seemed pleased to see me and over the next few years, selling me several thousand of these very useful items.

A decision was made to help cope with our new responsibilities, and we engaged Mrs. Wilkinson to keep the house clean, finishing the morning by cooking our lunch. She worked on the days that I worked and had days off when I did. This meant that Julia could give her time to the babies and on my days off, I could look after the household chores and food. We also found help for babysitting. Angela Drakes came for short periods so that Julia could occasionally get to the shops.

I continued to fit in work around home responsibilities. It was wonderful that the police station was just a short walk from the back door of our house, and that a telephone linked my office to the house through the police station switchboard. As the winter set in we had snow that made it difficult for Julia to get out with the twin pram we'd obtained for the boys. I was able to go to the Horncastle Fatstock Society Annual Dinner at Elsoms Restaurant.

Press interest in the birth of Horncastle triplets meant several photo sessions for us all. Pictures of us with our boys and stories about their birth appeared in the local papers and the Alert, which is the newspaper of the Lincolnshire force. The Horncastle News also decided to

A Policeman's Tale

do a feature on their local police, so we ended up with a double page spread about our section. The interest in our family continued for some time and photo shoots became something that happened quite often.

We wanted to have a family gathering for the baptism of John, Giles, and Peter. We were proud of our boys and wanted all the family to see them. We also wanted to use the occasion to say thank you to all of the family and friends who'd done much to help and support us prior to, and after their birth. The Christening was at the local Methodist Church on Sunday 7th March 1982. Godparents were carefully chosen for each child. We selected Susan and David Marshall for Peter, Anne and Arthur Platts for John, and Ruth Morris and Olga Yeates for Giles. Afterwards we enjoyed a celebratory do at Elsoms Restaurant for about sixty guests

The boys were growing quickly and getting too large for the twin pram. We needed something better. One solution was a buggy pushchair system. We connected a double buggy to a single buggy enabling all three boys to be wheeled out together. Car transport was another matter especially while they were still in carrycots. Julia's Renault Five had succumbed to rust and been replaced with a navy-blue Fiat. However, this wasn't equal to the task of transporting three little babies in their cots and on 1st May 1982, Julia became the new owner of yet another Maxi – a brown one. It enabled us to slot a cargo of three carrycots in the back quite comfortably with all the other bits and pieces required for a day out. We could go off to visit relatives and godparents much more easily.

The Leadership Trust required my services as a tutor for a week in October returning home in time for a party to celebrate the boys first birthday on 26th October 1982. We held the party on the Sunday, but on their actual birthday on the Tuesday, John developed a high temperature. Anne Woolman, who regularly looked after the boys while Julia went shopping, gave him first aid to cool him down. Then on doctor's advice he was taken by ambulance to the County Hospital at Lincoln, where he was fed ice cream and cooled by fans. He stayed for two nights and then came home, still sickly but very much better. During the following week, each of the three boys was poorly. It was a testing time for us all.

Meanwhile back at work it had been decided that two inspectors should be trained to set up the county murder room whenever this was needed, and, as I had experience in this area, I was nominated. Training in the systems used was given me and I waited for a call when the next murder occurred. The telephone rang on 7th December 1982, and the Detective Superintendent was on the other end. He told me a newsboy had been murdered that morning in Gainsborough and invited me to set up the murder room at Gainsborough Police station ready for the arrival of teams of detectives.

Inspector Chandler and I began readying the murder room with all the kit needed. Computer terminals were installed together with numerous telephones. Over the next days, we toiled with the heaps of paper generated by messages from the public and the police enquiry teams. The murderer, named Douglas Blastland, a 25-year-old local

A Policeman's Tale

baker, with previous convictions for indecency with four different boys in the Grimsby area, had strangled and assaulted the newsboy, Karl Fletcher. He was caught and put in the cells at Lincoln for questioning. An angry mob outside the police station attempted to get at Blastland. He was sentenced to life imprisonment with a minimum term of 25 years.

I'd just resumed my duties at Horncastle when another telephone call, this time from Detective Chief Superintendent Colin Bailey, sent me back to Gainsborough. This proved a disaster for our family Christmas arrangements. On Christmas Eve 1982, Julia and I had got our young boys to bed and had tidied up. We were sitting down in the lounge, and I'd poured us both a sherry. With the prospect of a peaceful evening ahead, prior to the excitement associated with the arrival of Santa Claus, we sipped our cheery tipple. Yet another murder had been committed, this time by two young men, who intent on stealing property from a house in the town at 54 Wellington Street, had killed old Mr. Clarence William Qualters. The murder room was quickly set up once more, and enquiries begun. A successful conclusion was reached with the arrest of those responsible and I was again free to return to Horncastle. One side effect of this activity was the accumulation of a satisfactory addition to my pay for the overtime worked, which helped with the household bills.

I was invited to the University of Hull from 11th to 13th April 1983 to attend a Police Federation study group. The Police Federation operates like a trade union, but without strike powers. I'd been the inspectors' divisional representative on the federation since arriving in Horncastle, attending occasional meetings at the Golf Hotel at Woodhall Spa, or sometimes at Headquarters. The study group at Hull proved interesting, especially when Lord Plant told us of his conversations with the Prime Minister (from 1976 to 1979), James Callaghan. These were about police pay and the Royal Commission on which he sat, which had been set up to determine pay and conditions of service for the police. Apparently, the Prime Minister had said to him, 'What do they want Planty?' Lord Plant had told him of the pay demands. 'Well give it to them, Planty,' Jim Callaghan was alleged to have replied.

The diary for Friday 15th April 1983, notes that Julia and I should have gone off in our black tie and long dress to a mess ladies' night. However, another murder room call came, and I found myself at Deeping St. James on the Cambridgeshire border. For the next three and a half weeks, I was involved in the investigation of the murder of a fourteen-year-old girl, Gillian Atkins, who'd been sexually assaulted and strangled. For the first time we used computers as indexing tools for all the statements taken and maintained huge indices of all the ongoing strands of the enquiry and the people and vehicles mentioned. The perpetrator, Robert France, turned out to be a fairground worker and my friend John Walkley, who was the author of a book on interrogation techniques for detectives, handled his interrogation.

Managing to get a couple of days off in the middle of the investigation (the other trained inspector covering for me), I came home to find Julia with a puzzle. The boys were walking now. They could no longer be allowed in our garden, as the front fence, which had once been chestnut palings, was now a ranch style with large gaps following the widening of Cagthorpe, the road in front of our house. If they were let loose it would be easy for them to wander onto the road. I asked the police administration for a better fence but was refused, so I went off to the agricultural merchants, Burgesses, on the Wong to look for an answer. Chicken wire was a favourite, but they showed me some sheep fencing, which had a much wider weave of wire, but still close enough to contain sheep (and triplets). I bought several rolls and lots of staples. Back home, I set about triplet proofing our fence so that Julia could have peace of mind and let the boys to play freely.

A couple of months later saw the end of my time as the Horncastle Inspector although I didn't know it then. I'd been nominated to attend the Police Staff College at Bramshill on a Junior Command Course. This course was generally seen as a prelude to promotion and although it meant leaving Julia to cope as best, she could for nearly six months, it was difficult to turn down the opportunity, and Julia was supportive.

I travelled down to Hampshire on Monday 27th June 1983 to begin the course. However, not long after starting, I was invited back to Lincolnshire on 8th July at 11.30am to receive the award of my medal for long and exemplary service presented by the Lord Lieutenant of the County, Captain Sir Henry Neville. Julia and I enjoyed the reception at force headquarters with several colleagues who'd joined when I did and who received their medals too.

The course was quite intensive, designed to fit us for command roles in the police force. There were many highlights. One of these occurred in connection with the psychology course. We did some interesting personality testing using the Myers-Briggs tests as well as others. Our tutor, a Hampshire Superintendent, took us on a visit to Broadmoor. This institution for the criminally insane resembled a prison but was run by the Special Hospital Service. We met many of the inmates and I was somewhat shocked to discover that the pleasant woman cleaning one of the dormitories had dismembered two babies and kept the pieces in her refrigerator. In the carpentry workshop, where there were a great number of sharp tools such as chisels, a huge black man with staring eyes was happily chatting to a group of us while waving a saw in the air.

Another outing was to visit a casino. I was amazed when our superintendent purchased one hundred pounds worth of chips and demonstrated his skill at the gaming tables. This area was a closed book to me, and largely still is. At least I got to see what happens in real life, rather than relying for my information on Bond films, which always seem to feature a casino scene. Other interesting outings included a visit to HMS Victory in Portsmouth Harbour, and to a drug rehabilitation centre where I was able to talk to people attempting to kick their drug habits.

There were numerous lectures, tutor sessions, and essays to write and submit. Once again, my trusty Imperial Good Companion 7 typewriter was severely bashed, after I'd done research in the library, to produce the required number of words. I was fortunate in having one of these papers added

A Policeman's Tale

to the collection of student work held in the library for reference purposes.

I greatly enjoyed membership of the Fielding Society, a literary club, with regular meetings in the old mansion. One evening we had an interesting encounter with Richard Ingrams who was editor of Private Eye, the satirical magazine, and another evening heard a talk by Colin Dexter, writer of murder mysteries especially the Inspector Morse series of novels.

There were some very enjoyable mess nights. We also played hard, and I did my best to contribute my volleyball skills towards the inter-syndicate championship competition.

About four weeks before the end of the Junior Command Course on 15th November 1983, there was great news as I was promoted to the rank of Chief Inspector. From that date, I learned, my posting was to the Administrative Department at Boston. The news was carried in the Grimsby Evening Telegraph.

As a family, we again appeared in the force newspaper Alert. Meanwhile even though the course at Bramshill had a month to run Julia and I turned our thoughts to moving to Boston. We'd considered the possibility of buying our own house. This was with an eye to the future, and eventual retirement, when a house of our own would be almost essential. We decided to take the plunge and visited estate agents to obtain details of properties for sale in Boston.

At the end of the Bramshill course I had to say goodbye to the syndicate friends I'd made. Back at Horncastle, Sergeant Bill Anderson had arranged a farewell gathering for

Julia and me at the Red Lion Inn at Baumber. We had a good social evening and the section presented me with a pewter tankard as a reminder of my Horncastle days.

XXIII Boston Chief Inspector

I caught up with a little leave at the end of my course at Bramshill so was able to spend Christmas with the family. Then on Tuesday 3rd January 1984, I drove the twenty miles from Horncastle to Boston. My first day there was occupied mainly with meeting the people I was to work with. My new boss was George Bulman. He had been one of the Headquarters Information Room sergeants many years before when I was there as a cadet. Now he was the Chief Superintendent in charge of Boston with Holland Division, which covered two local authority areas in the south of the county.

I began to discover what my work would involve as the Administrative Chief Inspector. My experience was based on a short period as acting sergeant at Spalding years before, when the mysteries of the imprest account had made an impression on me. Now I had a staff of several civilians to look after such matters, but before anything left the office, usually on the way to Headquarters, it needed my signature, so I had to understand what I was signing. This process began straight away. One of the other areas needing my attention was budgeting the expenditure of the division. Almost everything except pay and uniform was a matter for me. This was new in the force, as until then, Headquarters had decided how the budget should be spent. The new system of devolved budgeting was a great leap forward. It meant extra work, but this was compensated for by the ability to use money where it was really needed rather than having to be prized out of Headquarters by sending in reports pleading for a new desk, carpet, or redecorations to police stations or houses.

My first day in my new job was interrupted however around 4.30pm, when Mr. Bulman appeared in my office to tell me that Julia had had an accident at home, and I'd better get off there straight away. Of course, I did, and returned to Horncastle in some haste. Julia had tumbled down the stairs and hit her head on the telephone table at the bottom. She'd a severe wound above her eye and had been taken to hospital by the doctor for stitching. Neighbours had rallied round to look after the boys. Rushing round to the hospital, I tried to comfort her. However, I blurted out the words, 'You might have killed yourself'. Julia was not impressed, and I realised my choice of words was not the best. Even so, I tried to help and comfort her as best as I could. I decided that the best help would be to take the rest of the week off and help with the children.

Therefore, I didn't really get my teeth into my new job until the following week when I began to get to grips with learning the ropes of the job, I was to have for nearly three years. It seemed that the name of the game was financial management, with some personnel management thrown in.

Julia and I very quickly settled on buying a new home in Boston at 13 Bain Road. We put down a £1550 deposit on 20th January 1984 and were able to move in on 29th February. This was to be our home for the next six and a half years. We had good help from the family in making the move. While we had worked out the financial commitment needed to buy our house, we found that rising inflation and its effect on interest rates hadn't entered our calculations.

Initially, repaying the interest on our mortgage cost us monthly payments of £228, but within twelve months, these had risen to £258 on a £30,000 mortgage. My four-weekly salary income, including housing allowance, after tax, superannuation, national insurance, and Police Mutual Assurance Society payments came to around £610. The costs of living in our own house began to impose a severe strain on the family finances, as many homeowners are well aware.

Much of the summer was spent getting the garden in order. We planted roses called 'Blessings' along one border in the back garden. These were quite beautiful and very successful. The garden was great for the three boys to play in. At the bottom of the garden, there was a shed where they could hide among my tools. There was also a little lean-to greenhouse. It was just big enough for a few tomato plants. Despite the financial restraints, it seemed great to be a property owner. Of course, maintenance was now my responsibility and there were always jobs to be done. For instance, the branches of one of the apple trees had been rubbing on the shed roof and I needed to refelt it. The lawn cutting made plenty of compost. I enjoyed all this, often with help from three small members of the family.

Time passed swiftly at Boston. At work, I continued on a steep learning curve getting to grips with new computers for financial management and writing letters for the Chief Superintendent. I soon discovered one of his favourite phrases when writing to members of the public was 'it can do nothing but good'. I tried to get this into most of the letters I drafted for him, and he seemed to like it. One day while talking to my admin staff I unwisely said that I thought Boston was all 'sprout pullers and lorry drivers', which I thought was a generally accepted perception. However, one of the clerks soon pulled me up with 'Well my father is a lorry driver, and my mother is a sprout puller and I'm a Young Farmer'. I'm not sure if that made me right or wrong, but I don't think she thought much of my opinion.

Arthur Scargill, President of the National Union of Mineworkers (NUM), called on the miners to strike. On 12 March 1984, a strike started which was to last for nearly a year. The strike only began to crumble when the National Coal Board offered miners various pay incentives to return to work before Christmas. On 3 March 1985, the NUM's executive narrowly voted for a return to work, and the miners acknowledged defeat and returned to work two days later. The effect on the police was tremendous. Every police force sent contingents of officers to the pit areas. Boston Division regularly contributed, leaving a much-reduced workforce to carry out local policing. Various

A Policeman's Tale

senior officers went off to assist in command roles, and as a trained PSU commander I was keen to go too. It was made clear to me that I was expected to keep the division running by staying in Boston. My work was cut out processing hundreds of claims for overtime. These were very detailed timesheets compiled both by those who'd gone off to the strike areas, and by the officers covering for their absence. Huge amounts of overtime were paid it seemed to everyone but me. The general belief in the police force was that Mr. Scargill had done the miners no favours, but great benefit to police officers' pockets. This was perhaps one more example of unintended consequences.

Various things took me away from Boston from time to time. Again, I was fortunate to be selected to go off to Blackpool on another marking panel for three weeks in May 1984, and then once more in October the same year. No Swedish massages were on offer this time. I was on various working parties looking at aspects of the force such as the prosecutions system and had to tour the county researching practices in each division. There was also a spell in June 1985 at the Civil Defence College in Easingwold in Yorkshire for a short course. Afterwards I discovered that I was down to be in the Boston Borough Council nuclear bunker in the event of war, as the police liaison officer. Julia took a dim view of this! In October 1985, I travelled down to London by train to the Home Office in Queen Anne's Gate for a working party on the contents of police car boots. I contributed to the proceedings by stressing the importance of a good brush for sweeping up after road accidents. I'm not sure if this was useful in the determination of procurement needs for the future, but I felt it was a very practical contribution.

One nice thing about Boston Police Station was the provision on the top floor of a lounge for senior officers. This was equipped with a splendid coffee maker. It was my job to see it was filled and set to provide morning and afternoon supplies of freshly brewed coffee for we senior officers. It was a good opportunity to find out what was going on and discuss current developments. I always looked forward to the trip upstairs. The view across the river from the lounge of the Stump was wonderful and if we had visitors, it always impressed them. While at Boston great changes in the force resulted in substantial reductions in the management teams in divisions. The force was split into North and South Divisions. Boston lost its Chief Superintendent and the superintendent deputy. The traffic divisional chief inspector was removed, and we were reduced to one superintendent and three chief inspectors. The crowd in the coffee lounge was much reduced, but often we had visitors from the new divisional headquarters established at Bourne.

Regularly I was called away from Boston and the family. The year 1986 saw me at Bramshill again for a college course on financial management. It was good to discover that Lincolnshire Police were well ahead in devolved budget management.

John, Giles, and Peter were by now almost five years of age and in September 1986, they started school at Boston West Primary School. Julia had kitted them out in smart new school uniforms. They posed, like fashion models, for a photograph in our garden before being put in the tender care of their first teacher, Mrs. Oliver.

My parents celebrated their Golden Wedding on 21st September 1986 with family celebrations at the Lynton Hotel at Cleethorpes. It was a wonderful celebration which included their five grandchildren.

I'd been doing my administrative job now for nearly two years and on 29th September 1986, I was instructed to swap jobs with the Operations Chief Inspector, George Butcher.

As Operations Chief Inspector, I was in charge of day-to-day policing in the Boston and Spalding areas, with several inspectors to command, and around two hundred police officers. The police area covered 455 square miles with a population of about 120,000. Apart from this, it was also my job to deputise for the Superintendent in his absence, usually at the weekend. I used to receive a small addition to my pay each day I did this. This came about because of the Police and Criminal Evidence Act, which among many onerous provisions required certain tasks to be performed by an officer of at least the rank of superintendent. Since we only had one of these in the division, the chief inspector covering had to act up for the day.

It was one of my tasks to ensure plans were made for major operations such as the Tulip Festival in May at Spalding, and the New Year festivities in Boston. Extensive plans were prepared for these happenings and operational orders issued to all involved. The next step was usually a briefing session when all the officers, sometimes a hundred or so, gathered to hear the plans and raise any questions.

Patrick J. McNeill

Being in the lead police car for the flower parade at Spalding, ahead of the mile-long procession of beautifully decorated floats was very enjoyable. A less enjoyable event was always New Year's Eve. The tradition in Boston, which I mentioned earlier on, was to climb the Five Lamps in the Market Place at midnight to the cheers of the merry makers. This often resulted in battles between the police attempting to maintain order and safety, and people determined to carry out the tradition or assist the climbers. My preparations began several months before the event. One task was to ensure that no building site, or road works in the vicinity of Boston town centre provided loose ammunition for anyone minded to throw stones, bricks, or other objects. Leave had to be cancelled and a large number of officers assembled. I remember briefing a roomful of officers on the top floor of Boston Police Station at 10pm on New Year's Eve with my cunning plan.

Chief Superintendent Michael Follows had come along for the evening and listened as I explained that the Five Lamps would be left to its own devices and no police attempt would be made to interfere with any prospective or actual climbers. In fact, the police would fade into the shadows at five minutes to midnight and keep a low profile until a radio message announced the resumption of normal patrols. I was in the Market Place as midnight approached and watched the plan unfold. Several youths tried to climb the huge lamppost, but each failed and the crowd soon lost interest. After half an hour, no incidents had needed police intervention and relative peace reigned. It was judged a successful night's police work, much to my relief.

A Policeman's Tale

Mr. Follows used to visit the division regularly, unannounced, and carry out his inspections of our doings. These often resulted in me having to explain alleged shortcoming and I never looked forward to seeing him. He often told me not to be so defensive in my dealings with him. I always used to see him as a man with monkeys sitting on his shoulders. He would try to put some of these on mine, and I always tried very hard to prevent this. My superintendent, Bert Shaw, told me in one of my annual assessments, that I didn't suffer fools gladly. He advised me that I shouldn't let this show quite so obviously. When I asked him for an instance of this, he quickly called to mind some of my exchanges with the Chief Superintendent just mentioned. Now I can see he was quite right. Michael Follows was doing his duty as he saw it and I think he had a regard for me, as he certainly wrote me a pleasant letter on my retirement.

One of my deputising jobs was to become a member of the local Sea Cadet unit management committee. I regularly attended meeting and events connected with the unit and discovered a great deal about an area of life previously unknown to me.

In March 1987 I went off to Wakefield for short course in police firearms tactics, and then in May the same year spent a couple of weeks at Bramshill on a management support skills course. This was mainly about facilitating interactions between groups of people to get the best of them. This fitted in well with much of the leadership training I'd had and been responsible for passing on. In September of that year, there was a week at Ripley in

Derbyshire on a course for Police Support Unit commanders. This was designed for officers who would command several units on operations.

Following the birth of our triplets, Julia and I felt unable to take family holidays for a while, because of everything needed for a family of five on the move. Nevertheless, in 1987 we decided to dip our toes in the water and booked two weeks at a holiday camp in Brixham in Devon. The holiday was a success, and we all enjoyed the change of scenery, sun, sea, and sand.

Back to work, Julia and I sometimes enjoyed social events that the superintendent was unable to attend. On Friday 27th March 1987, we spent a splendid evening at a banquet in Boston Assembly Rooms as guests of the Mayor and Corporation, sitting next to the local Member of Parliament Sir Richard Body. Another interesting evening, on 16th September 1987, was at the Royal Air Force Station at Coningsby where the station commander entertained us to a reception and demonstration of the capabilities of the Phantom jets based there. Two of these fast jet fighter plans roared along the runway together with their afterburners glowing, making a deafening roar, and then shooting up into the evening sky. The noise was almost mind bending, but the experience exhilarating.

Julia's mother had passed away in 1985, on 17th November, at the age of 77 years. My mother had suffered from heart failure for several years and on 11th June 1988, at the age of 74 years she died. Both of us felt these losses greatly, as did our two bereaved fathers. In both cases, we gave what family support we could, but living away at

A Policeman's Tale

Boston, it was difficult for us to do as much as we wished.

Despite our loss, life had to go on, and we had already booked a holiday for the year. Encouraged by the success of our trip to Devon we'd decided to try foreign shores and headed for Brittany. We took a gite at Plogastel St. Germain, near Quimper for two weeks from 29th July to 13th August 1988. We all had a great time exploring this glorious part of France, and we enjoyed the beaches, sea, and scenery. I enjoyed being able to use the schoolboy French learned many years previously at Clee Grammar.

Back at home considerable effort had been made in the police force to introduce a national computer system to speed up the exchange of information between forces. This had resulted in the introduction of the Police National Computer. The computer was designed to assist in all manner of crime related matters. For instance, it was possible to check any registration number against a nationwide list of stolen vehicles, and names could be checked against lists of wanted people. In October 1988, I went up to Durham Police Headquarters for a short appreciation course on the use of this technology. I can't now remember much about it, but I do remember that there was a splendid swimming pool at the headquarters which I enjoyed using. An evening out had been arranged at a brewery and a civic reception at Sunderland Town Hall. For a short course, this seemed a very agreeable programme for the delegates!

In the autumn, Julia and I were invited to a concert in The Embassy Centre at Skegness with Orff's Carmina Burana as the main work. During the interval I completed an entry in a prize draw and was rewarded a short while later with the news that Julia and I had won a weekend in London. The opportunity was to attend the final of the young musician of the year competition at the Royal Academy of Music. We spent a splendid weekend, 26th and 27th November 1988, in the big city staying at the John Howard Hotel. Steve Race hosted the event at the Royal Academy, and during the interval, Julia and I got to mingle with notables such as Lady Barbirolli.

It was around this time that I was encouraged by the Deputy Chief Constable, Mr. Bensley, to apply for various Superintendent vacancies as they arose. One of these was at the Police College, and he seemed to think me suitable. I submitted my details for several of these positions, but each time received a polite rejection. I was now in my late forties and approaching thirty years' service. Both of these factors seemed to count against me, and I supposed that promotion beyond chief inspector rank was becoming increasingly unlikely.

Once again, my services were required on the marking panel for the promotion examinations, but this time the venue was Scarborough. The panel had taken over the Palm Court Hotel for a month and from 13th November until 9th December 1988 I devoted much of my time to scribbling little red numbers on a host of scripts written by policemen hoping to advance in the service. I was delighted to find the hotel had the benefit of a swimming pool, so that, whenever the little red figures danced in front of my eyes, I would get my trunks on, and do a few relaxing lengths in the warm water.

Chief Superintendent Follows saw me on my return and told me that he felt the post at Headquarters Community Affairs Department that was becoming vacant would suit me. I agreed, and in no time at all, I was informed that this was to be my new posting with effect from 30th January 1989.

Julia and I set about selling our house in Boston. On Friday, 13th January 1989, we were advised that a suitable asking price would be £84,000. The 'For Sale' sign was planted in the front garden, and we awaited results.

XXIV Headquarters Community Affairs Department

It was time to start anew. It was not very clear what my new job involved. Once again, my career in the police service had taken a path into areas not previously encountered, and there would be a steep learning curve. I quickly discovered I had a male inspector, Mike Draine in charge of Crime Prevention, and a woman inspector, Sue Chapman, responsible for Community Affairs throughout the county. My overall responsibilities ranged from advice to householders on locks and bolts, to race relations, and juvenile delinquency. In each of the five sub-divisions in the county were stationed a Community Affairs sergeant and two or three constables. I had to get a grip on this and find out all about these areas of police work. There were also some civilian clerks at Headquarters, and Community Affairs was part of the Operations Department under the command of a chief superintendent.

A Policeman's Tale

Beginning the daily routine, I drove fifty miles from Boston to Nettleham for work arriving before 9am each morning, with a similar trip home each evening. Little did I know that this was to last for eighteen long months. There were some good points about it and quite a few down points. Bad points were the time it took and the cost together with wear and tear on my car. However, on the good side I realised I had over two hours each day to myself, to think and unwind – a luxury that compensated a little for the downside. The drive from Boston was through the flat fenland, along the long straight roads with dykes on either side, to Coningsby, then Horncastle, over the Wolds, through Wragby, and then into Nettleham. This journey was reversed each evening. In the summer travel times extended as the part of my journey along the A158 between Nettleham and Horncastle included huge numbers of cars and caravans heading to or from the coast at Skegness or Mablethorpe.

Both Sue Chapman and Mike Draine, my two inspectors, knew far more about their jobs than I did. I learned quickly. One of the most puzzling areas related to burglar alarms. It seemed that the Association of Chief Police Officers had a national policy relating to these, which my department had to manage in respect of Lincolnshire. Some burglar alarms just sound a local bell or siren, but many are linked directly to police stations or central alarm stations operated by private alarm companies. If the alarm is activated, a police response is looked for. This would be provided normally on receipt of a call. However, when police officers responded they often discovered the call was a false one for various reasons. Generally, these were due to a fault in the system, or the alarm being set off by the householder or someone properly on the premises.

Our policy was that after three false alarms we stopped responding. We wrote to the person with the alarm, and their alarm company, and warned them of this. Of course, this needed a considerable amount of record keeping and letter writing. This was followed often by more correspondence, objections, explanations, and appeals. If I sought to cut off response to a gun shop, the owner would find that another police department would withdraw his dealer's licence. As you can imagine this was the source of considerable tension, which would hit my desk. On one occasion, I had to visit a huge manor house in the countryside to talk to the elderly occupant whose burglar alarm regularly went off in error to discuss the situation. I enjoyed the tour of the house and her hospitality, learning a great deal about the impossibility of maintaining such premises on a small income. Another time, Julia was visiting me in my office, when a gun shop owner rang in great distress over the proposed withdrawal of response to her burglar alarm. Julia had to listen to me trying to be firm, tactful, diplomatic, and coping with a very dissatisfied member of the public. She got a good idea of some of the stresses of the job.

I became a member of the Racial Justice Forum for Lincolnshire. Regular meetings, sometimes at Police Headquarters, extended my knowledge of the problems faced by minorities in the county. We organised conferences attended by the public to address these

A Policeman's Tale

problems and worked hard to quantify the size of problems in the county. This was an uphill task given the small number of minority citizens in the county at the time. One area where statistics were required was records of racial incidents. Any occurrence considered to have overtones of racist behaviour had to be recorded. Often this proved difficult as much reliance had to be placed on the perceptions of officers dealing with incidents, and then persuading them to submit an appropriate form. If I got three or four forms in a year, it was only by chasing them up. This may well have reflected the low level of racist behaviour, or only the lack of reporting by the public.

I joined the Assistant Chief Constable at regular meetings between the Probation Service and Social Services to discuss inter-service matters. These were mainly concerned with juvenile crime, but often covered other matters affecting our three organisations. I sorted out the relevant files and often did the minutes for the meetings held at the headquarters of each of the services in turn.

The summer of 1989 saw the family holiday taken in West Jutland in Denmark. From 4th to 19th August. We stayed in a summerhouse at Lønne. The overnight voyage on a car ferry from Harwich to Esbjerg was a new experience for the boys. We found Denmark a great place with wonderful beaches and the weather to go with it. Having our car, the Montego, with us enabled us to tour the countryside and to visit various summerlands. These are parks with lots of activities for children that the boys, Julia, and I thoroughly enjoyed. There was of course a trip to Legoland, which was a great experience for us all, and a must for visitors to Denmark.

Returning to work after the break, and throughout the summer, I helped promote and organise the countywide scheme aimed at giving youngsters activities during the long school holidays. The scheme was called 'Escape' and the police worked with Social Services all over the county devising events and activities. One of these was at Bardney where I hired a one-woman circus to teach children the skills of the ring. This went very well until I received her invoice. I passed it for payment to the county council as usual knowing it would take probably two to three months for the money to reach her. She was on the telephone within a week in a tearful state telling me she was relying on the money to pay her way and that she needed it immediately. This brought into sharp focus for me how much time it took to get any invoice paid and how patient most suppliers of services to the police and county council must be. I rushed off to the police accounts office and, between us, we managed to speed up payment of her bill, so she got her money after only three weeks. This was not bad for our painfully slow accounts system.

Our house had still not sold. Returning home one evening, Julia informed me that a Mr. Cheetham had made an offer of £79,000 for our house. This being somewhat less than the asking price we turned him down – a bad move, which, in hindsight, we should have accepted.

On 16th October 1989, I was at Blackfriars Theatre in Boston where we launched a crime prevention initiative. Mike Draine had invited celebrity BBC gardener, Daphne Ledward, along to say a few words from the stage, and I was

A Policeman's Tale

to introduce her. The event was designed to draw attention to doorstep conmen who talk their way into your house and steal property. It was to disseminate practical advice to combat this menace. I discovered that this was the usual pattern of crime prevention launches. Mike Draine was very good at dreaming up a new initiative to catch the public imagination and attention. We would find a celebrity and manufacture an event that would produce photographs and paragraphs in local papers. The aim was also to get a couple of minutes at least on the local television news programmes. Mike and I spent time trying to find suitable celebrities prepared to give their valuable time (preferably free) to the cause of crime prevention.

One benefit of my Community Affairs post was that I continued to receive an allowance to run my car for police work. Further, there was a scheme to obtain a car for use on a contract permitting private use. For three years I'd had a red Montego under this scheme and at the end of that contract on 24th October 1989 it was replaced with an oyster beige Montego. These cars, while not as versatile at the Maxis had been, were quite roomy and I was able to carry all five of us in reasonable comfort. At least that was the case until our sons reached their teenage years.

It was just as well I had a decent vehicle as I was now regularly attending conferences and meetings around the country. On 27th October 1989, I had a trip to Liverpool, and on 30th November 1989 to Dudley in the midlands for another meeting.

Christmas came and went, and the Boston house had still not been sold. Therefore, on 23rd January 1990, we reduced the price of our four bed-roomed detached modern residence to £72,000, hoping for a quick sale. This seemed to have a beneficial effect. On 10th March, we received an offer of £71,000 from Mr. & Mrs. Dave Roberts, which we accepted. Now we were able to consider seriously looking for a house in the Lincoln area. We'd already had some estate agents' brochures and now we began searching in earnest. I spent many lunch hours checking possible houses. Julia came over with me on a day off and we looked at several that generally were too small or too expensive. The chief problem seemed to be the difference in price between houses in Boston and Lincoln. They were about £20,000 higher in Lincoln for a four bed-roomed house than at Boston, and in Nettleham, they were higher still.

Disappointed by lack of progress, Julia rang several estate agents asking for details of any properties in Nettleham and the villages north of Lincoln. A sheaf of leaflets arrived. Over my lunch hour each day, I went out to look at the properties for sale. Then on 31st March, Julia phoned me at work to say a fresh one had come on the market in The Chestnuts at Nettleham. The price seemed right – would I look it over. I did this and was impressed. She rang to arrange a viewing, which was fixed for the very same evening, when, coincidentally, she was to attend a ladies evening with the Lincolnshire Police Officers Mess. We turned up at the Moulder's house with me in black tie and Julia in her long gown. I think they were impressed. A tour of the house made us both enthusiastic. It was smaller than our current house at Boston, being one room short, but had a good kitchen and garden. We decided to offer the asking price of £89,950, which was accepted. Now it was down to all the paraphernalia that is entailed in house purchase of surveys, solicitors, mortgages, and contracts. The new mortgage was for the sum of £50,000, requiring monthly repayments of £432 interest and another £100 towards endowment assurances to cover the repayment of the capital sum in twenty-five years' time. While the interest rate then was 12.45% this was gradually to reduce over the coming years as inflation subsided. Payments became more manageable.

Shortly before our house purchase, on 14th March 1990, we received the very sad news from Olga Yeates of the death of our friend, Ruth Morris, Giles's Godmother. Ruth had been suffering with great pain after an operation to replace her knee joint, but her death was a great shock to us all. We attended the funeral the following week, and I went to the Coroner's Inquest with Olga to give her some support during a very difficult time. I had been appointed as one of the executors of Ruth's will. This was a new experience for me, and, with Olga, I spent quite some time in conference with the solicitor sorting out Ruth's estate.

A couple of months later an offer came our way from Anne and Arthur Platts to join them on holiday in Hampshire. They were off in their caravan to Sandy Balls in the New Forest, and we took a chalet from 25th May to 1st June 1990 for a break. The chalet turned out to be quite luxurious with a good barbeque facility that we used to the full. Blessed with good weather we enjoyed walks by the river and trips to the Moors Valley miniature railway in the Dorset Country Park, and sightseeing in Christchurch.

Returning to work after the break, at Headquarters in Deepdale Lane, Nettleham, I settled down to my duties. The Moulders moved to Nottingham leaving the house in The Chestnuts empty. They had invited me to keep an eye on it while it was empty prior to the completion of the sale. In my lunch hour, I'd go around and check it over, picking a few raspberries in the garden as I did so. I looked warily at the Leylandii hedge at the back of the garden, about twelve feet tall and fifty feet long. Mr. Moulder had offered to sell me his electric hedge trimmer for £40, and I'd accepted. Close inspection indicated that I was going to spend a great deal of time looking after this hedge. It gave seclusion to the property, but the cost was to be three-day trimming sessions for both Julia and I. I was helped by Olga's kind gift of a tall set of aluminium steps that helped me get near the top of the hedge.

I had the keys and on looking in the empty garage, I saw the two wall cabinets that looked a handy place to keep garden chemicals and car polish. Opening up one of them revealed a strange conical shaped object suspended from the centre shelf. It looked as if it was made of paper. Curious, I poked it, and made a small hole in the side. Immediately out flew several wasps. Angrily they made straight for me. Fleeing into the garden, I was pursued by the wasps. Catching up with me, they landed on my shiny baldhead giving me at least six or seven stings. I returned to work, but in a very short time, my face and head began to swell. I took an antihistamine tablet hoping it would help, but it didn't seem to have any effect. My face was like a melon, so I went to the chemists, Krystals, in the village, to seek

A Policeman's Tale

advice. They told me that antihistamine was the only remedy. After soldiering on for the rest of the afternoon at work I headed for home, with an aching, swollen face. Julia and the family were very shocked when I got to Boston, and surprised I'd soldiered on in such a state.

Fortunately, the effects wore off, but I'd learned one more lesson in life. Now I'm very aware of what a wasp's nest looks like. I arranged for the pest control officer from West Lindsey District Council to come and remove the nest which he kindly and expertly did.

On 12th July 1990, we packed up our things at Boston and with two removal vans made our way to number 3 The Chestnuts at Nettleham. My father helped us clear up at Boston. I went off with the vans to meet them on arrival at Nettleham. My father followed with Julia and the boys. We found Susan and David Marshall ready to help us unload at Nettleham. They'd made us a picnic with strawberries for tea. This was very welcoming for tired folk. The day went well, and we looked forward to family life in the village. There were of course quite a number of things about the house to fix. These included fitting our cooker in a gap, which was half an inch too narrow, sorting out the plumbing for our essential washing machine, and removing a Belfast sink to make room for our tumble dryer. John, Giles, and Peter prepared themselves for starting at the local Church of England Junior School.

It seemed no time at all before we were off again on a family holiday. This time I'd taken up the offer of Sergeant Ian Simpson, the officer running the underwater search unit, who owned a holiday caravan, on the Isle d'Oleron, on the western coast of France. We hired the caravan for two weeks from 27th July to 12th August 1990 and set off in our Montego. We arrived in a heat wave and found the confines of the caravan a little like living in an oven while the heat was on. The island however was a splendid holiday venue and we all enjoyed ourselves, especially on the Atlantic Ocean beaches.

Back home, I got to grips with some of the outstanding jobs around the house that we were still settling into. One project was to make room for my model railway, which had been in storage at Boston. I'd begun planning there to provide a home for the lines in the loft but was overtaken by the lack of time after working and family chores. However, now I determined that my 00 layout would have a home. Julia and I decided to sacrifice one of the two raspberry beds and Mr. Kime, a builder in the village, arrived with his mate to put down a concrete base. Next, I had a shed made by Messrs. A. B. Creasey, a firm from Scotter. It measured ten feet by eight feet, with insulated walls, meshed windows, and a securely locking door. This was delivered and assembled. Nettleham electrician, Neil Caldwell, was asked to fix up an electricity supply for lights and sockets. With great ceremony on John, Giles, and Peter's birthday, Olga Yeates declared the railway shed open. Now remained the joinery, the task of making baseboards and scenery. This was to occupy me for many of my spare moments over the coming years. Sometime John, Giles, and Peter helped with ideas for the layout, and eventually operating the controls.

At work, I had a new Community Liaison Inspector,

A Policeman's Tale

Carole Rose. She arranged a presentation in the museum at headquarters to take place before an invited audience. A member of the House of Lords was to do the honours. I was asked to entertain her to tea and biscuits before the event, which I did, discovering that she had appalling bad breath. However, despite this problem, she was kind enough to help us and I managed to make my own little speech without too many nerves and fluffing my lines.

I needed to improve my understanding of minority communities. On 26th November 1990, I went off to Lancashire for a two-week course at Preston exploring various religions and immigrant communities. The course included an interesting visit to a Sikh temple where, after removing my shoes, I met temple members and saw the various shrines. This experience gave me a much better understanding of many aspects of the culture of other communities.

In December 1990, I reflected that I was approaching the thirtieth anniversary of my appointment as a constable. This is a defining moment in a police officer's career, and it is when most officers take retirement. At thirty years' service maximum pension became payable, and I was due to reach this point on 28th December 1990. Of course, I still had considerable family responsibilities with three ten-year-old sons at school, and a mortgage on the house with twenty years to run. Other factors to consider included the likelihood of promotion. I'd never heard of anyone being promoted beyond thirty years' service, so it seemed I needed to rule this possibility out. Furthermore, my car was on contract hire, and the contract period had another couple of years to run. All these factors pointed towards the need to continue to draw a regular salary rather than a pension.

Early in 1991, I had another visit to Bramshill for a two-week Staff College course on Crime Reduction using the community approach. Returning to Nettleham I discovered that Inspector Mike Draine had hired a hot air balloon to publicise a crime prevention initiative. We planned to launch the balloon from the police field as a media photo shoot opportunity. Radio Lincolnshire were invited along, and their presenter Dave Bussey came to the event. It turned out that balloons have to be launched early in the morning before the wind rises above five miles an hour, so we were all there around sunrise (although it was such a grey morning the sun was nowhere to be seen). It seemed a good idea for John, Giles, and Peter to attend before school so with Julia we all trooped along. Several attempts to get the balloon up in the air were made but the wind proved too strong and after a while the whole thing was abandoned. Even so, we'd managed to get some publicity for the crime prevention project, and John, Giles, and Peter had interesting news to share with school friends about their encounter with the world of hot air ballooning.

That year we planned and enjoyed a family holiday in Denmark in the same summerhouse at Lønne in Gammelgabsvey (Old Gap Road) that we'd visited in 1989. This time we visited some of the places not seen on our previous visit. We found several good swimming pools with extra facilities such as waterslides. The pool at Oksbol had two of these. One of them sent you down in a spiral while the other, which we called 'the zonker', seemed like a straight drop down at high speed. Julia emerged from it vowing 'never again', and I managed only one trip down. Scandinavia is noticeably cleaner than much of England. Standards of hygiene seem higher, and this was reflected at public swimming pools. On the way to the changing rooms, an area was set aside to remove footwear and socks, preventing mud getting onto a wet floor. Then you move into the main changing area where you disrobe and put on your swimming costume. I did this at Oksbol as usual and headed for the showers. A stern attendant, equipped with a whistle, called me back and instructed me, firmly, to remove my trunks before showering. He then saw that I took a soap-impregnated sponge from a large basket of these and joined the other people in the showers thoroughly washing myself. Helpful diagrams on the wall indicated all the areas where the sponge should go, so that nowhere was missed. After this and rinsing down, I was allowed to get into my trunks at last. I headed towards the swimming pool, but as soon as I glimpsed the water a female attendant shouted at me. I couldn't understand the Danish, but she soon made clear that there was a little shower foam still in my hair and that I should return to rinse it off in the showers. No wonder the water in the pool was sparklingly clean. After all this it was still great to be in the water and Julia told me the procedures in the ladies changing room were just as strict.

At work, I was privileged to meet several people well known in the entertainment world, while involved in activities designed to draw attention to crime prevention and improve the police profile in connection with other community matters. These included the actor Richard Todd (famous for his role as Guy Gibson in 'The Dambusters' film). He was slightly smaller than I expected, but very pleasant. Proudly he wore his Parachute Regiment tie and related the story of how he came by it. Another member of the acting profession I met was Peggy Mount, then appearing at the Theatre Royal in Lincoln. Her radio and on-screen persona was that of a dragon, but in the flesh, while certainly a large lady, she was delightful, helpful, and keen to help the project we were running, when she visited Police Headquarters.

We'd run a competition for young people on the lines of a well-known television quiz. The Blockbusters quizmaster, Bob Holness, kindly agreed to compere the finale of this competition and he duly arrived in my office at Headquarters where we went over the plans for the evening. His expertise and courtesy were very evident, and I added him to my list of very pleasant people I'd met from the world of stage and screen.

An annual event not mentioned so far was the Lincolnshire Show. The county agricultural event often attracts around one hundred thousand visitors over the two days in June when it is held. Very soon after my arrival at headquarters in January 1989, I discovered that I was on the committee to plan the police participation in the show. By this I don't mean the policing of the show, which in itself is a large operation, rather, the stand which the Lincolnshire Police took to show the public something of our operations, or alternatively to get a crime prevention, road safety or other message across to them.

A Policeman's Tale

I was surprised to discover that, not only was I on the committee, but it was my lot to organise the police stand with the help of my department. This entailed long discussions with my two inspectors, and consultations with the traffic department and the public relations department. A major consideration was always the budget for the operation. The hire of a tent or other exhibition facility was always expensive. Usually, the Agricultural Society wanted to rent out the space that we would occupy, and my task was to attempt through negotiations to get the space free, which I usually managed to do.

The County Council always felt the police stand should be close to their stands. They hoped to bask in our reflected glory perhaps. They certainly hoped we would coordinate our presentation with their own, leading to more discussions. Each of the years I was involved we managed something different and something people were keen to see. The preparation was very important of course with attention to detail, but after the hard work of putting the stand together prior to the show, there was two long days of at least twelve hours on your feet, meeting and greeting people.

When I first went down to the showground just north of Lincoln, I was offered the use of one of the force's mobile telephones. This seemed very useful to me. It must be remembered that the mobile phones of the late 1980s were very different from those in use now. They consisted of a heavy battery unit, a bit larger than a brick, and a normal telephone handset on a curly cord. There was no question of putting this apparatus in your pocket; you just lugged it round using the substantial handle to carry it. However, it seemed to work most of the time and came in useful when things went wrong.

Some of the show themes we cooked up involved eye-catching displays. One year we managed to bring three police cars from the continent with their crews. These caught the public imagination. The Dutch Porche car in orange livery was very smart, and the German car in green livery with two khaki clad officers was much admired.

We tried a French waitress theme one year to publicise 'no alcohol' beers for drivers and had Barry Sheen's racing motorcycle alongside an array of police motorcycles. Mike Draine arranged for an aircraft to circle the show towing an aerial crime prevention message. Another aspect was arranging for items to give away to visitors. To keep within budget, they needed to be inexpensive, but preferably useful with a message for the long term. I liked pencils with rubbers on the end with a crime prevention message, but we tried several other items. Of course, there were masses of leaflets to be given away, and children visiting seemed keen to fill a bag full of any leaflets they could find – prizes from their day out.

While the show was hard work, it was also a welcome break from the office. It was one of the few occasions when the community affairs officers from around the county got together to do something interesting – usually we only gathered for departmental meetings.

The Lincolnshire Echo regularly produced a spread in the centre of the newspaper devoted to police matters, especially crime reduction and road safety. I was always

A Policeman's Tale

keen to see that topics related to my department were featured and we arranged photo shoots and articles to appear in these supplements. Using commercial sponsorship, we managed to produce an edition of a newspaper for wide distribution throughout the county. We called it 'Neighbour'. After the work of filling the pages was over, I went down to the print works in Lincoln to see the presses roll. The huge machine was impressive to see. It must have been about fifty feet long. When it sprang into action, a huge roll of newsprint was quickly transformed into neat bundles of papers ready for distribution.

I was often asked to produce some words for something we wanted in the press. Usually, the reporter would ask if I had a photograph of myself to accompany the article and a 'bromide' of the police crest. I kept a little stock of police crest 'bromides' (just a very good quality print), and after a while I got the police photographic department to produce a stock of pictures of me in and out of uniform. There were two versions of each – in one I was smiling (for upbeat articles), and in the other I looked suitably stern to accompany items where the police were threatening to 'crack down' (as the press love to say), on something or other.

One of the activities I indulged in during my spare time was wargaming. I'd begun this when Julia and I moved to Lincoln in 1976. John McKay had introduced me to his Napoleonic model soldiers, and on returning to the area, he'd invited me to wargame with friends at his home in Sudbrooke on Monday evenings. In February 1992, I made one of several visits to Scarborough with John McKay and other friends to the Wargames Holiday Centre. We stayed in a small hotel in the town and each day travelled out to the centre where we played a variety of games with period model soldiers. I usually enjoyed these excursions when there was opportunity to play a large battle over several days, in contrast to the two- or three-hour battles at John McKay's home.

Julia and I had greatly enjoyed our two previous excursions to Denmark and this year we decided to try a visit to the east side of Jutland, booking from 7th to 23rd August 1992 at Sælker Molle. After crossing the North Sea, we drove to our summerhouse in a pine forest. We discovered the owners were very keen on candles, and these were liberally distributed around the house. We enjoyed very atmospheric evenings together in their soft yellow light. We were blessed with fine weather and enjoyed barbecues in the garden, and tours around the countryside. The town of Ebeltoft was very memorable, and for the first time for us, we saw a fine wind farm down by the seashore.

Returning to England and work my mind was now very concentrated on the prospect of retirement. With Julia, I'd attended two retirement courses over the previous five years and listened carefully to all the advice, particularly the financial suggestions. I'd calculated the probable income from my pension and the outgoings. It seemed that while my pension would be half my pay (if I commuted the maximum proportion), I'd pay less income tax, no national insurance, and the eleven percent pension contributions would also cease. Additionally, the commutation sum when invested would also produce an income. Overall, I'd not be much worse off retired than by continuing to work. This was an attractive prospect indeed. After much discussion with Julia on 1st September, I submitted notice of resignation effective from 25th October 1992.

I had joined the Lincolnshire Constabulary as a sixteen-year-old cadet in 1958 and worked for thirty-four years to the age of fifty, achieving the rank of Chief Inspector. The Chief Constable, Mr. Neville Ovens, presented me with a certificate of service; the Lincolnshire Police Authority gave me as retirement gift three model engines for my railway. Assistant Chief Constable Alan Goldsmith presented these at a buffet lunch for friends that Julia and I attended at Police Headquarters. A few weeks later, the Lincolnshire Police Officers Mess presented me with an inscribed figurine of a typical police chief inspector. It was a memento of my service and membership. In many ways it was a great wrench to leave the only job I'd known all those years. On the other hand, I had never felt that I had time enough for both my family and my work and I was always torn between the two. Now on retirement I hoped to see much more of Julia and the three boys – something only the great holidays we'd managed together usually achieved.

An essential feature of retirement of course would be managing the finances and to this end Noel Lancaster, who worked for Nelsons, the independent financial advisers, visited Julia and me at home. Under his guidance, after he'd completely reviewed our situation, we arranged for investments from the pension lump sum due on retirement, hoping that we'd stay afloat over the coming years.

XXV Nettleham in Retirement

I suppose I slipped easily into retirement – after all, hadn't my father said to me at the age of sixteen that I'd be able to retire on a good pension when I was forty-nine. I'd carried on a few years beyond that, but his prediction was close to the mark.

One of the first very pleasant tasks was to take my pension commutation cheque to the Midland Bank in the High Street in Lincoln and deposit it. The cashier looked closely at the green printed Lincolnshire County Council cheque and said, "In view of the large amount, I'll contact your branch at Cleethorpes to inform them that it has been deposited". This was a good moment, and the first part of getting my financial affairs in order to support us all until our sons were old enough to manage their own finances.

From 25th October 1992, for the first time in my life, I could look forward to days without the compulsory need to attend school or work. However, a new sort of timetable

A Policeman's Tale

for my week soon began to emerge. First, there were household duties that I was now free to help with, and then there were calls on 'Dad's taxi', which was now available for John, Giles, and Peter.

With three eleven-year-old sons living in the house, there was no time for Julia and I to become a 'Darby and Joan' couple. A pattern developed quite quickly, including household chores of 'Hoovering', as well as two clothes washes most days to keep up with the laundry produced by us all. This kept me on my toes. There was the weekly trip to the supermarket to stock up the empty fridge and kitchen cupboards. Usually sorting out the bills waiting to be paid followed this. I needed to ensure the bank account had sufficient funds to cover the direct debits for council tax, water rates and all the other regular demands. Helping with running the house, and all the necessary mundane tasks, allowed Julia to engage in some of the activities she enjoys. After a break of ten years, she once more found a little time to take up her cello and start a new string quartet.

Once the three boys had gone off to school on weekday mornings, Julia and I were able to enjoy a large pot of percolated coffee and catch up with the Daily Telegraph. Spare time could be spent in the garden keeping the lawn mown, or in the railway shed adding little touches to the scenery or just running the trains around. The railway shed was quite a pleasant retreat. It was warm and equipped with a radio. Julia would flash a torch from the kitchen window alerting me mealtimes were at hand.

I've always enjoyed swimming, and occasionally I went to one of the local Lincoln swimming pools for a swim, sometimes with the boys, and sometimes alone. Deciding that I should do more to keep in shape, I responded to an advertisement to join The World Gym. This was above a nightclub in Clasketgate in Lincoln. It was a basic affair and relatively cheap with an annual fee of a little more than one hundred pounds.

I had an initial session with one of the instructors who checked my weight, height, and measured my waist, upper arms, and thighs. He talked through the objectives that might be followed to improve muscles and fitness, and then he showed me how to work the various exercise machines. We agreed on a regime to follow, and I soon got into a routine of making two visits a week. After signing in, you changed into shorts, vest, and trainers. Then a warming up exercise on the cycle began the session, followed by a set number of repetitions on each machine to exercise different parts of the body. You carried a little card that you ticked off as you did each exercise, and then got the instructors signature at the end. Then it was into the showers, followed by ten or fifteen minutes in the sauna, and after another shower getting back into your clothes. The benefit of exercise soon began to show. Working in the garden, I found I could wield the heavy hedge trimmer much more easily, and my muscles were in better shape. I enjoyed the exercise but sometimes felt a little weak willed about actually putting the Daily Telegraph down and going to the gym.

Once there, I soon found that the other regulars welcomed a chat in the changing room before working out, and afterwards, while showering and getting dressed. The age range was from teens to late seventies, and the sessions

A Policeman's Tale

alternated between men's times and women's times. Some of the tales told were very interesting, and I found insights into other people's activities fascinating. I enjoyed the first year, and because of the health benefit signed up again at the end of it. I had a shock however in April 1996, twelve days after paying my £112 fee for the coming twelve months. Going down to the gym after Easter I found the doors were firmly locked and all the equipment had disappeared. The management had done a moonlight flit.

Legions of disgruntled customers had paid their fees and now couldn't use the facilities. The Lincolnshire Echo carried articles and updates about the affair and the police investigated.

I was in luck however, having paid my renewal fee by credit card. Fortunately, the law requires credit card companies to ensure that the supplier honours transactions over £100, and if not requires the credit card issuer to compensate the buyer. The Trustee Savings Bank reimbursed my money when I wrote to them explaining the circumstances and enclosing press cuttings and copies of my contract. I was pleased with this and resolved to use credit cards for large transactions whenever possible in the future, particularly if I had any doubts about the supplier. I looked at the possibility of joining another gym but found the joining and annual fees a little out of my league. I had to content myself with a resolve to concentrate on swimming for fitness and do crunchies (not the breakfast cereal variety) on the bedroom floor before getting dressed each morning.

Because of the unsatisfactory situation regarding swimming pools in Lincoln, I took a decision to join

Wragby Swimming Club. There were three swimming pools open to the public in the Lincoln area, but all of them were attached to secondary schools and, for the most part, only open out of school hours. However, the small pool at Wragby is open in the daytime, and I was introduced to regular visits by John McKay. Soon I struck up friendships with regular swimmers and the staff and decided to subscribe taking family membership of the club. Over the years, I've swum at least twice a week often taking John, Giles, and Peter along too. Generally, I go on a Monday evening to an adult's session, and on a Wednesday morning to the over sixties session. At the end of a few lengths, it's great to have a break for a short while, when I can chat to the regulars. Occasionally I meet one or other of them when out shopping with Julia, and some of them delight in saying to her, while pointing to me, something along the lines of, 'I didn't recognize him with his clothes on!' Julia is used to these quips now.

The club has no local authority funding and relies on income from swimmers. This barely covers staff wages, and oil for the boiler that heats the water. Various fund-raising efforts are always in progress and for several years, Martyn Hardy, one of the lifeguards, has organised an annual 'swimmerthon'. Relays of members attempt to swim the twenty-three miles of the English Channel. My effort is usually around fifty lengths of the pool (about half a mile), which Julia checks, giving plenty of encouragement, as I complete each length.

Another activity that filled Monday evenings most weeks was wargaming. John McKay, who at the time of my retirement was the superintendent at Gainsborough, West Lindsey Sub-Division. He regularly invited friends to wargame in his large double garage, or his dining room. He lives in a large bungalow at Sudbrooke and over the years, I spent a considerable amount of time fighting miniature battles from a variety of historical periods. The earliest battles were from the time of Marlborough, at the start of the eighteenth century, with the big set piece of the Battle of Blenheim, a favourite when time and resources allowed. Other battles from the Seven Years war, in the middle of the eighteenth century, allowed me to use my Austrian army.

John's own favourite period was the Napoleonic time at the start of the nineteenth century, when his hero, the Duke of Wellington, could take the field. At other times we re-enacted battles from the American War of Independence and the American Civil War.

A set of sixteen hussars was presented to me for my fiftieth birthday by the wargamers, and this was the start of my collection. I now have two large toolboxes holding white metal alloy figures – regiments of foot soldiers, cavalry, and artillery. These are all in as authentic uniforms of the period as it was possible to paint. Some of these are my son John's soldiers. My skill as a painter of miniature figures, already fairly good after completing railway figures, improved tremendously to the point where the little soldiers have details, such as the pupils of their eyes, and every gold or silver button, carefully picked out. For accuracy, it was necessary to obtain good reference books with detailed plates showing uniforms of the Austrian army during the Seven Years War. I managed to obtain some very good ones at Wargaming Conventions that took place at weekends, when I would go off with John McKay, or one or two of my sons, and spend a very enjoyable time browsing the stalls and exhibition wargames. It was possible to examine the exhibitors wargaming figures with a view to purchase, and also to see examples of superbly painted figures spurring on my efforts to produce painted figures, of the same high standard

The Wargames Holiday Centre near Scarborough was another attraction. Making several visits with John McKay and others, I stayed at the Sylvern Hotel near the seafront and travelling each day to the centre, in a nearby village, where a vast table was available to play major battles. The beautifully detailed model soldiers and the well-made scenery, including fortified towns added to the pleasure of doing battle. The other wargamers were from all sections of society and included an Austrian banker called Herbert, who had to be regularly reprimanded for 'clumping'. This is the term used for picking up several model soldiers in one hand, which can be the cause of damage to the paintwork or bend fragile tiny bayonets. Our eldest son, John, seems to have enjoyed wargaming more than the other two. He still enjoys this hobby, and he came with me on one of the trips to the Wargames Holiday Centre.

My railway shed, I think, deserves a few words here as I'm detailing my hobbies in retirement. Until the advent of a computer in 1998, the building of my model railway was my main hobby. Having begun as a simple circle of track with a few sidings, it developed over the years. When I had the opportunity to use the purpose built shed, I realised I'd

A Policeman's Tale

need a proper plan for the track and scenery. I pored over various track plans in the Hornby catalogue, and in the Peco book of track plans. Articles were studied in my favourite magazine, The Railway Modeller. Eventually I decided that the best design was a double track circle with a spur leading to a higher level, going to a station over a set of hidden sidings.

The result of this decision was much carpentry, although I was able to use some of the old baseboards I'd built for the layout at Horncastle. The design included an engine stabling facility at both main stations as well as limited goods yard accommodation. The model was to be set in the mid-1950s, and eventually I decided on a precise date of 17th June 1956. This enabled me to decide on the way the countryside was represented, allowing the correct type of wildflowers to be in bloom on the trackside. Photographs taken around Woodhall Spa of blooming wild roses helped me recreate a little bit of Lincolnshire in miniature. Indeed, the model was set in Lincolnshire on a supposed line from Louth to Lincoln (such a line did exist at one time, but my stations are imaginary). The station on the mainline is Halford, while the spur line leads to the terminus station at Thirsby. That station is modelled loosely on the one at Heckington near Sleaford. The hidden sidings will hold up to six trains, and at any one time, a maximum of three engines can be running. This allows for a couple of trains to run around the main lines while shunting or other movement takes place on the spur or in the sidings.

The model railway has given me much pleasure over the years, but, once I gained a computer, the railway fell into second place, and sometimes spiders took up residence in the tunnels weaving their webs over the rolling stock. John, Giles, and Peter were interested, but generally only when I was in the shed at the same time.

This brings me to computers. My interest stemmed back to the early home machines of the 1980s and when John McKay let me have an old Oric computer with a tiny 48k of memory. The only way to save programmes and data was to make a tape cassette of it and this was most laborious. However, this machine gave much pleasure, and the principles of programming were learnt. Later, again by way of John McKay, I came by an Amstrad word processor, which seemed a great advance on the Oric. I managed to keep some of my budget details on this machine, and to do letters and the like.

By 1998, dissatisfaction with these rudimentary machines had set in and I hankered after something more powerful – in other words a proper computer. Advertisements by Tiny Computers caught my eye. I visited their store, in the Waterside Shopping Centre in Lincoln, and mouth-watered over the array of machines on display. Eventually I spent around £1000 on a machine with all the trimmings of printer, keyboard, mouse, scanner, and a digital camera.

The boxes arrived home by courier a few days later. There was great family excitement as we set about opening them and setting up the machine on the sitting room table. Once we were satisfied that everything worked came the next problem. This was the positioning of the computer. Julia and I had great discussions about this and in the end

A Policeman's Tale

arrived at the solution. I bought a desk that would fit on the landing next to the door to Peter's room. By the time, the printer had been fitted in on a little table, there was not much spare space, but this served me well over the next seven years, until an alternative became available.

I would sit at the computer working or playing away whilst the lads, in their bedrooms, would emerge from time to time and pass comments. At first, before John, Giles, and Peter bought laptop computers of their own, it was necessary to run a roster so that each of us had a little time on the computer. This avoided arguments to some extent, but there was always reluctance when the current computer player or worker had to move over for the next in turn to have a go. Sometimes Julia would alert me to a cup of tea being brewed down in the kitchen, and from this very central position in the house, I felt like being on the bridge of a ship. Occasionally it was like the bridge of the 'Titanic' just after striking the iceberg, as vital, noisy communications between my sons took place around me.

Happily, time moved on, and so did my computer station, from the landing to the small front bedroom in 2006, but more of that later.

John, Giles, and Peter, at the time of my retirement had moved from Nettleham Junior School to attend the comprehensive at Cherry Willingham. We'd all spent several evenings visiting possible schools. The chief options were Christ's Hospital School, Yarborough School, William Farr at Welton, and the De Aston School at Market Rasen. Our lads eventually decided that Cherry Willingham suited them best, and financially it suited me since Lincolnshire

County Council provided free bus transport.

Julia and I did our best to support our three young men in their school activities attending the usual round of school events. I even responded to the invitation to the annual governors meeting with parents. To the embarrassment of everyone, I was the only parent in attendance and the various reports were given solely to me, fortunately in an informal manner. As parents, we were pleased to attend prize-giving ceremonies, when our sons' received recognition for hard work, and also school pantomimes and concerts. The school did much to encourage our lads' musical and theatrical talents as well as their academic side.

At the age of sixteen, having obtained their General Certificates of Secondary Education the three of them moved on to De Aston School at Market Rasen entering the sixth form for General Certificate of Education Advanced Level studies.

Julia and I continued to enjoy a variety of holidays. As a family, in June 1993, we enjoyed a long weekend in an apartment in York. One highlight was a cruise in a motorboat along the river Ouse, and of course there was a visit to the National Railway Museum to see favourites such as Mallard, the record breaking Gresley Pacific locomotive. The same year we made our first visit to Centre Parcs choosing Elveden Forest in Suffolk. The splendid facilities, especially the sub-tropical dome containing a wonderful swimming pool with wave machine, all in a woodland setting, appealed and we enjoyed riding around on our hired cycles.

We again visited Denmark staying at Skallerup Klit in the

A Policeman's Tale

very north of Jutland in 1994. This visit included the excitement of finding a washed-up sealed bottle with a message during a beachcombing walk after a storm. The message had travelled only fifty or so miles from Skagen and was a travel promotion competition. I returned the message but was not lucky enough to win the free holiday. We enjoyed visiting the northernmost tip of Jutland – a must for visitors. This involves a walk over the sand hills north of Grenen where we stood with one foot in each of the two seas, the Kattegat and the Skagerrak, which meet at this point.

We enjoyed the opportunity, while the lads were at school, to take day trips out around the county. These often included our good friend Olga Yeates. Many years ago, Ruth Morris and Olga gave us membership of the National Trust as a gift, and as longstanding members of the Trust, we were encouraged most years to visit perhaps Belton House, Clumber Park, or Tattershall Castle.

Other trips we made, included Springfields at Spalding, to see the wonderful plantings of bulbs, Rufford Park in Nottinghamshire, Sir Isaac Newton's birthplace – Woolsthorpe Manor, Hodsock Priory to see the snowdrops, Grimsthorpe Castle, and Belvoir Castle. For outings further afield, we would travel into Norfolk, a favourite spot being Walsingham and Wells-next-the-Sea, often stopping for a break at Sandringham, enjoying the wonderful parkland and perhaps taking a picnic before buying a few souvenirs at the gift or plant shop. We've stayed in Walsingham several times, at Elmham House where, although the accommodation is basic, there is always a warm welcome.

We usually visit the Roman Catholic and Anglican shrines, but I think my favourite is the Russian Orthodox Shrine which is housed in the former railway station.

Another enjoyable outing with Olga was to the Duke of Devonshire's great estate at Chatsworth. Yet another outing was to Barnsdale, the garden made famous by Geoff Hamilton in the television programme, Gardener's World. Peter had obtained some discount vouchers at the 2004 Lincolnshire Show for a visit to the Wensleydale cheese-making factory at Hawes in North Yorkshire. We went up with Peter, and Olga, and had a great day, not only seeing the cheese being made, but also sampling the delicious product.

We had enjoyed our Centre Parcs experience in Suffolk and thought we'd try the one in Nottinghamshire in 1997. It was great, and in 1998 we returned to the tropical dome in Sherwood Forest for another family holiday. Once again, I was able to indulge my love of sailing, and the excitement of swimming under the waterfall and then making the trip down the wild river. Some of the special treats on these holidays are visits to the excellent restaurants, and the special morning or evening events such as a Caribbean breakfast with jazz band, or a Robin Hood medieval banquet.

On 5th September 1998, my father celebrated his 86th birthday. Sadly, however, nine months later in 1999, he passed away at the age of eighty-six on 18th June. My sister, Susan, helped by her husband David, had been close at hand in Cleethorpes, with a helping hand for my father, as old age began to take its toll. My father had already had one short spell in hospital but was spared any serious illnesses until he was admitted, having collapsed suffering with diabetes. He responded to treatment initially but was then diagnosed with untreatable leukaemia. He died after six weeks in the Princess Diana of Wales Hospital at Grimsby. After the funeral, we spent a considerable amount of time sorting out his effects. We also needed to arrange the sale of the house at 43 Lindum Road, Cleethorpes, and deal with the will. After numerous trips from Nettleham, meeting Susan and David, we finally sorted everything out. In October, the family assembled in Stickney Churchyard, for the interment of my father's ashes close to those of my mother, his dear Bessie, in the Pickering family grave.

Keeping our house maintained was one of the things that kept Julia and I busy. We'd had it painted soon after we moved in, but in 1999, it was clear action was needed; especially since many of the window-frames were in a poor state. We succumbed to the sales talk of the representative from Staybright Windows and ordered double-glazing and new doors at front and rear. The windows were an expense but have given no trouble and we've been pleased we took the plunge and had the work done.

Later in the year, our sons achieved their 18th birthdays. We celebrated this in style with a large family gathering at the Inn on the Lawn Restaurant in Lincoln. I'd prepared family trees displays for both the McNeill and Boyers families. I put these up in the coffee lounge to provide a talking point for the family after the meal. Several folk took an interest and quite a bit of new information emerged to add to the records (at time of writing) of 387 relatives. This interest in genealogy lead to my taking a six-week course of lectures at Lincolnshire Archives on the subject and a continuing interest in the subject.

You may remember that I'd grown a moustache for a while in the middle seventies, and Julia now persuaded me that a beard would suit me, and as a bonus save all the trouble of shaving each day, especially over the winter months. After the boys' eighteenth birthday celebrations, I let my whiskers grow and by Christmas had a fine bushy beard. It was a little on the grey side for my liking and having proved I could do it I shaved it off as soon as the weather warmed up.

The year 2000 was notably the year most people celebrated 'the millennium'. Some argument accompanied this because it can effectively be argued that two thousand was the last year of the millennium and a new millennium only began with 2001. However, as 1999 turned into two thousand our family was confined to the house with severe coughs and colds. We stayed up for the midnight celebrations on the television and were rewarded with a huge firework display that brilliantly lighted the black night sky over Nettleham. Much controversy had arisen because it was feared that many electronic devices would be unable to cope with the change from years beginning '19xx' to '20xx'. It was thought computers and all clock-controlled systems might crash as the New Year was ushered in and everyone was urged to take precautions. This great 'Year 2000' problem was a non-event, needless to say, with very few difficulties being experienced.

A Policeman's Tale

Wednesday 14th June 2000 was the twenty-fifth anniversary of our wedding. Our Silver Wedding celebrations took place at the White Hart Hotel in Lincoln. We hired the Wellington Suite and were joined for lunch by close family. We were blessed with some lovely gifts, including flowers. Our guests returned with us to the Chestnuts for a cup of tea and a celebration slice of cake.

Not having taken a holiday in 1999 because of events, in July 2000 we flew from Manchester to Malta staying at Marsascala. The weather when we arrived was extremely hot and the rooftop swimming pool at our hotel provided a very welcome place to cool off. I was very taken by the colourful yellow and orange buses in Malta and one day we boarded one for a trip to Valletta. The harbour was both historic and interesting. Also well worth visiting was the Cathedral of St. John the Baptist, with its wonderfully coloured marble tombstones set in the floor commemorating members of the Order of St. John.

The year 2000 proved full of memorable events, including a mid-summer street party in the Chestnuts, and at the end of July, Olga Yeates invited us to her 80th birthday celebration at the Scold's Bridle Restaurant at Doddington. We enjoyed meeting her family and friends. Another adventure was a trip down to a BBC Henry Wood Promenade Concert in the Albert Hall. Peter chose the particular Prom we decided to hear, the main work being Holst's Planet Suite, performed with an added section for the planet Pluto.

The last family holiday together was another visit to Sherwood Forest, where we enjoyed the delights of the

Centre Parcs experience. The tropical dome with splendid swimming is a big attraction but I very much enjoy sailing the small dinghies on the lake.

In 2002, Julia and I took a holiday in Walsingham, and then in 2003 returned, after a break of thirty-two years, to Corfu. We stayed on the North coast near Sidari in the Loula Apartments, hired cycles for the first week, and a little car for the second week. We used the car to explore the island, revisiting some of the beautiful places we'd seen so long before, as well as new spots.

As previously mentioned, Julia and I try to enjoy the delights of Lincolnshire as well as having holidays abroad. We have always enjoyed swimming and visiting the coast for a day on the beach, so some of our outings on fine sunny days were to Jubilee Park at Woodhall Spa where the splendid surroundings to the well-heated outdoor pool can make a great day out. Our seaside trips took us sometimes to Mablethorpe, Anderby Creek, or Sutton on Sea, but most often to Huttoft, where a well-made car terrace on top of the sea defences provides convenient parking and easy access to the golden sands of the Lincolnshire coast. Although the North Sea is rarely as inviting as the Mediterranean, we both usually manage to bathe there at least a couple of times a year.

We had so enjoyed the experience of visiting Corfu that we repeated the holiday in 2004 staying once again in the Loula Apartments at Sidari.

Having had a great time again, we decided that we should try some of the other one thousand or so Greek islands, and in 2005 flew from Humberside Airport to Crete. Our first

A Policeman's Tale

impression was of a very rocky, barren landscape. Later though, we saw a great deal of the eastern end of this large island and visited some beautiful beaches. Although very mountainous, much of the island is agricultural and irrigation of the fields, in some cases using windmill pumps, is picturesque. We were lucky enough to see a family of the Cretan national bird, the lammergeier, a type of vulture with a huge wingspan, when visiting one of the monasteries in the mountains.

Lest you think that retirement is a period idleness, or endless holidays, I'd better say that finding things to do has never been a problem for Julia and me. We had the pleasure of travelling down to Surrey to take our friend Patricia Hagon and her late husband John to a family golden wedding celebration, staying in a splendid hotel near Dorking called the Burford Bridge Hotel. The open-air swimming pool appealed to me particularly, but I remember the room was excellent and the food very good. To come to the point however, during the pleasant hours spent in these surroundings, a headmistress friend of Patricia, commented to us that she couldn't imagine retiring, as she would wonder what to do each morning. Julia and I were shocked by this comment, and perhaps she wasn't being serious. Certainly, we have not found any problem filling our time, and usually complain to each other that we don't know where the time goes. Many other retired people I know tell me they don't know how they ever found time to go to work!

One day in 1993, I was relaxing and sunning myself in the garden when Julia brought a gentleman in naval uniform to see me. He introduced himself as a representative of the Royal National Mission to Deep Sea Fishermen and indicated that he was looking for a Nettleham house-to-house collector. Over a cup of tea, I agreed to help the cause, mainly because of my connections with Grimsby and knowledge of the good work done by the Mission for fishermen and their families. That first year I managed to collect £106.08, visiting nearly two hundred houses. With the help of Julia, I've carried out a further ten collections, although I've reduced the number of houses to around one hundred each year. I'm pleased to say we've collected about £700 so far and I hope to continue collecting for some time yet. One of the pleasurable parts of the exercise is the chance to meet and talk to neighbours. A downside is finding foreign coins in the little blue printed paper envelopes, or outright refusals by people claiming not to eat fish because they are vegetarians, or other vagaries.

Julia also helped mission funds, in another way, by arranging for her Appletree String Quartet to give a concert at a coffee morning event in our home, attended by friends and neighbours. This was successful and the proceeds were shared with Julia's favourite charity, the National Children's Homes. Julia had set up her quartet soon after we moved to Nettleham, in response to a request from John Walkley and his wife to provide music in the minstrel gallery at their new home, Appletree Cottage in Scothern. The success of this venture encouraged the quartet, which over the following years performed at weddings, church concerts, and flower festivals. The quartet also formed the basis of the small string octet that performed for the Lincoln Gilbert

& Sullivan Society production of 'Trial by Jury' in 2005.

It is important to keep in touch with friends and family but having moved away from many of them to Nettleham, it sometimes seems a long trip to visit each other's homes. We found that a meeting over lunch at a halfway house was a good plan for us. Sometimes we would meet Anne and Arthur Platts at Botts Restaurant, at Crowder's Nursery in Horncastle. Another meeting place, which turned out to provide excellent food, was the Hope Tavern at Holton-le-Moor. This old-world tavern, situated alongside the Lincoln to Grimsby railway line, is just halfway between Cleethorpes and Nettleham. We arranged to meet my sister and brother-in-law, Susan and David, there, and it's became a firm favourite. We meet other friends, like Pat and Derrick Rowbotham and Susan and Christopher Warren there too. A little further along the road, the Salutation Inn at Nettleton offered another good meeting place for us to revive friendships.

Each year the garden occupied my time with the usual mowing of the lawn and other regular tasks. One of the most onerous of these was the need to trim the fifty-foot long Leylandii hedge, which at about twelve feet high called for several days' hard work. Julia assisted greatly by holding the ladder, tidying up and general encouragement. For several years, we cut both sides of the hedge, but eventually gave this up as neighbours sometimes helped by cutting their side. In addition to the hedge, there were nine individual Leylandii trees around the garden, the remnants of old boundary hedges. These needed cutting to prevent them becoming excessively large. Julia and I had to set aside a week in the autumn, after all the birds' nests had emptied, to deal with this. Following the cutting sessions, we made several trips to the household-recycling depot at Great Northern Terrace with loads of green composting material.

Eventually we decided this annual round was getting too much, and looking into the future, we felt it best to take positive action. Each year a pair of Irishmen would visit us, offering to trim trees. Using their services, we gradually reduced the number of Leylandii from nine to nil. Having done this, we asked them for a quotation to reduce the hedge to about seven feet high. On our accepting their figure, they spent almost a day on the job bringing along a couple of young lads to help them and carting away a lorry load of hedge.

Despite the travails of hedge and tree trimming, I enjoyed having a good display of pelargoniums, fuchsia, and other colourful plants at the front of the house and on the patio at the back. Hanging baskets are planted up each year. I try to over winter many of these plants in the garage when the frosts threaten and have managed to keep several prize plants going for many years, some obtained at the County Show.

Every so often haircuts were needed for the men of the house. This meant a Saturday trip, just after lunch, to see Mr. Peter Rushby. Pete had a salon on Monks Road in Lincoln and the four of us would go down by car and spend about an hour in his shop as he wielded his expert scissors, trimming our locks. My haircut was usually over very quickly, but John, Giles, and Peter, having full heads of hair, and young men's styling, wanted a little more attention.

A Policeman's Tale

When Pete retired after forty-four years of snipping away, he began home visits, and it was always good to see him and catch up with the news every other month.

Once our young men had taken their Advanced Level examinations at De Aston School, it was time to look at possible university places for them. This meant travelling to universities offering suitable courses in their chosen subjects for open days. Julia and I travelled to Keele University in Lancashire, Coventry, Hull, and Birmingham in search of suitable politics and mathematics departments. Each of these trips was something of an adventure for us and opened our eyes to the world of higher education. We particularly liked the campus at Keele and the splendid restaurant. Choices were made and when results came through Peter went off to Birmingham to read mathematics, while John went to Hull to read politics. Giles decided to have a gap year.

The ensuing years were taken up with much travelling with our sons to set them up in student accommodation in halls, and later in shared houses. Peter completed a year at Birmingham, but his results lead to him taking a gap year the next year. Meanwhile Giles had decided to join John at Hull, also to read politics. The following year Peter went up to Hull to read Mathematics.

We discovered that Hull University also sported an excellent restaurant in Staff House. The Jubilee Restaurant, oak panelled, and bedecked with oil paintings of the university chancellors, was excellent value and served fine meals on our visits to see our lads. Some of these visits were for productions put on by Hull University Gilbert and

Sullivan Society, in which each son played a leading role.

As proud parents, we saw each of them graduate in turn at very impressive and colourful ceremonies. John and Giles each graduated with honours as Bachelors of Arts (Politics), while Peter completed the hat trick in 2006, graduating as a Bachelor of Science (Mathematics).

When Giles left university, his enjoyment of Gilbert and Sullivan, encouraged him to revive the Lincoln Gilbert & Sullivan Society. The old society had been wound up a few years before, and Giles set about starting a new one, the first concert taking place at Lincoln Drill Hall in the spring of 2005. A production of Trial by Jury, at the Broadbent Theatre, Wickenby, was mounted in December the same year.

Julia has always enjoyed the gentle ambient light of candles. We took stock of the Danes, who liked candles in their homes and began to use candles during winter evenings in our home. I'd visited a candle-making factory in Denmark on holiday and seen the dipping method, and the moulding method in use there. Obtaining library books on the subject, I set about making some candles of my own. My methods gradually improved as I gained experience, and I've had great fun making batches of fifteen or twenty coloured and scented candles for our use and for our friends. Susan and David often bring me stubs of used candles, some of them from Bridget and Sally, and these are melted down to make new ones.

Noel Lancaster of Nelsons Money Managers visited our home regularly to update us on our retirement savings. He always took his time discussing our financial affairs as well

A Policeman's Tale

as many other subjects, often giving us an insight into his own affairs. Nelsons invited us to road shows given in hotels in the region. We enjoyed these events, where we learned much about how the company was looking after our money. Also, we heard about the effect that government taxation was having on it, together with strategies to ensure we could take advantage of any schemes to avoid paying more tax than necessary. When Noel left Nelsons, and they were taken over by Close Brothers, we continued to use their independent advisors, but we very much missed seeing Noel each year.

The Montego that had been my police contract car lasted a number of years into retirement, but, by 1998, was undoubtedly well past its prime. Small rusty pieces had dropped off it and had been found on our drive. In addition, John, Giles, and Peter were getting larger. Once, two of them made me sit between them on our sofa and squeezed up to me. It was very uncomfortable, and they explained this was how they felt in the back of the Montego on family outings. It was time to look for a new vehicle. We went around the various dealers looking for something roomy. I had it in mind to find a second-hand car for around £5000. Eventually at the Rover dealers, R.M. Wright & Son, I was despairing. All the larger Rovers had room for five people, but in each case the rear seat had an uncomfortable centre seat, clearly meant only for occasional use. The salesman dragged me a little unwillingly towards a white car parked outside the showroom. The three young gentlemen were already sitting in the back. They enthusiastically invited me to consider buying this one because it had plenty of room for them. It was a one-year-old Renault Megane Scénic multi-purpose vehicle. A trial run out to Cherry Willingham convinced me that this was a splendid family car. It was about eight inches higher than the average car, and, since the rear seats could be removed, or folded down, promised versatility when moving furniture. The drawback was the price, which was £12,000. With a little encouragement I arranged to fund the purchase and the car proved excellent when the whole family were on the move, or when a generous gift of a bed (from Bridget) was donated to Giles. The Scénic was very useful moving our sons to and from their university accommodation. It was economical as far as petrol use was concerned, usually managing around forty miles to the gallon of expensive and highly taxed fuel.

All went well until August 2003 when I was about to taxi our sons into Lincoln for the evening. I started the engine. Clouds of noxious smelling steam from the exhaust filled The Chestnuts, neighbours came out of their houses and there was general consternation. To cut short a long story the engine head gasket had blown, and worse, the main block was cracked. A replacement engine was ordered, followed by fitting, and a large bill of around £2000. About the same time, I had another problem, concerning the immobiliser system, which relies on infrared remote control by the ignition key of the car. The two keys went wrong and had to be replaced (for £112 each), and the car couldn't be started and was towed to the dealer's workshop by the Automobile Association. These problems didn't affect my old 1938 model Austin Big 7 – but things were much

A Policeman's Tale

simpler then!

Over my life, I've loved listening to the radio, or as I prefer to call it (to some derision from John, Giles and Peter, the wireless). Early memories are of Dick Barton, Dan Dare, Wilfred Pickles, Tommy Handley, Ray's a Laugh, Take it from Here, and PC 49. Later I followed the Archers, loved The Goon Show, Round the Horne, Hancock's Half Hour and other comedy shows. I was always a very keen listener to the news (my father generally had the news on during mealtimes), and other favourites over the years have been Any Questions, and Gardeners Question Time. More recently such programmes as I'm Sorry I haven't a Clue, Just a Minute, Dead Ringers and The Now Show, have entertained me. Julia and I both keenly listen to Radio Three concerts, and sometimes enjoy the music on Classic FM, (even though the advertisements often spoil things).

I suppose I hear much more radio than I do television. There was no television at home before I left at the age of sixteen, and over the years, my watching has declined. I always enjoyed Morecambe and Wise, Doctor Who, and the original series of Star Trek with Captain Kirk. In recent years, however, my main watching has been news programmes, the Antiques Roadshow, and Working Lunch (the mid-day business programme). An exception to all this has always been anything to do with Star Trek and with all the family I've closely followed and made special arrangements to see episodes of The Next Generation, Deep Space Nine, Voyager, and Enterprise. Additionally, we've made family outings to see the ten Star Trek films as they've been released.

I've already mentioned Pat Hagon in connection with our trip to the Burford Bridge Hotel. She was the instigator of Hagon Happenings, a theatrical group for all abilities, which she started in Surrey when she lived there. Pat was the writer of the lyrics of the shows and her talented son, Richard, the composer of the music. She continued with Hagon Happenings when she moved to Welton, near Lincoln, and drew John, Giles, and Peter into a production of her musical version of Little Women. Later she involved them in a musical film, about witches in Lancashire, called Pendle Hill. Pat also produced a musical evening at Our Lady of Lincoln Church with the Appletree Quartet, so it was no surprise when she asked Julia and I to participate in a musical production about Sir Thomas Moore at the Old Hall at Gainsborough. Julia played the part of a serving wench, and I was a beefeater. My main task was to execute poor Sir Thomas with my great axe. I suspect we shall be involved with Hagon Happenings again over the years.

Following the death of my father in 1999, linked to diabetes, which my sister also began to suffer from in mid-life, I went to see my doctor for a check-up. Fortunately, there was no sign of the disease in me, but I was told to watch my weight, and to eat sensibly. Subsequent checks indicated raised levels of cholesterol and in June 2005, I began to take statin tablets, a small daily dose, successfully reducing these levels.

Late in 2003, Julia, with the Our Lady of Lincoln choir mistress, Theresa Inman, decided to record the church choir in which our three sons sang regularly. The compact disc would include four of the hymns Julia has written, she was to accompany some on the piano, and the Appletree Quartet would accompany another of the hymns. What we believed to be a straightforward undertaking proved to be much more than that. Choir rehearsals went ahead, and Julia and I sought out a recording studio that could visit Our Lady of Lincoln Church, do the recording, and produce the finished discs. Steve Hawkins of Ice Studio was contracted, and recording took place in the summer of 2004, mostly over two very full evenings. All the family were engaged in this process, my chief role being porter of heavy recording equipment, and car park attendant, with strict instructions to keep everything around the outside of the church quiet. This proved difficult with the slimmers club members slamming car doors, ice-cream van chimes, and sundry ambulances with their sirens, passing close by. After recording, the various tracks were edited and put together.

It was November before the 300 CDs were ready for sale, but this was in time for the 40th anniversary of the building of the church. Julia and I, set about fulfilling advance orders and making sales to the church congregation. We sold some through Ottakers bookshop, and the composer of the music for one of the hymns, Thomas Rookes, managed to sell a number for us. The venture cost around £1200, which Julia and Theresa put up initially. Eventually our sales meant the venture recouped its costs, and into the bargain, Julia and I learned many lessons about the process of making a compact disc.

The engagement of our eldest son John to Alice Lamming, the fourth daughter of John and Sheila Lamming took place on 27th August 2004. John and Alice began house hunting, and, in October 2005, John moved into a semi-detached house in Market Rasen. Aided by Alice, Julia and I, and the rest of the family he began furnishing and decorating in preparation for the wedding.

The consequence of John moving out was to free up his bedroom for occupation by Peter, who had always had the small front bedroom in our Nettleham house. Peter made the most of this opportunity, but it also gave me the chance to move my computer station off the landing into my very own office early in 2006. I'd often found it hard to concentrate when working on the landing, especially when racking my memory for incidents for this piece of writing. The move to a dedicated office gave me a little more thinking space and the chance to spread around items, such as cuttings and photographs, to help me organize a little better. Giles has some space in the office for his work as the president of the Lincoln Gilbert & Sullivan Society.

Moving to Nettleham turned out to have been an excellent thing in retirement. The village is very self-contained having most services close at hand, or only a short distance away in Lincoln. Not only that, but much of the village is constructed of honey coloured oolitic limestone, which is a very attractive building material. Long ago, the village had its own quarry for this material, and a row of interesting cottages remains, which used to be occupied by the quarrymen. Julia and I often enjoy walking around the village, or occasionally using our cycles for quick trips to the Co-operative Supermarket, Troika (the card shop), or Krystals (the chemists). The stream, known as the Beck, meanders through the middle, making an attractive feature.

A Policeman's Tale

The Beck begins at Riseholme, crosses the main A.46 Grimsby – Lincoln Road, and then through the grounds of the Police Headquarters, being fed there from the large lake, which was one of the old quarries. After this it emerges into the village by the old watermill, crosses a ford, and then a couple of hundred yards later passes the church, goes under the road and wanders through the rest of the village.

The Beck attracts ducks and from time to time, the numbers of mallard in the village seems to reach huge proportions. At these times, the ducks seek gardens in which to rear their ducklings, and our own garden has seen several broods over the years. The Parish Council has felt obliged to try reducing their numbers and has tried several methods from time to time. They have transported them away many miles but have been most successful by asking people to stop feeding them.

One of the favourite summer pastimes of the family during the summer is having a barbeque in the garden. Inviting family and friends to join us for a leisurely lunch, cooked over the hot charcoal, accompanied by a good wine, or a glass of cider has giving us much pleasure over the years. Our old barbeque, which was a gift from Susan and David while we lived at Boston, was replaced by a new larger one, also a kind gift from Susan and David after they'd been invited several times to join us for our al fresco feasts.

Getting the charcoal going was usually an exercise that John, Giles, and Peter wanted to get involved in. Eventually Peter decided that he would become the barbeque expert. He is very good at lighting up and often I leave him to get on with it while I see to bringing out the food Julia has prepared. The weather is important when we eat outside, and over the years there have been anxious moments as raindrops began to fall, and I was left to finish the cooking while everyone else retired to the house for cover. On the other hand, many very warm, sunny days have blessed us, and then quite often we have to use sunshades as we dine.

Since coming to Nettleham, we have enjoyed Christmases most years, except when sickness has laid us low. Latterly, Giles has become our culinary expert, and cooked our special lunch. He always makes an excellent Christmas pudding several months in advance ready for the big day. Our friend, Olga, who normally stays at least for the Queens Speech, usually joins us for dinner.

During 2005, Olga gave us cause for concern. She had to give up driving her much-loved Mini in the spring, because of problems with her sight. We helped by collecting her most Thursday mornings on our way to the supermarket for a joint shopping expedition. She managed very well, but in the autumn began having problems walking, even with her stick. In November, she had to be taken to hospital having fallen at home and spent five weeks in an intermediate care home. Julia and I undertook to inform friends and relatives of her progress and helped look after her home in Broadway, Lincoln. When she returned home, we assisted with the arrangements and the extra care needed to settle her and help her cope. Her first outing was to us on Christmas Day. We did her weekly shopping, and I began regular visits to deliver the shopping, and to help with various tasks, such as paperwork, and simple maintenance. I enjoyed helping, and it gave me plenty of chances to talk over family doings with her.

This brings me to the present day. I am looking forward to drawing my state retirement pension at the end of this year (2006) when I reach the grand age of sixty-five. I have joined a local gym with excellent swimming facilities and am intent on seeing more of the Greek islands on holidays with Julia.

These memoirs have been interesting for me to set down, and I hope you've found things of interest, dear reader, among the 87,000 words. There is some insight into how a baby born in a rural county police station grew up and spent his life in Lincolnshire (with occasional excursions elsewhere), working as a police officer, and raising a family. It has certainly been a varied sixty-five years, sometimes exciting, sometimes just dull routine. I hope I've captured some of the funny, and often embarrassing moments, although friends have kindly pointed out some omissions which they remember clearly, but which (perhaps wisely) I've forgotten to include.

It's been good fun writing this story of my life, and I'd encourage everyone to tell their story, setting down their memories as a record for the benefit of future generations.

Printed in Great Britain
by Amazon